MISSION

MISSION

An American Congressman's
Voyage to Space

by U.S. Congressman Bill Nelson

with Jamie Buckingham

Harcourt Brace Jovanovich, Publishers

San Diego   New York   London

Copyright © 1988 by Bill Nelson and Jamie Buckingham

All rights reserved. No part of this publication
may be reproduced or transmitted in any form or
by any means, electronic or mechanical, including
photocopy, recording, or any information storage
and retrieval system, without permission in
writing from the publisher.

Requests for permission to make copies of any
part of the work should be mailed to:
Permissions, Harcourt Brace Jovanovich, Publishers,
Orlando, Florida 32887.

Library of Congress Cataloging-in-Publication Data

Nelson, Bill, 1942–
Mission : an American congressman's voyage to
space.

Includes index.
1. Nelson, Bill, 1942–   . 2. Astronauts—United
States—Biography. 3. United States. Congress—
Biography. I. Buckingham, Jamie. II. Title.
TL540.N37A3 1988   629.45′0092′4 [B]   87-33605
ISBN 0-15-105556-4

Designed by Kaelin Chappell

Printed in the United States of America

First edition

A   B   C   D   E

A report to the American People
and their representatives in Congress

One of the things Christa McAuliffe carried with her aboard the ill-fated flight of the *Challenger* was a copy of the poem "High Flight," written by John Gillespie Magee, Jr., a Canadian combat pilot who died over the white cliffs of Dover in England in 1941. It expresses the sentiments of all who reach out—and up.

Oh, I have slipped the surly bonds of earth
   And danced the skies on laughter-silvered
      wings;
Sunward I've climbed and joined the tum-
      bling mirth
Of sun-split clouds—and done a hundred
      things
You have not dreamed of—wheeled and
      soared and swung
  High in the sunlit silence. Hov'ring there,
I've chased the shouting wind along, and flung
  My eager craft through footless halls of air.
Up, up the long, delirious, burning blue
  I've topped the windswept heights with
      easy grace
Where never lark, or even eagle flew.
  And, while with silent, lifting mind I've trod
The high untrespassed sanctity of space,
  Put out my hand, and touched the face of
      God.

Contents

NASAese   xi

PART ONE: THE FLIGHT   1

Columbia   3

On Hold   21

Getting Ready   27

Training   40

More Training   53

Still More Training   79

Scrubs   92

Straight Up and Accelerating   104

On Orbit   118

Whither Earth?   144

Coming Home   157

PART TWO: THE CHALLENGE 173

The *Challenger* Is Down 175

Space Research 186

Space People 204

International Cooperation in Space 227

Entrepreneurs in Space 248

Space Spin-offs 268

Understanding Our Beginnings, Charting Our Future 278

Tragedy and Triumph—Reaching for the Stars 288

SHUTTLE FLIGHT HISTORY 299

Index 305

NASAese

A glossary of acronyms, abbreviations, and special terms used by the people of the National Aeronautics and Space Administration. (Condensed from the more than 10,500 acronyms in the NASA vocabulary.)

AFB   Air force base, as in Edwards AFB (EAFB) or Patrick AFB (PAFB)

Airlock   The small compartment on the shuttle capable of being depressurized without depressurizing the orbiter cabin

ALS   Alternate landing site

APC   Armored personnel carrier. Tank-like vehicle, which waits at the bottom of the escape slide-wire.

APS   Acute phases of spaceflight

ASP   Astronaut support person. Astronaut designated from team of "Cape crusaders" to make final checks on board the shuttle before launch.

Attitude   The position of an aircraft or spacecraft deter-
                        mined by the relationship between its axes and
                        a reference point (as the horizon or a particular
                        star)

Barbecue mode   The orbiter in a slow roll as it circles the earth,
                        allowing the sun to evenly heat the orbiter

CAPCOM   Capsule communicator. Astronaut assigned to
                        monitor all spaceflights from Mission Control in
                        Houston and communicate with the astronauts
                        in orbit.

Cape crusader   Astronaut assigned to support test and check-
                        out activities on shuttle before launch

Cargo bay   The unpressurized mid-part of the orbiter fu-
                        selage behind the cabin, where the payloads
                        (primarily satellites) are carried

Deployment   The process of removing a satellite from the
                        cargo bay and putting it into orbit

DOD   Department of Defense

DSO   Detailed secondary objectives. Primarily medi-
                        cal and scientific experiments in the shuttle that
                        are secondary to the primary mission.

ECS   Environmental control system

EI   Entry interface. The time and place the shuttle
                        reenters earth's atmosphere—at about 400,000
                        feet altitude.

ELV   Expendable launch vehicle. Rocket that flies into
                        space and does not return for reuse

EMU   Extravehicular mobility unit. Space suit to be
                        worn outside vehicle for spacewalks or work in
                        cargo bay.

ES   Egress slide. Part of the orbiter that allows as-
                        tronauts to make hasty exit if there is an emer-
                        gency while still on the ground. Uses an
                        inflatable slide similar to those on airliners.

ETA   Estimated time of arrival

EVA	Extravehicular activity. Space walk.
FDF	Flight data file. Seventy-five pounds of printed paper detailing activity to be carried out in space as well as operation of shuttle.
Flight Day	A 24-hour period of time that measures each day in flight. Different from on Earth since day and night do not apply in space, nor do time zones. Also referred to as MD or Mission Day.
Gs	Measured gravitational force
GCA	Ground controlled approach
GPC	General purpose computer
HUD	Heads up display. The flight instruments readout is reflected at the level of the front window so the pilot does not have to lower his line of sight.
ICBM	Intercontinental ballistic missile. Military rocket capable of virtually circling the globe and exploding an atomic warhead on an enemy.
JSC	Johnson Space Center in Houston, Texas
LCC	Launch control center at KSC
KSC	Kennedy Space Center located near Cape Canaveral, Florida
Mach	Velocity relative to the speed of sound
Max Q	Period of maximum dynamic pressure on launch vehicle
MCC	Mission Control Center, at JSC
MET	Mission elapsed time. The time elapsed after lift-off.
Mission specialist	Astronaut responsible for payloads and other shuttle systems
MLS	Microwave landing system
MMU	Manned maneuvering unit. Propulsion system backpack worn in space.

MS-1   Mission Specialist One

NASA   National Aeronautics and Space Administration

O&C   Operations and Checkout Building at KSC. Crew quarters are on the third floor.

OES   Orbiter escape systems

OFT   Orbital flight test

OMS   Orbiter maneuvering system. Rockets aboard the shuttle that fire to change orbital altitude and orbit shape (i.e., circular or elliptical).

Orbiter   Manned orbital flight vehicle. The space shuttle.

PAM   Payload assist module. Rocket on satellite that fires to boost satellite into higher orbit.

PAPIs   Precision approach phased indicator. Lights at the runway's threshold that indicate whether the shuttle is high or low on final approach.

Payload   Space equipment, hardware, and consumables carried in the orbiter. (A satellite to be deployed in space is a payload.)

PI   Principal investigator. Earth scientists in charge of DSOs and other experiments.

Pilot   Second in command on the shuttle, assisting the commander from the right seat on the flight deck

Propellant   Material used to power the RCS and OMS on the shuttle. Usually two components, a fuel and an oxidizer.

PS-1   Payload specialist one, usually a career astronaut; responsible for various experiments in space.

PS-2   Payload specialist two. The second payload specialist.

RCS   Reaction Control System. Rockets (thrusters) on the shuttle that primarily control spacecraft attitude while in space.

RMS	Remote manipulator system. Robotic arm that reaches into cargo bay on shuttle and deploys payloads in space.
RTLS	Return to launch site. Emergency procedure to be used by shuttle to land at KSC following lift-off.
SAS	Space adaptation syndrome including space motion sickness
Simulator	A heavily computer-dependent mock-up of the shuttle on the ground at JSC that imitates spaceflight and is used for training
Sleep Restraint	Space sleeping bag with harness
SPOC	Shuttle position on-board computer, affectionately referred to as "SPOC"
SRB	Solid rocket booster. Reusable solid fuel rockets strapped to the side of the external tank.
SSME	Space shuttle main engines
STA	Shuttle training aircraft. Airplane used by astronauts to simulate shuttle air maneuvers.
STS	Space transportation system. The space shuttle.
TCDT	Terminal countdown demonstration test. Practice countdown that each crew goes through at KSC prior to launch.
TDRSS	Tracking and data relay satellite system. Satellite communication system providing coverage for all STS flights.
UCD	Urine collection device. Fitted cup to collect urine.
VAB	Vehicle assembly building. One of the largest buildings in the world, located at Kennedy Space Center. The shuttle orbiters, external tank, and solid rocket boosters are assembled here and rolled out to the launchpad three-and-one-half miles away.

WCS   Waste collection system. Space toilet.

WETF   Weightless environment training facility. Huge
                    water tank at JSC in Houston where astronauts
                    practice weightless activities underwater.

Zero Gs   Weightlessness

PART ONE

THE FLIGHT

Columbia

It was cold that Thursday morning in December. Intensely chilly for tropical Florida. There was frost on the roof of the crew's van. I shivered, more from excitement than from the weather as I boarded at 4:00 A.M. I was on my way to the launchpad—I was going into space.

The night before, my wife, Grace, and my staff had hosted a bon voyage party in Cocoa Beach. I was not able to attend. The seven members of our crew were in quarantine at the astronauts' quarters near the launchpad at Kennedy Space Center. But Grace had called and told me about it. A number of my friends in Congress had flown in to attend the party and to witness the dawn launch the next day. They were joined by a Science and Technology Committee delegation led by the chairman and fellow Floridian, Congressman Don Fuqua. Several of the astronauts also had attended, as had NASA associate administrator Jesse Moore.

At the close of the party Grace had called on our pastor to lead in public prayer, asking God to bless and protect our mission. "You handle the weather," Jesse Moore had joked as the minister stood to pray. "NASA can take care of everything else."

It was a friendly josh, but it was indicative of the pride NASA had in its ability to make things work. It was also a statement that would come back to haunt NASA many times.

Thursday morning, December 19, 1985, we were awakened at 2:35 A.M. Each astronaut had his own small room in the quarantine quarters at KSC. Mine was a ten-by-twelve-foot cubicle with dark blue carpet, a double bed, lamp, phone, two small dressers, a bookcase, mirror, and a fan. Actually, the room looked almost austere, but it was comfortable and sufficient. NASA spends a huge amount of money on technical equipment, but there are no luxuries when it comes to personnel.

I showered and shaved with the other astronauts in the men's bathroom down the hall. After a hearty breakfast with the crew in the dining hall, we suited up. I stuffed my pockets with all the things I planned to take along. Since *USA Today*'s announcement that I had been selected to fly the *Columbia* mission into space, I had been bombarded with requests to carry items aloft. One couple wanted me to carry a marriage manual so I could marry them from space. Another lady, a widow, requested I carry her husband's cremated ashes. NASA, fortunately, had strict regulations that defined the number and type of items that could be carried aboard the space shuttle. I had chosen the few things that I felt were representative of my community, state, and country.

Most of these items had been packed aboard the shuttle. They ranged from fresh Indian River grapefruit to pieces of the old Florida capitol in Tallahassee.

But that morning I was concerned with the items I would cram into my pockets. I had a voice-activated recorder in a zippered pocket by my left ankle, and a pocket Bible on my right side. In another pocket I had a special tape of songs that my little girl, Nan Ellen, had made for me. Also, I would wear my wedding ring. Besides this, I had the regular equipment: a pair of scissors, a knife, a small flashlight. Sooner or later, I had been told, I would need a flashlight in space—if for no other reason than to find my way to the space toilet in the dark.

Leaving the crew quarters, the seven of us boarded the elevator and descended to the ground floor of the huge building where the crew had been housed, seven miles from the launchpad at the Kennedy Space Center. I looked around at the men I had grown to respect and love.

Commander Robert L. "Hoot" Gibson, a Navy officer and copilot on the first shuttle mission to land at Kennedy Space Center, was married to fellow astronaut Rhea Seddon, a medical doctor with a special interest in surgical nutrition. Rhea had made her first spaceflight as a mission specialist on mission STS 51-D eight months before. Hoot had flown fifty-six combat missions in Vietnam as a Navy pilot. Later, he was a test pilot on the F-14A development project before joining the astronaut corps in 1978.

Our pilot was Charlie Bolden. A graduate of the U.S. Naval Academy and now a Marine lieutenant colonel, Charlie had come up the hard way. A black, he grew up in segregated South Carolina. Charlie was an outstanding pilot and extremely personable. He taught Sunday school in his Episcopal church in Houston. Just seeing him standing calmly in the elevator, a slight smile on his handsome face, gave me confidence.

There were three mission specialists, all Ph.D.'s. Doctor Steve Hawley, who was at that time married to Dr. Sally Ride, the first American woman to orbit the earth, was chatting with Dr. Franklin Chang-Diaz. Hawley, whose degree is in astronomy and astrophysics, was serious, talking business-as-usual. Chang-Diaz, small, dark haired, and a native of Costa Rica with a doctorate in applied plasma physics from MIT, was listening intently as Steve ran through items on the flight checklist.

The third mission specialist was Dr. George "Pinky" Nelson, a disciplined athlete with a doctorate in astronomy. Earlier, I had interviewed him on the monthly television show I hosted in Florida. Quiet and intense, he'd offered some great advice

The astronauts of Mission STS-61C. Left to right, Bob Cenker (payload specialist), Charlie Bolden (pilot), Bill Nelson (payload specialist), Steve Hawley (mission specialist), Pinky Nelson (mission specialist), Hoot Gibson (commander), Franklin Chang-Diaz (mission specialist). [NASA photo]

to young people interested in the space program. But he had also warned them that there are too many interesting things to do in life to set goals on a single achievement. He'd urged them to keep their eyes open for the many other opportunities the space program presented besides being an astronaut.

The final member of the crew was Bob Cenker. Like myself, Bob was classified as a payload specialist—a fancy name for a nonprofessional astronaut who is along for special reasons. Bob, an RCA engineer, had been invited by NASA to accompany this flight because RCA was NASA's "customer" on the mission—paying NASA seventeen million dollars to launch its satellite.

My task as payload specialist was to learn as much as I could in order to help with my work as Space Subcommittee chairman, and to assist in a number of medical experiments, some of which were important to cancer research.

The elevator stopped and we walked down the hall. A guard opened the door and we stepped outside to an explosion of flashbulbs and the glare of television lights. I had never imagined so many press people being up at 4:00 A.M. We were all grinning. We had been in quarantine for eight days. That meant we were not allowed out in public; and only select visitors, who went through strict medical exams each time they came—were allowed into the crew's quarters. Suddenly being out in public again gave me a shot of adrenalin. The astronauts were all private people and had no problem with the quarantine. I, on the other hand, had spent nearly all my adult life in politics, first as a state legislator in Florida and then as a United States congressman from the district that includes Cape Canaveral and the Kennedy Space Center. To remain quarantined from the public was a real discipline for a "people-person" like me.

Through the glaring television lights I spotted Bob Osterblum, who worked for NASA. Bob's infant son, Ryan, had made national news following a successful nationwide hunt for a liver transplant.Bob's presence at the door was a big boost for me. I flashed him my thumbs-up signal.

The crew of Columbia *on orbit. [NASA photo]*

We boarded the crew van, a modified camper designed for us and our equipment, and headed down the road toward the launch site. There was playful banter among the crew and with two other passengers in the van, George Abbey, our coordinator, and astronaut John Young.

Born in 1930, John Young was a graduate of Orlando High School and Georgia Tech. He was the first person to fly in space six times. A former Navy captain, he had retired from the Navy in 1976 after thirty-five years of active military service. At five feet nine inches tall and 165 pounds, he remained—at fifty-five years of age—in peak physical condition. He was one of the nation's top test pilots, had flown with Gus Grissom on *Gemini 3*, was command pilot on *Apollo 10*, and had walked on the moon thirteen years before with Charlie Duke. He had also been spacecraft commander on two shuttle missions—including the first flight of the *Columbia*. Since 1975 he had been chief of the Astronaut Office, controlling the activities of more than one hundred astronauts. No man in the world knew more about space than John Young. That morning he would be flying the weather plane over the Cape.

Leading and following the little procession were two security cars. Their flashing blue lights cast an eerie reflection on the faces of the other astronauts seated in the van. We were also under constant surveillance. A powerful telescopic video camera on top of the Vehicle Assembly Building (VAB) had picked us up when we left the Operations and Checkout Building (O&C) and would track us all the way to the pad. We drove past the *Saturn V* rocket that was on display at the side of the road. It was the *Saturn V* that had taken our men to the moon twenty years before. To the left I could see the Launch Control Center (LCC), a huge white building where, later in the morning, Grace, Billy, and Nan Ellen—along with the wives and children of the other crew members—would gather on the roof to watch our launch.

The procession stopped and John Young got out. Next, we dropped off George Abbey near the LCC. A car was waiting at an intersection to take John to the shuttle landing strip, where he would climb into the G-2 jet and take off to begin his morning weather surveillance. He would remain aloft until we were in orbit, continually circling the Cape to check on the weather.

The conversation grew quiet as George departed. To our left, hidden in the predawn darkness, were the 160 acres my grandfather and grandmother, Charles Hart and Jane Ellen Nelson, had homesteaded in 1915. I remembered the times when, as a boy, I had tramped over that marshy land, listening as my family told me stories of bull alligators, water moccasins, deer, and black bear. Now, from that very place I had known as a child, I was getting ready to orbit the earth.

Then, ahead I saw it—the *Columbia,* poised and ready for takeoff. It was beautiful, bathed in brilliant xenon lights. The spaceship was sparkling white, the lights picking up the brilliant colors of the American flag on the top of its stubby wings. From the side it seemed to be holding on to the huge, apricot-colored fuel tank as a koala bear hugs the trunk of a blue gum tree. On each side of the big, colorful fuel tank were the solid rocket boosters (SRBs), glistening white and reflecting the lights. The SRBs were fastened to the tank and would ignite on command to thrust us into space.

The whole rocket seemed alive. Even from three miles away I could sense its power. A huge cloud of vapor came from its innards like the breath of a giant on a winter morning.

I remembered other instances in my life when I had felt the same way. One afternoon when I was a boy, alone in the pasture on the back of my pony, for an extraordinary moment the pony and I seemed to be acting, moving, feeling as one. I had felt it another time, too, as a man, when I was climbing Mount Sinai in the predawn darkness. My companions had spread out and I was climbing alone, perhaps going up the same rocky ascent used by Moses. That morning, I had felt joined in a living, breathing union with the mountain. The psychologists call it "participation mystique," the moment a boy and his pony, a man and his mountain, or an artist and her work become one. Now, I was gripped once more. The space-ship and I were two parts of a single whole.

Far to the right of the road were the spectator bleachers where a number of my friends were shivering under blankets and coats in the intense predawn chill. I knew that Grace had arranged for a couple of buses to leave from the Hilton Hotel in Melbourne at 4:00 A.M. to carry my family and her family to the space center that morning.

We rounded a curve and ran parallel to the brown, gravel crawlway the shuttle had used when it was rolled out from the vehicle assembly building (VAB). Consisting of twin tracks separated by a green grassy strip down the middle, it was one of the most remarkable roads in the world. Wider than an eight-lane superhighway, it was designed to withstand loads previously unheard of. The road-builders had dug down nine feet, lined the bottom of the trench with large rocks, poured in seven feet of aggregate, and topped it with eight inches of super-hard pebbles imported from Alabama. The three-and-a-half-mile road had cost about 20 million dollars; its gigantic size had been necessary to support the massive tractor that held the rocket as it moved from the VAB to the pad. Slow, huge, creaking, grinding its massive cleats into the gravel, the tractor carried the entire vertical rocket on its back as it crept from its nest in the VAB to the launchpad on the edge of the world.

We continued to move in closer to the pad. I knew that after we were strapped in and the final countdown began, all safety personnel, including the firefighters, would pull back to a safety radius at least one and a half miles from the tower. From that point until lift-off, no one would be allowed to approach the rocket. We would be out there alone, the seven of us, strapped into a fragile spaceship bolted to 6.9 million thrust pounds of luminous fire.

We arrived at the launch tower early. Troy Stewart and the other suit technicians greeted us at the base of the tower. The astronauts hooted and laughed as the suit techs, wearing red-and-white Santa Claus hats and shouting, "Merry Christmas!"

opened the door of the van. The tension breaker was excellent
medicine. We all had a good laugh and boarded the creaky
elevator that took us up to Level 195—195 feet above the base
of the gantry, or platform. Since we were a few minutes early,
we had time to walk about the gantry, most of us just staring
at the beautiful spaceship. Now we were up close, the uncanny
sensation of its being alive was overwhelming. It was as if I
were standing beside a huge, resting animal. I could hear it
breathing, creaking, groaning. I wanted to linger on the gantry just to look at this magnificent machine, to gape at the
liquid hydrogen vaporizing from the nozzles of its three main
engines, and bleeding off at the top of the external tank.

Waiting in that cold, crisp, early dawn on the small, steel
grate walkway that extended from the launch tower to the door
of the shuttle, I stepped off to one side, away from the other
men. To my right was the Atlantic Ocean. To my left was the
state of Florida. I looked out over the expanse of the Cape,
toward the land where my family had put down its roots. Step-
ping aside, I moved behind a large beam and knelt on the steel
grate floor and mouthed a simple prayer thanking God for
this opportunity and asking Him to protect our mission.

Somebody was yelling for me, calling my name. It was 4:40
A.M. and time to board the spaceship.

From the tower we walked single file across the sixty-foot
gangplank called the access arm. I looked down through the
grate and could see the concrete pad, 195 feet below. To my
right, at the base of the rocket, was the huge concrete flame
pit, soon to be filled with a million gallons of water, where the
flames from the initial blast-off would roar out to the side. At
the end of the access arm was a tiny door through which we
climbed into what was known as the White Room, a room where
we were outfitted in our space suits. The suit techs here had
attached reindeer antlers to the tops of our helmets. Several of
them, dressed in their all-white suits, had polished the sides of
their white bunny booties a bright red to get us in the Christmas spirit.

I waited in line as Hoot and Charlie, our commander and pilot, boarded. Then I squeezed through the small hatch into the shuttle. The crew compartment was cramped, and I had to crawl to my seat. I had been in the shuttle mock-up many times during training at Johnson Space Center in Houston. But this time the shuttle was not horizontal; it was vertical— in takeoff position. Everything seemed strange, out of place. I had to be careful not to hit any of the hundreds of switches— all of which, fortunately, were protected by switch guards. When I was in position on my back, I was strapped into the seat. I was already wearing a prefitted harness that had my name on it. It had a chest belt and straps across the crotch. Built into the harness were two inflatable life preservers for flotation in case we came down in the ocean. Beyond that, I knew, there was no provision for escape once we were off the ground.

The hatch door banged closed. It was one hour fifty-four minutes to launch. The huge support structure had already been swung away from the shuttle, leaving the rocket standing free on the launch platform with only the narrow access arm still reaching out toward us. I imagined I heard the sound of the elevators as the men descended—leaving us alone to the task ahead.

We were now pressurized and the countdown was proceeding. I found myself reciting the Twenty-Third Psalm, which I had memorized as a boy.

The night before, most of our crew had ended up in the sauna to try to relax before we went to bed. We started talking about all the things that could go wrong—and, of course, there were many. Any crew member could accidentally unlock the door, and the pressure inside the shuttle would blow out the hatch into the vacuum of space. If we lost two of our three engines during the first seven and a half minutes of the eight-minute-thirty-six-second ascent, we would not be able to make an emergency landing and would have to try ditching in the ocean. It was clearly understood by all of us that we probably would not survive the impact of the water.

In fact, the more I thought about it, the more I became aware of the mission as an enormous interlocking web of calculated risks, any of which could prove fatal.

NASA had done its best to provide an escape system, but it was crude. If there was an emergency on the pad, we were to evacuate the ship and run across the access arm (if it was back in place) to where a set of baskets was mounted on the opposite side of the tower. Jumping in the baskets, we would hit a trip lever and slide down long cables to a concrete bunker a quarter of a mile away. If we had time once we reached the ground, we would jump in an armored personnel carrier called "the tank" and crash through the fence to safety. That procedure had been practiced in our preflight training, but all of us knew that an explosion on the pad, or in the air on takeoff, would be so devastating that no escape system could save us.

My mind raced back to January 27, 1967. About 1:00 P.M. three astronauts, Air Force Colonels Virgil "Gus" Grissom and Edward White and Navy Lieutenant Commander Roger Chaffee, had climbed into the *Apollo 1* capsule perched 218 feet above Launch Complex 34. They were undergoing a full-scale simulation of the scheduled February 21, 1967 lift-off, helping the nation reach President Kennedy's goal of landing a human on the Moon before the end of the decade. This was the first time the Apollo spacecraft was to undergo a complete checkup at its pad with the crew aboard.

The rehearsal countdown had reached ten minutes from simulated lift-off. The hatches had been sealed from the inside, and the technicians waited at the pad to practice emergency procedures if needed. At 6:31 P.M. the emergency happened.

A single spark, caused when a Teflon-coated wire struck a vent door under Grissom's left foot, ignited the capsule's pure-oxygen atmosphere. "There's a fire in the cockpit!" Ed White had screamed. In twenty-five seconds, the thousand-degree fire snuffed out the astronauts' lives—and almost extinguished the nation's space program at the same time. It was eight hours before the charred bodies of the three men were removed from the launchpad.

Former astronaut John Glenn, now a U.S. senator from Ohio, summed up the reality of the dangers astronauts face when he said, "Everybody is aware of the danger. . . . You feel it's important enough to take the risk, and that's the way the people feel here. Everybody's aware that in anything when you're using power, speed, and complexity the way we are, somebody's bound to get hurt sometime."

Although all the other missions had been carried out without fatal accident, the *Apollo 13* mission almost ended in disaster when an oxygen tank exploded two days into the flight to the moon, and the astronauts barely made it back to earth, relying on the lunar lander that was on board to sustain them. And while all twenty-three of the shuttle flights had returned safely, the astronauts knew the many things that had gone wrong—things the public knew nothing about, that could have caused a tragedy far worse than the one that killed Grissom, White, and Chaffee. The solid rocket boosters, the main engines, the computerized flight controls, the silica heat resistant tiles—all had to work nearly perfectly for a safe mission.

Were we operating on borrowed time, as many of the astronauts suspected? Or, had the technical ability of NASA become so practiced that a mission like ours was now simply a matter of routine? Lying on my back in the shuttle, I wondered.

Listening to the chatter on my earphones, I looked around as everyone went through their final checks. Above me were banks of lockers. The containers for my blood experiment were over to my left. My apparatus with the proteins for the crystal growth project was in the top locker. My clothing locker, numbered MF71K and color-coded to my assigned color, purple, was to my right. Above it was apparatus for some medical DSO experiments. Right in front of me was the treadmill I planned to use for my cardiopulmonary experiments. Bob was on my right. Franklin was at my left.

I glanced at my watch. I knew that Grace had arrived at the center and would be getting ready, along with the wives of the other astronauts, to gather on the roof of the LCC. I struggled with my mixed feelings. We were scheduled to return to earth on December 24 and land at Kennedy Space Center. I very much wanted to take off on schedule but could not shake the thought that a day's delay would mean spending Christmas in space. I gave an involuntary shrug. That decision was no longer mine to make.

Again, I was conscious of how "alive" the spaceship seemed to be. Now, strapped in the bowels of the great animal, I could hear its body sounds—the circulation of the fluids, the groaning and creaking of the skeleton, the slurping sounds of liquids and gases moving through the miles of pipes and tubes. The ship seemed to be breathing deeply, as a runner at the blocks inhales and exhales to prepare his lungs for the race.

Twisting my head, I could see light coming through the small window in the side hatch. Visibility seemed good. I wanted to be able to see everything when we blasted off. I knew John Young was up there somewhere, circling and checking the weather for us. It was a good feeling—all those people taking care of us.

From time to time there was more chatter and laughter on the intercom. At six o'clock someone said there would be a wake-up call in fifty-five minutes and we wouldn't sleep through it. Everyone laughed into their mikes.

Thirty minutes away from the launch, we got a call from Launch Control. We were on time and would go down to T-9 minutes and hold there to see what the weather was going to do. I thought about all those people out there who had come so far to see the lift-off. I didn't want them to be disappointed, and in that moment, I understood all too well the public pressure that was on NASA to get the bird in the air. No one wants to look bad, even if it's the weather that causes the delay. I breathed another prayer of thanks that NASA had never—to my knowledge—let that kind of pressure determine whether they should proceed with a launch or not.

And as I lay strapped in my harness atop that huge incendiary, my fate in the hands of others, I knew, too, the deep concern all astronauts must feel for their loved ones. I was no different. My mind raced outside the vehicle to Billy and Nan Ellen. And to Grace.

The countdown reached T-9, and we went into an automatic hold. The weather had closed in. The overcast was thickening. We heard John Young on the radio talking from his plane as he circled above the shuttle landing strip eight miles north. Minutes ticked by until the hold had extended beyond a half hour. I knew the people out there in the stands were freezing. Then, Hoot Gibson and Charlie Bolden said they saw blue patches of sky from their seats next to the front windows. Someone shouted into the mike of the crew intercom, "Come on, John, give us the go!"

I was surprised how relaxed I was. At one point I almost dozed off. Word came through my earphones that our "launch window"—the allowable time to launch in order to get into proper orbit—was forty-nine minutes. However, we had to deduct forty seconds for a "collision avoidance." How ironic that space had become so crowded we had to wait, as if at a four-way stop sign, for the Soviet space station *Salyut 7* to pass by because it had the right of way. I had been excited, for we had hatched a plan for me to talk with the cosmonauts while both crews were on orbit. It was a symbolic gesture that earthly adversaries could indeed cooperate in space, even though we may not be very successful at cooperating on Earth. The cosmonauts, however, were not in *Salyut.* The Soviet commander had become ill, and the cosmonauts had returned to earth.

Mission Control in Houston came over the earphones once again. They had extended the launch window to 8:10 A.M. That gave us forty-seven minutes. My tailbone was beginning to hurt from lying on my back. I decided to get involved in the conversation and asked Hoot how many technical people were supporting us.

"None," he laughed. "We're all alone out here. They've all left the pad, and there's not a soul within one and a half miles."

Finally, the weather broke. John gave us the go, and the countdown resumed. I cinched up my seat harness, and at T-minus-4 minutes we lowered our visors and began breathing oxygen stored on the orbiter and piped through our helmets. I reached back for the knob that tightened the entire helmet on my head so as to ensure a tight seal. Almost automatically, my left hand fingered the switch on the emergency air supply I would use if I needed to switch from orbiter oxygen.

On cue, the access arm retracted and we were freestanding on the pad.

I could feel the movement of the spaceship under me as the computer program gimballed the engine nozzles and checked the flight control surfaces. I could feel the huge engine nozzles moving.

At T-31 seconds we reached a critical point, because it was then that the automatic countdown switched to *Columbia*'s four on-board computers, with a fifth serving as a backup. From there on, we were in a "go" configuration.

I turned back the sleeve of my left glove so that I could look at my watch, a nineteen-dollar stopwatch set to start at zero countdown. Within seconds the three engines in the tail of the shuttle would ignite. If they didn't throttle up properly, the computer would shut them off automatically before the solid rocket boosters ignited. The solid rocket boosters—the two big Roman candles on either side of the orbiter—have to ignite at precisely the same moment. If they don't—if there is as much as a second's delay—then one booster would thrust while the other remained idle, causing the freestanding rocket to cartwheel into a giant fireball. Once the solid rocket boosters ignite, that's it. You can't shut them off. An explosion on the pad, or following takeoff, would mean I was on my way not to outer space but to eternity. I wasn't sure I liked trusting my life to a computer.

At T-25 seconds I felt my body began to brace for the ignition of the main engines, which would occur at T-6.6 seconds. My teeth were clenched. I tried to relax my jaw, but when I concentrated on my jaw muscles, I felt my whole body tighten. All I could do from that point was hang on.

"T minus twenty seconds."

"T minus fifteen seconds.

At T-14 seconds a computer flashed a signal to the launch control center: Something was wrong. The first indications were that a hydraulic pressure unit in one of the solid rocket boosters was faulty.

Launch Control said we had been recycled back to T-9 minutes. I felt my stomach sink. Surely, we hadn't come this close— only fourteen seconds from blast-off—to quit? At first I thought we could still make a lift-off because our launch window extended to 8:10 A.M. But reality sank in, and I realized the launch would have to be rescheduled. Hoot and Charlie were as professional and cool as anyone I had ever seen. Without skipping a beat, they immediately began shutting down the spacecraft. I sat silently, numb. To have gotten that close . . .

The access arm swung back into place, and the launch tower's automatic water sprinkling system turned on to quench any fires. We waited, and much later clambered out of the shuttle to return to our quarters. Since NASA assumed the hydraulic power turbine unit would have to be replaced, they decided to give the space center launch team a rest for the Christmas holidays and reset our launch for January 6. We were to report back to Houston on December 30 to begin quarantine.

It was several days later before I learned what NASA had discovered. Investigation by NASA engineers determined there was nothing wrong with the hydraulic power unit (HPU). The problem involved a faulty sensor sending the wrong signal to the computer.

By noon I was on a NASA flight to Washington, D.C., where I would be on time for votes in the closing session of Congress. That afternoon I would address the House of Representatives on what I had just experienced. But making the switch from astronaut back to congressman was one of the more difficult things I had ever done.

On Hold

As we left the launchpad in the crew van, we picked up George Abbey where we had dropped him off four hours before. He said he thought the problem lay in a faulty sensor, and that we would probably go the next day. We drove back to our crew quarters, where we had another breakfast—this time, oatmeal, rye toast, and orange marmalade. During breakfast we got the word that the problem was not a sensor but a faulty hydraulic power unit that overspeeded the turbine. The technicians were going to have to exchange it.

"That means," George Abbey said with a grin, "you are all free to spend Christmas with your families. We'll want you to report back to Houston on December 30 to resume quarantine. Of course, you'll maintain your training schedule through the holidays."

I flew back to Washington before the final session of Congress adjourned that night for Christmas. Even while I was in training at Johnson Space Center in Houston, I had tried to return to Washington to attend every congressional vote pos-

sible. I knew, of course, that I would have to miss many votes
while I was in quarantine and in space. Now, the scrub meant
I could catch the NASA plane back to Washington and be on
time for a series of votes on the reconciliation bill that would
cut $83 billion of spending out of the federal budget. The first
vote was scheduled for 2:30 that afternoon.

By noon I was aboard *NASA 1*, sitting in the backseat beside
Jesse Moore. I faced additional frustration when the control-
lers at Washington's National Airport would not give us a direct approach on landing, but put us into a holding pattern.
That caused me to miss the preliminary vote on the continu-
ing resolution bill by ten minutes.

A member of our staff met me at the airport, and I was able
to get to the House floor by 2:45 P.M. A vote was then in progress on the reconciliation bill. After the vote, from the Majority Table, I asked unanimous consent to proceed out of order
and share with my colleagues what had happened that morning.

Afterward, Ike Pappas of CBS interviewed me for the evening news. Instead of asking me about the technical aspects of
the mission, he seemed more interested in my feelings. I told
him that I seemed to express the sentiment of all the astronauts when I shouted up to Hoot, "I don't want to unstrap
and get out of my seat. Let's go!"

I was unwilling to leave the congressional floor because there
was a significant difference of opinion between the Senate and
the House over a proposed value-added tax. The big vote could
come at any time, and the bill kept being stalled into the night.
By 10:00 P.M., however, sheer fatigue was making me lose touch
with reality. I accepted an offer from a fellow congressman to
spend the night at his nearby apartment. I had just started to
climb into bed at 11:00 P.M., when he called back and said
another vote was in progress. I put my clothes on and walked
back to the Capitol building, doing my best to keep my eyes
on the traffic in the street and not look up into the sky, where

I felt I should really be—circling the earth every ninety minutes. The session continued until 1:00 A.M., and I finally crashed on my fellow congressman's couch for eight hours of sleep. I had been up for twenty-three hours. Friday morning I caught an Eastern Airlines flight back to Melbourne, Florida, so I could spend the day in my district office before going home to fall exhausted into my own bed. The weekend would be spent with Grace and the children.

The next ten days were Dickensian: the best of times and the worst of times. They were the best because it meant being with my family over Christmas. They were the worst because even though my body was still on earth, my spirit was past ready for outer space. In my mind and in my dreams, I was still sitting out there on Pad 39-A, waiting for lift-off. Grace knew this, and so did the children. They did everything they could to make it easy for me.

Unfortunately, however, my ten-year-old son, Billy, came down with the flu. I checked with Dr. Ken Beckman, who said Billy had a virus that had been going around the county and caused nothing worse than head and body aches, fever, and upset stomach. I was concerned for Billy, but realized I was far more concerned about myself. The KSC doctor had told me to stay away from anyone contagious. If I did catch the flu, I would know in about ten days, and the virus would probably last for about five days. That would mean I would be knocked out of the launch—they would never risk having me back in quarantine if I were sick, much less have me and my germs isolated in the shuttle for the duration of the flight.

Grace and I talked it over. Our plans were to spend Christmas with her folks in Jacksonville. We decided I should rent a car and drive up separately. I could not put myself in jeopardy by riding in an enclosed car for 180 miles with my family, all of whom had been exposed to Billy's virus.

Everyplace I went I could hear people coughing and sneezing. I stayed out of crowds, and at the gathering on Christmas night with Grace's extended family—a group of about fifty people—I felt I had no choice but to wear a surgical mask. The children thought it was hilarious, and I felt like a fool. (Despite my efforts, I still caught a mild virus. However, it lasted only a couple of days, and the only aftereffect was some physical weakness. I quickly regained my strength when I started back into my training cycle.)

Alone in the rented car as I drove up to Jacksonville, I tried to analyze what I had learned since the scrub. It was hard to pull all the pieces together. For months I had prepared for launch day, going through intensive training in Houston and at KSC, separated from my family; living my dual existence as astronaut and congressman; preparing physically, mentally, and emotionally to orbit the earth. Now, it was December 23, the day we should have been approaching our descent. But instead of traveling 17,795 miles an hour, 203 miles above the earth, I was in a rented Chevrolet driving north on I-95.

What had I learned from this?

For one, I had learned something about my ability to react to adverse conditions. I discovered I could still get uptight and anxious. I discovered, too, that the stress had left me exhausted.

But there was also one obvious and fundamental discovery: NASA's systems are exceptional. The automatic sequencer, for instance (the computer working during the countdown), had successfully detected a signal of the hydraulic power unit overrevving in its turbine and had cut off the countdown. Had the hydraulic unit failed, it could have completely thrown off the gimballs on the nozzles of the SRBs, which would have thrown us off course once we launched, and caused a disaster. For me this was a clear confirmation of the basic competence of the system. Errors could creep in—as we were later to learn—but fundamentally, the NASA program is an extraordinary feat of complexity and design.

I had a new appreciation of that unheralded team of NASA technicians who developed and operated the various systems.

The professionalism of America's space team, both launch and mission support people, is truly remarkable.

The professionalism of the crew continued to amaze me. There had been no hint of disappointment in Hoot and Charlie's voices as they read out their checklists over the air-to-ground radio, coolly and methodically going through their procedures for shutting down the spaceship. They followed a lengthy list of instructions to push buttons, flip switches, and read data from the on-board computer screens. It was not until they had finished and were eating breakfast that they expressed any personal disappointment. I had learned from them and knew I was a better man for it.

I also had new respect for the other astronauts, the men and women who wait for years outside the limelight for the opportunity for spaceflight. I had become impatient after waiting only a few months, but these men and women had been preparing and waiting for years. The frustrations they felt when passed over for a mission crew had to be enormous.

From the lessons I had learned, I made some new resolves. One was the resolve of self-discipline. Even though my body nearly collapsed from exhaustion after the scrub, I knew it was possible to bounce back if I was in good physical shape. We had lost the chance to launch on December 19, but I was determined to do my part to see that we made our next deadline. Of course, I could not do this by myself; in fact, I knew I was but a minor player in the carefully orchestrated space team. But if I was out of tune, the entire "orchestra" would suffer. Thus, despite the fact I had Christmas at home, I was determined to discipline myself through the holidays and maintain physical conditioning.

I soon learned that astronauts get a lot of attention. Senator Jake Garn, who had flown on an earlier shuttle flight, told me of the struggle he had had with his newfound celebrity status after he returned from space. He spoke of an encounter at a fish fry with a lady who came up and wanted his autograph for her child. "The woman wasn't at all interested in the fact I was a United States senator," Garn laughed. "She wanted her child to have the autograph of an astronaut."

I had experienced the same thing myself when I walked into the congressional chamber the afternoon after our scrubbed flight. The Congress had given me a standing ovation—and I hadn't done any more, so far, than be strapped in a shuttle that hadn't moved an inch.

Getting Ready

Almost all the high-school students in America today have been born since we landed on the moon. As a result, most of America's youth take the space program for granted. Things were different when I was growing up.

As a boy, I never dreamed of being an astronaut. Even though I grew up in the shadow of Cape Canaveral where the names John Glenn, Al Shepard, and Deke Slayton were part of daily conversation, I never thought I would fly in space. I wanted to be in government.

I was in high school when the Soviets orbited the first satellite, *Sputnik*. Our nation united behind its own space program, and finally, after several failed attempts with a Vanguard rocket, we succeeded with an Army Redstone rocket in launching the first American satellite, *Explorer*.

It was an exciting time for me as a student at Melbourne High School, just twenty miles south of Cape Canaveral. The eyes of the nation were focused on Brevard County, Florida. Many of the children of the Cape's scientists and technicians were my classmates. Because of an innovative high-school principal who knew how to obtain foundation money, Melbourne High School was ranked as one of the ten best high schools in the country.

Even as a student I knew our nation was entering a new era. The state of Florida, long known for its citrus and beaches, and often called the vacationland of the nation, was being thrust into an age of high technology. We could be, literally, the launchpad for the future of the world.

Like most Americans, I was listening as we launched *Apollo 11* to the moon. As a first lieutenant in the Army, I was on leave in Hungary and had to travel to the highest hill outside of Budapest with my short-wave radio to tune in to the BBC, which cut in to NASA Control. I was a proud patriot that day behind the Iron Curtain as I cheered the sound of the *Saturn V* rocket lift-off.

And, like most Americans, I stayed up late on July 20, 1969, watching on television what was taking place 240,000 miles away. Mission commander Neil Armstrong, clad in his bulky spacesuit and reflective helmet, lumbered down the ladder of the lunar module and stepped onto the moon—fulfilling President Kennedy's mandate to land a man on the moon before the end of the decade. I listened as he planted his foot on the dusty surface of that dead globe and said, "That's one small step for man, and one giant leap for mankind." The success of the *Apollo 11* mission signaled the end of one space era and the beginning of another.

Curiously, my own roots had become entangled with the roots of the space pioneers when, in 1915, my paternal grandparents had homesteaded on land that is now the Kennedy Space Center. Back then, under the Homestead Act, if you "squatted" on the land for two years, the government would deed the real estate to you. No one really wanted that mosquito- and snake-infested land on north Merritt Island. My grandparents were brave enough to settle on it and build a house,

The natural Florida landscape at the Kennedy Space Center as interpreted by artist Kent Sullivan. [Photo courtesy Congressman Nelson]

swatting mosquitos and fending off rattlesnakes. That property is now adjacent to the north end of the space shuttle runway at KSC.

My family first moved to the panhandle of Florida in 1829. When I asked my ninety-seven-year-old maternal grandmother if she had ever thought of spaceflight when she heard of the Wright brothers' airplane in 1903, she replied that no one could imagine such things back then. Next, I asked her if she ever thought that her grandson would be flying in space. She quickly replied no, and allowed as how she didn't want him up there, either.

When I left the Florida State Legislature and was elected to the U.S. Congress in 1978, I was assigned a seat on the House Science and Technology Committee—which has jurisdiction over the nation's space program—including the aerospace activity at the Kennedy Space Center and at the Air Force's Eastern Test Range, which was part of my congressional district.

Then, in 1981, the nation began a new chapter of space exploration as it launched the shuttle. I was in the congressional delegation that came down from Washington to see the launch and landing. The group was so elated at the technological achievement that we spontaneously burst out singing "God Bless America" when the *Columbia* landed. In 1983, a NASA task force reported on the possibility of carrying private citizens on space shuttle missions. The idea that ordinary citizens—those not part of the professional astronaut corps—might go on future journeys into space immediately fired my imagination.

The report by NASA administrator Jim Beggs concluded that it would be feasible to fly such persons by the mid-1980s, when seats would be available and individuals could be flown without undue risk to crew safety or to the mission. Furthermore, the report stated, it was desirable to fly observers on the shuttle to increase the public's understanding of spaceflight.

The Space Act passed by Congress had authorized NASA to provide the "widest . . . dissemination of information concerning NASA activities. . . ." Beggs's task force concluded that flying observers would meet the intent of the law.

NASA realized that the moment their recommendation was made public, people by the thousands would be applying to go into space. Therefore, the task force recommended that among the first should be an observer-communicator who would provide written and verbal reports of the flight in order to communicate this experience to the public or apply it in classroom teaching. According to the report, the candidate should be—

· highly motivated to fly on the shuttle as evidenced by how he or she would use this opportunity;
· able to accomplish one hundred hours of training;
· pass both medical and mental examinations;
· able to adapt to the living quarters and working relationships required by a mission;
· willing to accept federal employment during mission-related activities, including the waiving of personal profits as a result of the flight.

In looking over these qualifications, I realized I could meet them all. It seemed to me that shuttle guests would fall into three categories: engineers for private companies with cargo aboard the shuttle; foreign dignitaries interested in cooperating with us in joint projects; and special communicators, such as teachers, journalists, and those politicians who had specific reason to fly into space—other than to take the ultimate junket.

The task force stated that rigorous qualifications would be set. In addition to the medical and psychological screening, they recommended orientation rides in high-performance aircraft, high-stress training exams, and emergency procedure drills. Whether I was ever selected or not, I knew I should begin the process of getting ready. I started training and decided to learn everything I could about the space program. That meant more than simply reading books and visiting the Cape. If I was going to speak about the space program accurately in Congress, I wanted to feel what the astronauts felt.

I started a regimen of physical conditioning that included running at least four miles every day, plus workouts in the gym. I also flew in America's hottest high-performance aircraft to accustom myself to a stressful physical environment. In an Air Force F-16 jet, flying over the bombing test range in south Florida, I asked the pilot to pull the max Gs—that is, to put the plane into a maneuver that would make me feel a centrifugal force many times the force of gravity. As a boy I had attended carnival shows and ridden in various rides that flatten you out or crush you into your seat. But they were nothing compared to what the pilot did to me that afternoon as I was riding in the backseat of the F-16. For fifteen seconds in a left turn, we pulled nine times gravity. The pressure was so intense that my oxygen mask was sagging off my face.

Later, in an Air Force F-15, with afterburners thrusting, the pilot pulled straight up, and I experienced the tremendous exhilaration of vertical flight—flying straight up toward the heavens.

I wrote a letter to the NASA chief requesting to fly but did not talk to top NASA officials because I did not want there to be a perception that I was using political pressure. I heard nothing for two years, but continued training just the same. In my heart I knew the opportunity would eventually present itself.

Following the 1984 elections, NASA announced it was going to limit the number of congressional participants on the shuttle to four. Those who would be considered were the two Republican chairmen of the Senate subcommittees that have jurisdiction over the space program, and their counterparts in the House of Representatives—the two Democratic chairmen of the House subcommittees. The first invitation to be extended was to Republican Senator Jake Garn of Utah, an experienced pilot.

It was well known on Capitol Hill that the two people in Congress who wanted to fly were Jake Garn and myself. Now Jake had his chance.

At that time, I was only a member of the House Subcom-

Bill Nelson in training, about to take a check ride in an Air Force F-15 jet fighter aircraft. [Photo courtesy Congressman Nelson]

U.S. Senator Jake Garn, a payload specialist aboard Discovery, *STS-51D.*
[NASA photo]

mittee on Space Science and Applications—not the chairman. But the chairman had announced his intention to accept the leadership of another subcommittee, and I was next in line to fill that spot. The election of the subcommittee chairman takes place at the beginning of each new Congress and is done by a caucus of those Democrats on the Science and Technology Committee. Election is according to seniority and is usually routine.

Much to my frustration, a week before the election, a senior member of the full committee decided to give up the subcommittee chairmanship he held on another committee and take the chairmanship of the Space Subcommittee. I was crushed. Just when it seemed I might be in line to take over the subcommittee's leadership—a position I really wanted, since the space center is in my district—it seemed to be snatched away from me. I was deeply disappointed. I also knew I had to be chairman to be considered for flight in the shuttle. Under the House rules, the senior committee member had the right to do what he announced—but I knew I had no choice but to oppose him. I had been patiently waiting my turn for the leadership of this subcommittee.

Breaking with precedent in the Democratic caucus, I challenged him and forced the issue to a vote. When the vote was taken, despite the institutional preference for seniority, I won.

I waited several months after Senator Garn completed his flight in April 1985, then went to see NASA chief Jim Beggs. Beggs told me he was planning for me to fly, and an invitation would be forthcoming. I received the following:

Honorable Bill Nelson, Chairman   September 6, 1985
Subcommittee on Space Science and Applications
Committee on Science and Technology

Dear Mr. Chairman:

As you know, the space shuttle has long enjoyed the support of Congress and, in particular, your support both as a Member of the Committee on Science and Technology and as chairman of the Subcommittee on Space Science and Applications. Given your NASA oversight responsibilities, we think it appropriate that you consider making an inspection tour and flight aboard the shuttle.

We believe the shuttle to be the space transportation system of the future, capable of meeting all presently projected NASA and DOD, as well as foreign and commercial, requirements. It will provide the means by which the United States will maintain its world leadership in space, providing capabilities to build a space station and explore commercial opportunities.

While we will be flying quite often in the coming year, we will have to work out with you a mutually acceptable date. There will be a relatively short period of training which we can work out between your office and the Johnson Space Center to fit your schedule.

As you know, we do require that individuals flying with us develop an appropriate experiment or activity in pursuit of the objective of furthering the overall program. We would appreciate your giving consideration to the activity that you would like to pursue.

The maturing of the space transportation system to the point where we can fly private citizens, as well as engineers from private companies and representatives of foreign governments, is, of course, the beginning of a broadened participation in our space program by many in the United States and abroad. It will culminate with the development of the permanently manned space station in the 1990s. It is therefore appropriate for those with congressional oversight to have flight opportunities to gain a personal awareness and familiarity, and because of your well-known interest, we are pleased to invite you to fly.

Please advise as soon as possible of your availability, and we will work together on the necessary arrangements.

Sincerely

James M. Beggs
Administrator
National Aeronautics and
Space Administration

At the same time, because of President Reagan's interest in the program, America's first civilian in space was also being chosen. The president had requested that a schoolteacher be the first bona fide civilian to fly. The selection committee finally decided to invite Christa McAuliffe, an elementary-school teacher from Concord, New Hampshire, with Barbara Morgan from McCall, Idaho as her backup.

I agreed with the President that her selection would enthuse an entire generation of American students about space technology because they could identify with her as an ordinary schoolteacher. Through their fascination with spaceflight, they would develop new interest in science, math, and technology—all subjects in which our country has been woefully lacking. It is no secret that America is far behind the leading technological nations in producing our share of mathematicians, scientists, and engineers.

I would add, parenthetically, that I strongly support the program that calls for Barbara Morgan, Christa McAuliffe's backup, to fly in the shuttle now. There are many mixed feelings about this project—not the least of them having to do with Barbara's safety and NASA's image if there was to be another accident. However, I feel Barbara should be allowed to fly to fulfill a promise to American schoolchildren that a teacher will "teach the classrooms of America from space."

Cynics will scoff at this notion, but there is much to gain from the Teacher in Space Program. Barbara has completed her training, although it would be necessary to do much of it all over again, and she and the other finalists are willing. Like the other astronauts, they all realized the danger when they volunteered.

However, I have changed my mind about other civilians in space. There will be plenty of opportunities after the space station becomes operational for journalists, artists, writers, and other observer-communicators to fly. For now, they should wait, even though interest in riding the shuttle remains at an all-time high. (A nationwide poll by *USA Today* one year after the *Challenger* disaster discovered the percentage of those who would ride the shuttle was down only slightly from the program's early days—46 percent in a 1982 NBC/AP poll, compared to 43 percent in January 1987.)

Thus, I agree with current NASA chief James Fletcher that only astronauts should fly as the flights resume. My one exception, of course, is Barbara Morgan, who should, for the sake of America's schoolchildren, be aboard one of the missions. By and large, however, as NASA recovers, with limited resources and only a few manned vehicles, flying the shuttle and conducting the experiments must be a job for full-time professional astronauts. Pilot astronauts are trained to fly the spacecraft. Mission specialists—each an expert in his or her discipline—are trained to operate the myriad systems on board and to conduct the experiments. This is as it should be for the forseeable future until new technology, new machines, and many more missions take place. Then, the call can go out again for additional "payload specialists."

No doubt it will sound like a self-serving declaration on my part to say that no more politicians should fly soon. But reality has overtaken perception. Senator Garn and I were invited to fly as chairmen of the respective space subcommittees in the Senate and House at a time when most NASA management thought that the shuttle had become "operational." The risk was considered acceptable and the flight opportunities were many.

Other invitations went out to many aerospace firms, offering to fly one of their engineers or scientists as a gesture of goodwill for giving NASA the business of launching a satellite. It was, in essence, a free ride. The exceptions were Charlie Walker of McDonnell Douglas, who was the acknowledged expert on the process of electrophoresis, and a few other scientists on specialized missions. At least for the forseeable future, however, these specialists should come from the ranks of the full-time astronaut corps and not from the civilian sector.

In 1985, of course, it was all very different. NASA said I should begin thinking about the experiments I would like to conduct. I responded that I wanted to select carefully those experiments that would need an experimenter's unlimited attention on orbit—experiments that had not always been possible for the professional astronauts who flew and operated the spacecraft. I was pleased that NASA had given me a choice.

Training

Today's astronauts don't have to be super athletes. The shuttle offers a relatively benign environment that makes it possible to place everyday people into orbit. At no time during shuttle flight, for instance, is one required to do fifty pull-ups. But it does take stamina to perform several days of intense experiments in microgravity; naturally, being in top physical shape makes it easier. I was glad I had begun running years before the flight. There would have been too little time for physical preparation had I waited until the opportunity finally arrived. As it was, the training began as the first session of the ninety-ninth Congress was winding down to a very busy finish.

I knew the training would be demanding and I knew that good physical conditioning plays a major role in maintaining mental alertness and emotional stability. The training NASA required would pack years of learning into a few months, and move me a quantum leap ahead in my knowledge of America's space program.

I realized that my assignment to a mission, the timing of the

40

flight, would become an important issuc for me. I talked with Jim Beggs and told him that my best time to fly—to allow me time to vote in Congress on important bills I knew were coming up—would be in December 1985 or early January 1986. Beggs promised to do his best, suggesting I might have more time for preparation on the flight of the *Challenger,* scheduled for January.

The extensive preparation needed to become a payload specialist began with a make-it-or-break-it physical examination at the Johnson Space Center, the home of the astronauts. I could hardly sleep the night before. It was 12:40 A.M. before I finished filling out the medical forms in the hotel room. I prayed that I didn't have some hidden problem that would force me off the flight. Again, there was nothing I could do but hope for good results.

Early the next morning, after fasting for the required twelve hours, I reported to the clinic at JSC. A technician drew a lot of blood and sent me off for my cardiopulmonary exam—all calibrated by computer. The stress test began with my running on a level treadmill. The machine slowly sped up and tilted more and more uphill. It wore me out, even though I had been running daily for more than three years. Sixteen electrodes were stuck to my chest and back, along with a blood pressure tourniquet that checked my blood pressure every minute of the run and while I was cooling down. I also breathed into a mouthpiece that calibrated my oxygen intake and my carbon dioxide exhalation.

The run was fun compared to the next step—the proctoscopic exam. NASA, thank goodness, no longer used the old-style proctoscope that was about the size of the handle of a pool cue, and almost as long. Their state-of-the-art proctoscope was smaller and flexible, equipped with laser and computer enhancement. It showed clearly the inside of my colon. Although I was uncomfortable, I was able to look up from my awkward and embarrassing position and actually see the inside of my colon as the proctoscope flashed its findings on the TV

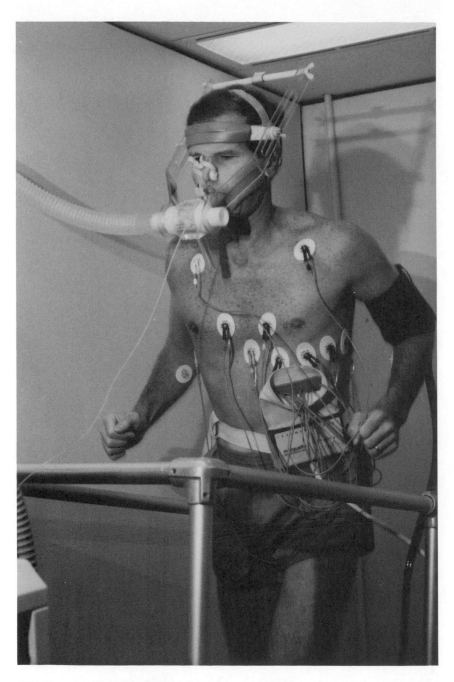

The stress test. [NASA photo]

screen before me. The doctors and nurses confirmed that the proctoscopic examination was everyone's least favorite, but it was often requested by NASA personnel since President Reagan's bout with colon cancer.

After an eye test, a hearing test, and a written psychological questionnaire were completed, I was told to get ready for "the bag." I had already heard about this experiment from others and was expecting to be closed up in a small bag for four hours to see if I would go nuts from claustrophobia. It was explained, however, that the bag was a facsimile of the Personal Rescue Sphere, an inflated ball thirty-six inches in diameter, similar to those vinyl bean bags people sometimes have in their dens to relax on. In case an emergency in space made it necessary to send up a rescue shuttle, the bag would be used to transfer the astronauts, one at a time, from the disabled shuttle through outer space to the rescue vehicle. Only two space suits were kept on board the shuttle, and they would be worn by the astronauts responsible for ferrying people to safety. The rest of us would crawl, one at a time, into this round, windowed bean bag. We'd be supplied with oxygen, zipped up, and then pulled by a tether from our spaceship to the rescue shuttle—guided by the two men wearing space suits.

I was delighted to learn that there was a real purpose for the bag. There was little chance a second shuttle could be launched in time to save the crew, but just the existence of the bag held out some hope of rescue for future flights, if an emergency were to happen. I crawled through the opening, was outfitted with electrocardiogram sensors, and was zipped into total darkness. My knees were up to my chin, and my arms were around my legs in a fetal position. It was as if I were back in a dark womb, only this time the umbilical cord ran to my chest sensors rather than my belly button. I realized I was going to be there for a while, so I relaxed and started to doze off. The men monitoring my condition apparently concluded from my slumber that I was not claustrophobic, and they terminated the test.

Those minutes of undisturbed rest were the last I would have for several days. The majority of my pretraining tests were finished that Monday, and that night I caught a flight from Houston to Denver, where I caught up on my congressional duties.

Tuesday, I chaired a field hearing of the Space Subcommittee at the University of Colorado campus in Boulder, and then toured Martin Marietta's aerospace plant in Denver. Afterward, the subcommittee members went inside Cheyenne Mountain at the North American Air Defense Command Center under eighteen hundred feet of solid granite, where General Herres, the NORAD commander and Space Command leader, briefed our committee on America's early warning system.

Our nation's Department of Defense is a major user of NASA technology. Defense systems such as surveillance satellites, highly accurate satellite positioning and directional systems, and enhanced radar all were developed from NASA research.

Thursday, I flew back to Washington because the Congress was back in session and working on farm legislation. That evening, I eagerly returned to Johnson Space Center.

The last medical hurdle, on Friday, was the psychiatric exam. I had never been to a psychiatrist before, but it turned out to be one of the most engaging two hours I ever spent. Dr. McGuire was warm, friendly, and articulate. He had interviewed all the astronaut candidates since the early space days, so his experience was enormous. It showed.

As we talked, I tried to analyze his analysis—picking up the trends of his questions and the consistency of the conversation. It was a fun game. Afterward, he told me I had passed the test in the first fifteen minutes, and he had used the following two hours of questions merely to corroborate his conclusions.

I recalled the old political joke about the candidate who had been discharged from the army, years before, with a ten-percent mental disability. He quipped that he was the only candidate in the race who had a certificate to prove he was ninety-

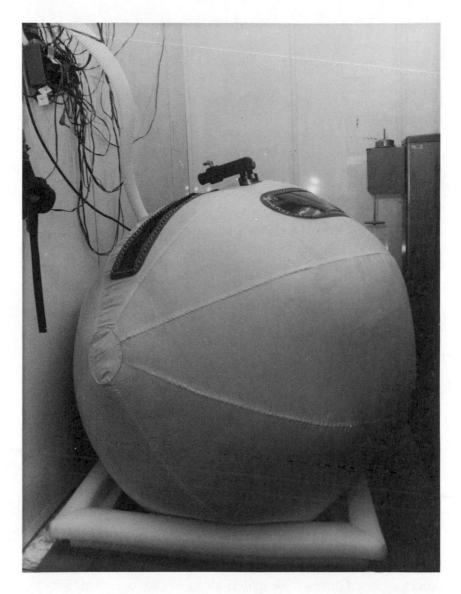

Personal Rescue Sphere for astronauts aboard a stranded space shuttle. The PRS, which is 36 inches in diameter, is also known as "The Bag" in a test for claustrophobia. [NASA photo]

percent sane. Now, at least, despite my desire to fly in space, I had the official seal of approval.

Long before that day I had known it was possible the Pentagon might inform me that a major defense contract had been awarded to my district. Now, of all the times to have to attend to congressional duties, the call came right in the middle of the psychiatric exam. I had been waiting for months for the announcement, wanting it to coincide with the further announcement that Grumman was going to locate its new plant in my hometown of Melbourne. I had even prearranged for city officials and the Chamber of Commerce to be notified, and as a result they were called to gather at the Melbourne Hilton for my announcement. But instead of being there in person, as I had hoped, my announcement was now going to have to be made by speaker phone.

I asked Dr. McGuire if we might recess the examination long enough for me to make the phone call. He had never had an interruption quite like this before, but he willingly obliged. He merely requested to listen in on my end. Once the call had been completed, we resumed the exam. He confessed it had been a diverting break from his rather routine task of examining astronauts.

So much for all the poking, prodding, and questioning. The remainder of the day was spent being measured for the myriad items of space gear I would use during the flight. Besides the familiar light blue flight suit, astronauts carry a number of items with them on board the shuttle. These include slacks; several dark blue, short-sleeved shirts with collars; short pants; and a jacket. Gloves were issued along with wool slipper-socks, a personal kit of toiletries, a knife and flashlight, scissors, pens, a leg-mounted clipboard, and small tape recorder. NASA had thought of most everything.

The next item, an orange G suit, was familiar to me from previous flights in high-performance aircraft. But this time its purpose would be a bit different. In the microgravity of space, blood tends to rise from the legs into the torso and head. Flight physicians require astronauts to wear a G suit during reentry into Earth's gravity to prevent blackouts caused by blood rushing from the brain back into the legs. The bright orange suit was fitted to me and inflated for tests.

The space helmet was a marvel of engineering. It was in two parts, hinged at the top and latched behind the ears. It was attached to an oxygen supply, and the interior formed a perfect seal around the face to keep the pure oxygen in and any noxious gases out. It was to be worn during launch and reentry and contained a communications system.

My biggest surprise came when I tasted space food. I had expected it to be bland; instead, it was quite tasty. Many of the foods were actually available on grocery store shelves. Seventy-two different food items were available, ranging from beef Stroganoff with noodles, to Mexican scrambled eggs, to shrimp cocktail. The dietitian told me I was allowed to design my own menu so I would not have to eat foods I did not ordinarily like. Each crew member would be supplied with three balanced meals a day, providing 2,800 calories with all the recommended dietary allowances of vitamins and minerals necessary to perform in the environment of space.

I was particularly impressed by the packaging for the food. The rehydratable items were sealed in square, nestable containers designed to maximize storage space. Each individual package, such as sweet-and-sour chicken, had been precooked and all the water removed. Then it had been sealed in a small, rigid, plastic bowl with a flexible, see-through film lid. Mealtime preparation was simple: Water was introduced into the package without breaking the seal through a hollow needle inserted in a septum in the base of the cup. After the water had mixed with the food and the food had been reconstituted, it could be heated in a convection oven in the galley. (A microwave oven was not available on the shuttle because it used too much electrical power.) When it was ready, all you had to do was remove the package lid with a knife or scissors and eat with conventional utensils—knife, fork, and spoon. Similarly,

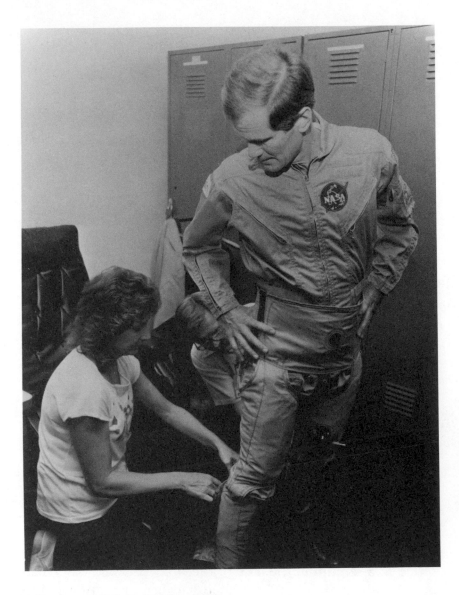

Adjusting my G-Suit. [NASA photo]

Astronaut Charlie Bolden in the pilot's seat on orbit. [NASA photo]

beverages were prepared by adding water and inserting a polyethylene straw into the container. I was warned to pay special attention to the clamp on the straw that prevented the fluid from flowing back along it and out of the container in zero gravity. Nothing like having to recapture four hundred individual droplets of orange drink floating freely in the cabin of the shuttle, the dietitian said.

I tasted the food and made my selections. For instance, my meals for Day Five were:

BREAKFAST: MEAL A
Applesauce
Oatmeal with raisins
Grits with butter
Orange drink
Decaf coffee with cream and sugar

LUNCH: MEAL B
Beef almondine
Cheddar cheese spread
Rye bread
Peach ambrosia
Chocolate-covered cookies
Dry roasted peanuts
Lemonade
Hot tea with sugar

DINNER: MEAL C
Mushroom soup
Teriyaki chicken
Potatoes au gratin
Cauliflower with cheese
Butter cookies
Chocolate pudding
Apple drink

Like everything else aboard the shuttle, each dish I selected had my own color-coded purple dot on the package to distinguish it from foods selected by the other astronauts. Each dish had its own Velcro strip attached so it could be fixed to either the meal tray (which was held to one's lap with more Velcro) or to one of the many other Velcro strips on the flight uniform or in the cabin. Items such as the chocolate pudding, cookies, and nuts were the same kind of packaged foods you find on grocery store shelves.

On September 30 I spent three hours in an altitude chamber at Andrews Air Force Base outside of Washington, D.C. While the test could have been done in Houston, I used the Air Force chamber in the Washington area so that I could also attend to my congressional duties. This was my first foray into trying to juggle the demands of NASA and Congress. The juggling act was to become an increasingly complex, and at times frustrating, game of logistics.

Andrews is located in suburban Maryland and is the closest Air Force base to Washington. It is the home of the President's plane, *Air Force One*. The Air Force runs an entire department for physiological flight medicine there, where aviators are taught the varied effects of high-performance flying on the body.

The doctors who briefed me before I entered the chamber explained that the majority of military aviation accidents are caused by pilot error, with a substantial portion of those attributable to *hypoxia*, a lack of oxygen. The purpose of the altitude chamber was to make me aware of my particular symptoms of hypoxia so I could recognize the condition when it occurred and correct it by supplying myself with 100-percent oxygen.

Once in the altitude chamber I was required to breathe pure oxygen for thirty minutes to flush the excess nitrogen out of my bloodstream. At high altitudes, the flight surgeon said, the nitrogen in the body would form bubbles in the bloodstream, causing "the bends," a dangerous condition familiar to deep sea divers.

The sergeant who accompanied me into the altitude chamber instructed me in the procedure. The test started with a rapid "ascent" to the equivalent of thirty-five thousand feet, followed by a quick drop to eight thousand feet. This allowed me to equalize the pressure in my ears. Next, the pressure returned to twenty-five thousand feet. The sergeant told me to take off my oxygen mask. Within moments I began to feel dull and lethargic. When the sergeant asked me to calculate simple math, I was confused. I put the oxygen mask back on, and after four or five deep breaths I was feeling normal again. I had just seen a training film in which a pilot, because of hypoxia, was unable to get his mask back on his face. Fortunately, my hypoxia was slight.

Afterward, the flight surgeon told me this exercise was only marginally related to shuttle flight. The spaceship's cabin was pressurized at all times, and we would be breathing a combination of oxygen and nitrogen pumped into our space helmets, should an emergency occur.

Three days before I took the altitude test, Jim Beggs called me in Houston to say he had decided I should fly on the *Challenger* with Christa McAuliffe. He wanted me to commit myself to two months of training and was concerned I could not be ready for the December flight because of my congressional duties. I told him I respected his judgment and accepted what he was saying. However, I thought I could be ready for the Christmas flight on the *Columbia*.

Then, in a strange turn of events, Hughes Aircraft Company decided to pull its satellite off the *Columbia* mission. Hughes had experienced two failures on its previous two satellites and wanted to do some more design analysis before it launched another. Greg Jarvis, the Hughes payload specialist who was originally supposed to fly with the Hughes satellite on the *Columbia*, was then reassigned to the next mission on the *Challenger* to depart in late January 1986.

On October 4, Jesse Moore called me in Washington to tell me of the change. I would not be flying on the *Challenger*, as I had thought, but was now assigned to fly aboard *Columbia* on December 18.

More Training

Along with the flight assignment came my introduction to the people who would be my coadventurers—the crew of professional astronauts. They would prove to be a source of information about how NASA operates at the grass roots—something I wanted to learn. It was part of my responsibility as chairman of the subcommittee that authorized funding for NASA.

During my first full week at JSC in late October, I set a goal of getting to know these people as well as possible. I was happily surprised at their friendliness. Their technical expertise was immense, but they were also just a great bunch of guys.

Mission commander Hoot Gibson is a master of his trade. But his expertise is almost concealed by his quiet, unassuming demeanor and his closely controlled emotions.

I never heard Hoot raise his voice. His low-key leadership didn't include the stiffness people often associate with career military officers. Hoot proved to be a thoughtful leader, accepting of idiosyncrasies, and adept at finding ways to bring out the best in all of us. His manner was casual, but he always got the job done. I sensed he would be very cool under pressure.

Hoot was the first to talk to me about how frustrating it was for the astronauts to interact with NASA management. As the Rogers Commission investigating the *Challenger* accident would later point out, suggestions and complaints from the astronauts were often pushed aside. In the reorganization of NASA that followed the accident, however, these professionals were finally assigned to areas where their voices of experience had long been needed.

Hoot spoke, for instance, of his frustration with the brake system on the shuttle, a concern aired publicly by astronaut Henry Hartsfield, commander of the mission that flew before *61-C*, (the official designation of our flight). During a lunch break in November, Hoot said astronauts repeatedly had complained that the brakes could jam when touching down on the shuttle runway. On the KSC runway, which lacks the almost unlimited landing space of Edwards Air Force Base, this represented a significant danger. In fact, Hoot told me he never let up on the brakes once they were applied for fear they would bind, causing the shuttle to veer off to one side. A frequent joke among the space workers at KSC is that the pilot of the shuttle had better be right on the money when he lands, because there are hungry alligators all around the landing strip. The guys at the shuttle landing facility have a picture of a fourteen-foot alligator that lives in an adjoining canal, sunning himself next to the runway—smiling.

That concern, and others I learned about while training, were the type of things I had planned to report to Congress following the flight. But as events were to turn out, the in-depth investigation that followed the *Challenger* accident disclosed them before I could report them.

Flight *61-C* was the first spaceflight for pilot Charlie Bolden. Although he performed the duties of copilot to Commander

Gibson, he was the pilot in NASA terminology. Charlie and Hoot had spent hundreds of hours on the flight deck of the shuttle simulator, reviewing every possible scenario expected during the upcoming flight. A Marine lieutenant colonel and graduate of the U.S. Naval Academy, Charlie has a frank, engaging manner. His laughter was often heard during training sessions, and he always had a spark of humor in his eye.

Although Charlie grew up in segregated South Carolina, he was fortunate in having a father who was an outstanding football coach at a black high school, and a mother who was a school librarian. His parents taught him the value of education and that to succeed, he had to work hard. But despite his brilliant record as a student and as an athlete, the South Carolina delegation refused to consider him for appointment to one of the military service academies—because he was black. Since his qualifications were outstanding, the White House, under President Johnson's direction, arranged for Charlie to get an appointment from a Michigan congressman. In 1964 he entered the United States Naval Academy at Annapolis and was promptly elected the Naval Academy's first black freshman class president.

During a break in the lengthy briefings that filled my first full week at JSC, I watched Hoot and Charlie practice their skills. They were joined in the simulators by the other professional astronauts in the crew—mission specialists George "Pinky" Nelson, Steve Hawley, and Franklin Chang-Diaz.

There are two types of simulators, housed in a top-security building at JSC. The *motion-based simulator* actually tilts skyward and shakes during a mock lift-off. The reenactment is almost identical to the real lift-off. The windows on the simulator are computerized so the pilots actually see what they would see during a real launch. As the engines ignite, they see the tower disappearing as they move heavenward, followed by the outline of the Florida coastline as the shuttle rolls over on its back. Next come the stars, with an image of the earth disappearing below, and finally the sun as the shuttle breaks out of

A crew press conference at pad 39A, Kennedy Space Center. [NASA photo]

Commander Hoot Gibson and Pilot Charlie Bolden at their seats on the flight deck during the mission. [NASA photo]

Mission Specialist Steve Hawley with the commander, checking a procedure in the flight data file. [NASA photo]

the darkness. This is accompanied by all the sensations of lift-off except the G force and, of course, the final breakthrough into weightlessness.

The simulated touchdown includes a view of the runway in the front window. In fact, there are several runways that the computer can select, ranging from the unlimited desert run-way at Edwards Air Force Base, to the shorter runway at KSC, or one of the emergency landing strips, such as the one in Senegal, West Africa. A slight jar is felt as the main landing gear touches the ground, and a second bump as the nose wheel touches.

There was a second simulator in the same room called the *fixed-based simulator*. This was a mock-up of the cockpit, with images of the cargo bay. It was used primarily to practice launching satellites from the cargo bay and other tasks per-formed while orbiting the earth.

Franklin Chang-Diaz is a study in determination. Born in Costa Rica in 1950, he decided at an early age to become an astro-naut. To prepare himself, he moved to Connecticut, where even though he spoke very little English, he finished high school in 1967. He was a quick learner, and by 1977 he held a doctorate in applied plasma physics from the Massachusetts Institute of Technology, where he had become an innovative expert in the design and development of fusion reactors. Finally, in order to become an astronaut for America, he became a U.S. citizen.

Franklin's abilities were not limited to science, however. For two and a half years, he worked as a house manager in an experimental community residence for deinstitutionalizing chronic mental patients and was an instructor at a rehabilita-tion program for Hispanic drug abusers in Massachusetts.

Small, with straight, dark hair, Franklin loved to scuba dive in the Caribbean. His somewhat shy smile often flashed quickly and then disappeared behind his normally serious gaze.

I found Steve Hawley to be warm and friendly, with a quick wit. Steve was taken seriously by his fellow astronauts, however, as the team member who knew the flight rules and procedures better than anyone. He held a Ph.D. in astronomy and astrophysics and had flown aboard the orbiter *Discovery*. He was, at the time of our flight training, still married to astronaut Sally Ride. I was amused listening to Hoot and Steve talk about their wives. They called them Dr. Seddon and Dr. Ride—a playful honorific, but still a measure of their affection and respect.

Steve came from Kansas and often spoke fondly of his home state. He was an engaging conversationalist who invariably had us laughing in no time. Steve's father was a minister and later was selected by the astronauts to speak at the memorial service in Houston for the *Challenger* crew.

Dr. George Nelson, or "Pinky" as he was called, had performed the famous spacewalk, during which he managed to snare the Solar Max satellite from its orbit and then, with the help of astronaut "Ox" van Hoften, repaired it in the shuttle cargo bay. On that occasion his peak physical conditioning had come in handy; he had needed every bit of the physical strength he developed as a high school football player and a weight lifter in later years. Pinky went out of his way to help me; the simulator trainers started referring to us as the Nelson brothers because both of us have blond hair.

Pinky's roots were in Wilmar, Minnesota, a place popularized by Garrison Keillor in *Lake Wobegon Days*. During our extended quarantine period, I often heard Pinky laughing out loud as he read this book about small town life in his native state.

My first chance to get to know the other payload specialist on the flight, RCA engineer Bob Cenker, came during the taking of the official crew photograph. Bob was one of the chief de-

With Franklin Chang-Diaz and Pinky Nelson. The launchpad in the background. [NASA photo]

Payload Specialist Bob Cenker and me, as we arrive at KSC for the mission.
[Photo courtesy Astronaut Jim Adamson]

signers of the communications satellite we would launch into
orbit. He also was the only crew member not accustomed to
being in the public eye and was uncomfortable with the public
interest in him back home in New Jersey. He also was unused
to being away from his family, often commenting on how the
mission had taken away much of his time at home. But he took
to the training with a youthful enthusiasm—even if it was
tempered by a healthy restraint at public functions. Over the
course of our months together, however, I was amazed at his
rapidly acquired ease in the spotlight. He became quite articulate in public and now frequently gives speeches in his home
state. I grew to appreciate Bob for his quiet competence and
for the engineering talent he represented—so important to
our country and its technological future.

During the first week I found myself falling into a regular
routine. At age forty-three I was in the best physical shape of
my life. Before I went to the space center at 7:30 A.M., I would
run, do some calisthenics, and eat a breakfast of grapefruit,
rolled oats, and apple juice. Then I would leave to spend my
day at the space center, either in briefings or practicing the
experiments I would perform in space.

One day after training, Hoot suggested a crew run. All were
ready except me, because I had already run four miles that
morning. But I went along and ran more than eight miles that
day. Charlie Bolden kept saying he liked to run slowly; however, I had a feeling he was holding back because of me. After
I learned he had run in several Marine Corps marathons, I
knew it for certain.

Our running together continued through the quarantine
period. One morning, when a cold front hit Houston, I had to
run in the predawn darkness with a towel wrapped around my
head for warmth. Once, at the doctor's request, I ran with a
recorder strapped to my waist, attached to sensors listening for
bowel sounds as part of one of NASA's many medical experiments.

———

One of my first tasks on arriving at JSC was to learn more of the specialized terms that pepper the conversations of the astronauts and their support personnel. Most of the NASAese was a totally new language of acronyms, all standing for different items and procedures. To the outsider it made the astronauts and their technical support teams sound a bit exclusive, almost arrogant. Yet the acronyms were a necessary part of the flight data file—a huge mastersheet of the crew's activities, detailing every minute of the mission, down to specific instructions for the switch positions. Learning the facts contained in a foot-high stack of workbooks filled my evening hours. Together, they contained technical descriptions of how every shuttle system worked, from the airlock to the toilet. I felt like I was in college again.

My first taste of weightlessness came during zero-gravity training in a KC-135 airplane. The plane, a modified Boeing 707, performed a flight maneuver called a *parabola* to create about twenty-five seconds of weightlessness. Cruising at twenty-six thousand feet over the Gulf of Mexico, the pilot would pull the nose up, ascend to thirty-four thousand feet, then tip the huge, four-engined jet over and dive back down to twenty-six thousand feet in free-fall. This topsy-turvy flight pattern, repeated up to forty times, gave the passengers in the padded fuselage time to perform experiments and experience zero gravity for about half a minute each time.

Before I got on board, I was trained for emergency exits using parachutes and oxygen masks. Also, Pinky warned me I would have to reorient my thinking substantially because in weightlessness there is no up or down. During the first three parabolas, I simply sat in the cockpit and watched the horizon slip in and out of sight.

At the bottom of each descent, the pilot opened up the throttles of the four engines, seeking maximum thrust to break out of the dive and start the ascent again. As he pulled back the stick and gravity returned with a vengeance, the passengers had to be careful not to tumble back onto the experiments they were doing during their previous twenty-five seconds of weightlessness. On the pullout from the dive, a force equal to twice the pull of gravity pinned everyone to the floor.

From my initial vantage point in the cockpit, it seemed an amazingly violent maneuver, especially in such a large aircraft. However, those back in the fuselage, surrounded by padding on the floor, walls, and ceilings, didn't mind the maneuvers, especially when the plane reached the top of the parabola and they suddenly started floating freely.

Air sickness was always a problem on these flights because of the repeated roller-coaster motions; hence, the plane's nickname, The Vomit Comet. Some experts are convinced there is a correlation between getting sick in the KC-135 and getting sick in space. Others dispute this theory. I saw it as a good sign, nonetheless, when I was able to function more or less without discomfort.

There were six experiments aboard that flight, mostly conducted by NASA personnel from the Marshall Space Flight Center in Huntsville, Alabama. The experiments included tests of spring-loaded releases to be used to deploy a planetary sciences experiment during an upcoming mission. Another experiment was designed to study how molten metal solidified without gravity to disturb it. Interestingly, the John Deere Tractor Company had their eye on this one. They were hoping to put an experiment on a future shuttle mission that would show how to make a better alloy—obviously, a big advantage in a highly competitive marketplace.

After several maneuvers I left the cockpit and entered the padded fuselage, where I strapped myself to the floor next to Dr. Larry DeLucas from the University of Alabama at Birmingham. Our job was to work with a mechanism I would use in space for the research experiment I would be handling.

It was then that the fun really began. When I felt the plane dip and my body lighten, I unstrapped and pushed off—too hard. I sailed upward, crashing into the ceiling. But before long, and with some practice, I was effortlessly turning flips.

It took very controlled movements and a soft touch to keep from ping-ponging off the walls of the plane.

The experiment stations were spread throughout the passenger area to keep weight evenly distributed, and as I was adjusting to zero gravity, I frequently floated over them. Inevitably, in spite of my precautions, I was on my head or over a station on several occasions when the weightlessness ended and the Gs returned. It was a wonder I didn't break something.

Pinky, Charlie, and Steve obviously loved flying in the KC-135. As old hands, they were sailing and laughing all over the plane, hanging upside down and spinning in the air.

After my first week at the space center, I decided to follow Jake Garn's advice and ask one of my staff to come to Houston with me. I needed a helper at JSC to coordinate the training schedule with my congressional work and requests from the press. I asked my press secretary, David Dickerson, to join me in Houston. He arrived on the day before Halloween and shared the two-bedroom apartment I had rented near JSC for the next six weeks.

While I was busy training, David set up what soon resembled a remote congressional office.

Much of my time at JSC was spent in the cavernous Building 9A, located near the center of the university-like campus. Under its forty-foot-high ceiling, crews practiced many on-orbit routines in exact mockups of the orbiter's crew compartment and its sixty-by-fifteen-foot payload bay. Every part of the orbiter's interior was replicated, even down to the placement of individual screws. A working replica of the remote manipulator arm was used to practice capturing mock satellites and gently moving them within the grasp of astronauts stationed in the payload bay. The "satellites" were actually gray, helium-filled plastic bags the size of Cadillacs, which when not in use, stayed tethered near the center of the building. For though the mechanical arm, designed for use in zero gravity, could easily snatch an orbiting satellite weighing several thousand pounds, in Building 9A, under the full force of Earth's gravity, the weight of a single astronaut would break the delicate machine.

I had seen the mockups of the shuttle interior on previous tours of the space center, but my first real introduction to this duplicate of my future living quarters came during a lunch-time training session when we practiced preparing a meal. It certainly couldn't have been called cooking. Most of the time all we did was inject hot or cold water into food, as previously described, and wait for it to assume a recognizable form. My surprise came when we collected the wrappers and other trash— I couldn't believe the size of the pile. As with everything else, every piece of plastic had to be stowed out of the way. For the United States has always "packed out" its space trash to keep the low Earth orbit paths as clear as possible of debris. At one time, the Soviet cosmonauts dumped trash from their space-craft, but international agreements have now slowed the pace of space littering.

Space trash is more than an aesthetic problem. NASA esti-mates that 4 million tons of man-made debris is currently or-biting the earth and the amount is increasing at the rate of almost 2 million tons a year. Most of this debris burns off in reentry, but by the year 2000 a shuttle will still have to con-tend with 9.5 million tons of space garbage floating in orbit.

About half of the debris that floats in space is the wreckage of satellites that break up. Another 25 percent is made up of spent rocket stages and discarded equipment. North American Air Defense Command, at Cheyenne Mountain, Colorado, is currently tracking seven thousand orbiting objects the size of baseballs or larger. It estimates there are another thirty-five thousand nontrackable items the size of marbles, along with trillions of paint flakes and even smaller particles of aluminum oxide.

Because of the speed of objects in orbit—twenty-five thou-sand feet a second—even a tiny object could damage a satellite or pierce the skin of a manned spacecraft. A one-ounce paint chip, for example, has almost twice the impact of an automobile traveling at fifty miles an hour. A window in an earlier shuttle mission was cracked when the shuttle, moving at 17,795 miles an hour, collided head-on with a paint chip traveling at 17,795 miles an hour in a different orbit. I shuddered to think what would happen if we collided with an apple core at thirty-five thousand miles per hour—or a pair of pliers.

Fitting seven people into the surprisingly small middeck and flight deck was quite a chore on Earth. But once outside the pull of gravity, the living area would become far more comfortable since the amount of usable work and living space is significantly increased. It would be just as easy to "stand" on the walls, and if need be, we could work "head-to-head," using the roof as a second floor and thus doubling the available "floor" space.

Equipment designed for each mission was first tested in our mockups to make sure it fit. I practiced in the shuttle mockup to become familiar with the locker system and to get a general feel of the space available for the treadmill and the other equipment I would need. All experimental equipment had to be unpacked, assembled, repacked, and stowed once more in the replicated stowage bins. This mockup also was the best place to get oriented, learn how the various systems worked, and remember where all the other space gear was stowed. The workbooks Bob Cenker and I studied at night gave us the details, but there was nothing like hands-on experience.

A system of codes precisely defined the location of every storage bin in the wall of compartments at the rear of the middeck. For example, "MF28E" would mean a bin in the front portion of the middeck, 28 percent across, going from left to right. The *E* meant the storage area was thirty inches from the top, as each letter in the alphabet meant a drop of six inches from the ceiling.

Storage is a major concern on the shuttle. It took a clever and very adaptable storage system to contain all the food and clothes used by seven people in the course of a week—not to mention the garbage and toilet waste. When all the equipment for the mission and the individual experiments was added, the wall of storage lockers on the flight deck quickly filled up. Moreover, each locker was packed with a variety of items, and to work efficiently each of us had to locate exactly what he needed without difficulty.

Building 9A was one of the few areas where the public could watch crews training for their days in space. Under the curious gaze of tourists, the *61-C* crew did one of its first team exercises by practicing emergency escapes from the orbiter mockups. NASA, of course, had its own term for getting out of the shuttle in a hurry—*emergency egress.*

There never had been a need for a real evacuation of the shuttle, although an aborted launch on flight *41-D* had the crew hustling out of the orbiter and down the elevator while being doused with the fire-suppression water system. If an emergency happened before lift-off, crew members could leave through the side hatch. If necessary, they would slide from the launch tower to the ground in the padded slidewire basket— though the slide had never been tested with crew members aboard for fear the abrupt stop would injure its occupants. Finally, of course, there was the armored personnel carrier at the base of the slide to drive farther away from danger.

To practice for an emergency at the launchpad, the crew used a mock-up of the crew cabin and flight deck in Building 9A. But instead of leaving the mockup in its horizontal position, as I was used to seeing it, the replica was tilted nose up. We all lay on our backs in launch seats installed specially for this drill. This new position had the curious effect of "rearranging" the crew compartment, and it left me oddly disoriented for a few minutes until I grew accustomed to the change. I was somewhat taken aback that the human brain could become so confused by an environment that had simply been moved through a ninety-degree tilt.

All seven of us were set to escape, when Hoot gave the

Franklin Chang-Diaz and me in the slidewire basket, which is intended to provide a quick escape from the launch pad. [NASA photo]

"emergency evacuate" order. In fifty-eight seconds, we unstrapped from our seats, pulled down our visors, and switched
from the shuttle oxygen system to a portable air supply carried
on our belts. Then, we opened the hatch and crawled out. I
knew that in reality we could be fried in those few seconds. I
also knew we would have moved even faster had there actually
been a fire in the shuttle.

Among my new experiences was a half day of firefighting
training. This drill taught us how to extinguish fires during an
emergency and how to work together as a team. I suspected,
however, that the latter purpose was all the exercise was really
good for. We drove out to a remote section of the Johnson
Space Center, where we were met by trucks from the Houston
Fire Department and firefighting personnel from JSC. After a
thorough orientation and explanation of the equipment, we
practiced with hand-held extinguishers and put out several small
fires. Next, the fire chief said he was going to teach us how to
walk through fire without being burned.

I watched with interest as fuel oil was poured on top of a
shallow pond about the size of a large swimming pool. This
was then ignited with a great whoosh and began to burn fiercely.
I was a little concerned, however, when I noticed that the crew
trainer was wearing a shiny aluminum, heat-resistant suit, while
the rest of us were wearing only our flight suits.

The crew chief handed me the fire hose with instructions to
turn the special nozzle to "Fog." Instantly, a great cloud of fog
spewed out in front of me, and I was able to walk right up to
the blazing inferno without being scorched. "Now," the chief
said, "if you turn the nozzle to a steady steam, and direct it at
the base of the fire burning on the water, you can actually part
the fire—just like the Red Sea was parted for Moses." The
object was not to try to put out the fire, but to keep swishing
the steam of water back and forth and walk forward through
the flames. In theory, the other crew members were to stick
close to me, following through until we reached the other side.

Fortunately, we did not put this part of the experiment to the test but were permitted to back away with the nozzle still on fog and let the fire truck put out the fire. When I asked the fire chief if this method would be effective in a fire at Level 195 on the tower, he just rolled his eyes. I sensed he knew that any fire on the top of the tower would not resemble fuel oil burning on a shallow pond. However, the experience in team-work seemed valuable, and I left the firefighting exercise with a feeling of preparation, if not exactly readiness.

Two weeks before our scheduled launch date, the crew traveled to KSC to practice the last leg of the prelaunch escape plan, as well as do a dry run of the launch countdown. Some tried their hand at the wheel of the escape "tank." The only way for the driver to get a clear view of the road ahead was through a hole in the roof. The tank, while noisy and cramped, would go up to thirty miles an hour. But speed was far from my objective. I knew the press would have a field day if I crashed the tank into something. I didn't push my luck and maintained a careful pace when it was my turn to drive.

The more we practiced all these escape procedures, the more one thing became certain: If there was a real danger, a fire or explosion, there was little likelihood of getting out of the spaceship. I began to suspect that things like the firefighting exercise, the basket slides, the tank, and the talk I kept hearing about installing inflatable escape chutes, such as those on large airliners, were all for public consumption, to try to calm the alarmists who were constantly being stirred by articles in the press about NASA's poor safety standards. We all knew that an explosion on the pad, or shortly after lift-off, probably would be fatal—regardless of anything NASA did to provide escape mechanisms.

The mock countdown at KSC was my first time inside the space shuttle while it was sitting on the pad. "It now becomes real," Hoot said as we rode in the crew van to the launchpad.

Up close, the shuttle looked enormous. The apricot-colored

tank that carried fuel for the main engines dwarfed nearby workers who were preparing the system for launch. We rode the gantry elevator to a White Room, where the cargo was undergoing a final contamination-free processing. We roamed up and down the work levels to inspect it.

A worker set the mood for us all when he yelled, "Go get 'em and God bless!" We did, indeed, feel ready to go.

The prelaunch escape procedure had at least the semblance of sophistication. The escape plan we would use after a landing, however, seemed uncharacteristically low-tech for NASA. We were told we would crawl from the orbiter, drop to the ground, and run like the dickens for safety. On the other hand, this was probably more effective than some of the more elaborate schemes I'd seen, such as the baskets that were supposed to slide us down from the top of the tower.

We had practiced our postlanding escape options at JSC. Our first was to open the side hatch, hang from a special hatch handle, and drop eleven feet to the ground. The crew simulated this while breathing their independent emergency air supplies. During the drill, however, we dropped only a few feet, onto the elevated platform. Previously, the crews had practiced the full eleven-foot fall—until an astronaut had injured his ankle on the padded floor. We all wondered what would happen if an astronaut had to make that drop after a week in zero G.

If the side hatch was jammed shut, escape became a complicated task. The procedure called for Hoot to make us a new escape path by blowing out the top left window above the flight deck. The crew would then clamber out through the hole onto the roof of the shuttle after attaching a rope to a special harness which went over our shoulders and tightened across the groin. We then slid thirty-three feet down the rope to the ground. A friction brake on each rope and handle system was provided to slow our descent. Nevertheless, the drop still began with a jolt sharp enough to have made *61-C* an all-soprano crew if our harnesses had been improperly adjusted. I hadn't anticipated the sharp drop and was glad I had the straps pulled tight.

As in a real emergency, our tight-fitting helmet visors were closed to keep out any toxic fumes. But the close fit was a liability this time. We had already used our personal air supplies in the other egress drills and were all now low on compressed air. As we were sliding down the ropes, several of us had to open our visors to avoid asphyxiation.

Fortunately, there was only a slight chance a crew would have to evacuate this way. But if our brakes malfunctioned, or if the tires blew while we were landing at KSC, the orbiter could veer into the wilderness on either side of the massive landing area.

Immediately after landing at Edwards Air Force Base in California, I did several orientation experiments on myself which included violently shaking my head from side to side. The results convinced me of how easily an astronaut could become disoriented and unbalanced if he quickly moved his head vertically and laterally immediately after landing.

Only after our flight did the NASA doctors finally conclude that a crew's disorientation after six days in space would be so great that had we tried to follow the escape instructions, there would have been an immobilized pile of dizzy astronauts on the ground beneath the shuttle, unable to run away from danger. Such a scene could have been tragic in the case of *61-C*, because we were scheduled to land with deadly explosive hypergolic fuel aboard in the nose of the shuttle—right next to the crew. Fortunately, the procedures now are being rewritten according to data gathered during our flight.

As important as the practice of the simulations was, there was always the less obvious purpose of getting the crew to work as a team. When astronauts were all military test pilots, teamwork came as a second nature to the crews. But the new breed of astronaut included scientists often used to working on solitary research projects. The time together was valuable to us all as we gauged each other's personalities. In the cramped quarters of the shuttle, it was important for each of us to be able to depend upon the others. There was no room for uncertainty about fellow crew members during spaceflight.

This team feeling extended to the trainers and other members of the ground crews who made the system work. We all realized that it was their expertise that made spaceflight possible. We were just the public face of an enormous human endeavor.

During this time I had my second encounter with Christa McAuliffe. I had first met America's "teacher in space" with her backup, Barbara Morgan, and Greg Jarvis on one of the KC-135 flights. Once we had all become accustomed to the parabolas, we enjoyed the feeling of zero G. On one occasion we joined hands and floated in a chain along the cabin. Christa had great eagerness to learn and a high sense of adventure.

Christa had been declared the winner of NASA's teacher-in-space competition in July, and had arrived in Houston together with Barbara, the first runner-up, about the same time I had to begin training. However, since they were part of a different crew, we saw each other only from a distance. Christa was scheduled to take 114 hours of intense training in her role as a temporary astronaut, as I was. One of the things she joked about was her life insurance company, which had canceled her policy when it heard she was going to fly on the shuttle. Eventually, another life insurance company gave her a million-dollar policy.

While my assignment was to conduct various medical research experiments from my location on the shuttle's middeck, Christa had been assigned two jobs on mission 51-L. First, she was going to videotape six science demonstrations that NASA was to edit and then distribute to schools across the nation after she landed. Second, she would teach two live television lessons from space.

As I had, she immediately ran into both personality and bureaucratic problems. It began with a clash with her educational

A flying human chain in zero gravity aboard a NASA aircraft during training.
Left to right are Gerald Magilton (backup for Cenker), Christa McAuliffe, me,
Barbara Morgan (Christa's backup), and Bob Cenker. [NASA photo]

coordinator, Bob Mayfield, a science teacher from Texas. Mayfield didn't think Christa was qualified as a science teacher. He
also found himself chafing at Christa's seemingly curt New England accent. Christa acknowledged she was not an expert in
science, but she considered her mission to be primarily socio-
logical.

There were also problems with NASA. Christa made it plain
from the beginning that she would teach the live lessons the
way she wanted to. She was having difficulty learning NA-
SAese and did not feel she could communicate effectively to
schoolchildren using a jargon known only to a few elite members of the space community. NASA disagreed. Also, in true
bureaucratic fashion, it wanted Christa to write out her lessons
word for word so they could be approved before she presented
them on live television. Christa balked. All a good teacher needs,
she said, is a lesson plan and a room full of students. If it
worked on Earth, it would work in space. Her stubbornness
paid off, and NASA eventually backed down.

Of course, she couldn't just wing it. She spent a large amount
of time in the simulator practicing where she would stand (or
float) and what she would say. No sooner would our team leave
the simulator than Christa's team would appear for rehearsal.
"Good morning, this is Christa McAuliffe, live from space in
the shuttle *Challenger*. . . ."

Her lesson plan called for her to start on the flight deck by
introducing Commander Dick Scobee, who would talk about
his job flying the spaceship. Then the pilot, Mike Smith, would
talk about the on-board computer. Floating down to middeck,
she would point out various features, such as the bathroom,
the treadmill, and the galley, where she would show the camera
some of the space food. In a voice-over, she would continue to
talk as the camera focused through the back window into the
huge payload bay, big enough to hold a railroad boxcar or a
school bus.

Her second lesson, to be delivered ninety minutes later, was

titled "Where We've Been, Where We're Going, and Why."
She planned to use a small model of both the *Kitty Hawk* and
the *Challenger* to help describe some of the differences between flying then and now. She was also going to do a few
experiments so the children could understand the benefits of
space research compared to research on earth. One demonstration I was particularly interested in had her shaking a clear
plastic bag filled with marshmallows and M&Ms, then a jar
filled half with water and half with oil. This was to allow the
children to see that neither solids nor liquids separate in zero
gravity as they do on earth. She was to explain that the benefits of this phenomena for industry would be astonishing. Once
the space station was in place, scientists could then mix metal
alloys in a way never possible on Earth. In fact, using a simple
procedure, more than seventy new combinations of metals could
be created in space, ranging all the way from metals that would
stretch to incredible length in tiny wires to metals with unpar-
alleled strength and flexibility and new kinds of armor for military and police use.

As I listened, I became aware that there was no limit to what
we could do in space. Each day Christa's lessons and demonstrations, as well as my own experiments, seemed to be taking
on new and expanded importance.

Part of an astronaut's training was maintaining flying skills
through regular flights in the high-performance T-38 jets. These
were hangared at Ellington Field, about fifteen minutes away
from JSC. The flights served as good escapes from the more
routine aspects of an astronaut's life. As our launch date drew
near, the training schedule provided more opportunities for
the shuttle commander and pilot to sharpen their skills in the
T-38 and in the shuttle training aircraft, used to simulate the
special feel and the sharp descent of a shuttle landing.

In late November, I had to check the box on the training
checklist that required my flight in the T-38. Before I left for

Ellington Field, the astronauts gave me a hard time, putting in bids for my personal belongings in case I didn't make it back. I laughed with them. I wasn't worried about my safety. Hoot was my pilot.

Still More Training

The T-38 flight had two purposes. The first was to get me comfortable with the feel of high-performance flight. An unspoken purpose, however, was to build my confidence in Hoot's piloting skills. After all, my life would be in his hands during the landing. His self-confidence showed in the precise way he handled himself and the keen glint in his hazel eyes.

After the sleek, needle-nosed jet was pulled out of the hangar, a side ladder was hung from the cockpit, and I clambered up and into the back seat. Crew members made certain I was strapped in and that the parachute mechanism was in place. One of the men pointed out the handle that worked the seat ejection in case we had to bail out. My "thanks a lot!" brought grins from the other pilots who had come to see me off.

After a final instrument check, Hoot adjusted our intercom system and rolled us out to the end of the runway. I listened as he talked to the control tower, and at last the words came back, "Cleared for takeoff." The machine began to tremble under me as Hoot pushed the throttle all the way forward to

"Afterburner." Raw jet fuel spewed into the giant turbines of the engines, and the little plane roared to life, leaping off the runway and climbing skyward at an incredible forty-degree angle, heading south out over the broad expanse of the Gulf of Mexico.

There are few experiences in the world like being strapped into the center of a high-speed aircraft. Gravity pulls at your cheeks and droops your lower lip as the plane pulls out of a rapid dive. Performing aerial acrobatics, practicing dogfight maneuvers, and simulating shuttle landings were all part of Hoot's repertoire in the sky.

Hoot talked me through most of the maneuvers. "Here comes a slow roll," he called, and I watched the earth slip over on top of the plane then reappear on the other side. Next was a four-point roll. Then Hoot said, "All right, Bill, feet on the rudders and hand on the stick—it's all yours."

The hardest way to fly, an instructor once told me, is straight and level. This is especially true of a tiny jet with wings smaller than the back seat of a car, whistling through the air at almost the speed of sound. Just a touch on the stick and it wiggled this way or that. "Keep the pointy end forward and the dirty side down," one of the pilots had joked as we closed the canopy. Now I understood why. The T-38 was just as happy with the dirty side up as it was with the dirty side down.

I felt Hoot's steady hand back on the stick as he took over the controls. "This little baby can do a double roll in less than a second," he said. Even before I was able to grasp his meaning, I felt the little plane twist, and the earth zipped in front of my face as if someone had snapped a window shade.

"I thought you said a double roll," I complained.

"Aw, Bill, you must have blinked your eyes. That was twice. Count this time."

I felt the plane jerk, and within a second we had completed a 720-degree roll. It happened so fast that had I had a glass of water on my lap, not a drop would have spilled as the earth flipped past the canopy two times and we snapped back to horizontal flight.

I asked Hoot to replicate a bombing run like those he flew over Vietnam. We quickly descended, and the lightness in my head told me we had outrun gravity. Then Hoot pulled up, and the massive G force flattened us into our seats. I thought, if they could recreate this experience at Walt Disney World, every kid in the nation would beat a path to their door.

Barrel-rolls, wingovers, loop-extensions, and pitchbacks—we did them all as we made vapor trails at near supersonic speeds above the Gulf of Mexico. Previously, I had flown in the military's hottest jets—the F-16 and the F-15. But I had never danced in the sky like I did that day with *Columbia* commander Hoot Gibson.

Prior to landing, Hoot streaked down perpendicular to the runway, and at the last minute pulled sharply left. After a soft circle into a final approach, we touched down with a feather touch. However, instead of rolling us to a stop, the engines surged with power, and once again we leaped into the sky. Circling the airport and coming back down, we did four more "touch-and-go" landings before turning toward the hangar. Each landing was made with a different simulated problem: one engine out, inoperable flaps, instruments not working, etc. On the last landing Hoot even turned the controls over to me for the landing cycle, taking them back just before we touched down.

That evening, back in my apartment, I sat at the kitchen table trying to assess what I had experienced that day. I knew that several of my congressional colleagues were jet pilots: John McCain, Barry Goldwater, and of course, John Glenn. Maybe the sensations grow old after a while, like driving a car. A sixteen-year-old boy driving for the first time is tantamount to becoming an adult all in one moment. That afternoon I felt as if I were sixteen again.

———

On October 30, 1985, I watched the launch of the space shuttle *Challenger* on the TV screen at Johnson Space Center. Normally, during a launch, I would have been in Florida hosting a congressional delegation at Kennedy Space Center. But this time it was different. My perspective was different.

As the countdown proceeded for *Challenger*, the myriad details of the crew checklist ran through my mind—procedures already learned as part of my training. It was finally becoming real to me. We were not Boy Scouts preparing for an overnight camping trip. Every procedure and conceivable malfunction had been thought out in advance and simulated in lengthy training sessions. Each activity on the mission was documented in the voluminous flight data file—seventy-five pounds of paper carried on board. This included checklists, cue cards, and reference manuals. It was as thoroughly prepared a mission as any before it.

Yet, watching the shuttle lift off the pad and thunder toward the sky, I wondered what would happen if a fuel tank ruptured during those first few seconds after lift-off. I knew there was no manual procedure to cover something like that. I also knew that all the astronauts thought about the possibility from time to time—as did their families.

During my training, I was trying to accommodate more press interviews than I had ever experienced in my life.

A press conference was held at the mock-ups in Building 9A. The conference had been called to announce the main experiment I would perform, the cancer research project sponsored by the University of Alabama at Birmingham. But most news organizations sidestepped this opportunity in favor of one-on-one interviews in later weeks. These later meetings presented their own problems, as NASA rules restrict press access to the crew as the launch date draws near.

The main preflight press conference was held November 21, with each crew member describing his individual assignments for the flight.

The press wanted to hear me say I had seen many problems with NASA during my weeks of training. But while I had noted some areas of concern, I decided it would be better to make such pronouncements after the flight was over and I had a total picture from launch to landing. Fortunately, they were accepting of my role as a crew member, and once again I silently thanked Jake Garn for paving the way.

But I was paving a new path, too; one I wasn't even aware of at the time. For my space menu I had requested that some citrus be on board—specifically, Florida citrus. I have eaten a grapefruit every morning for most of my life. Rita Rapp, the dietitian, had told me I could pick out my own menu, within reason. It seemed reasonable to have some Florida citrus aboard the shuttle. Therefore, David Dickerson wrote a press release saying I would carry Florida orange juice in crystal form into space (rather than the somewhat bland, freeze-dried "orange drink" that was standard fare on the menu), along with some fresh Indian River grapefruit. Well, that just sent NASA into a tizzy.

Because it is a federal agency, NASA wanted to avoid endorsing any commercially competitive product. I had already annoyed their bureaucratic system by requesting that I take an American-made Harris-Lanier or Dictaphone tape recorder with me into space, both of which are located in my home district, rather than the foreign-manufactured Sony that NASA issued to all the astronauts. Now I had further agitated them by asking for Florida grapefruit. It wasn't the grapefruit that upset the system; it was the fact I had specified *Florida* grapefruit. I was from Florida, the orange juice crystals were from the Florida Citrus Commission, and the grapefruit was coming from Florida's Indian River region—all of which combined to overload the bureaucratic circuit and blow a number of fuses. They anticipated all kinds of flak from citrus growers elsewhere in the nation, so they vetoed the idea.

Good did come from it, however. As a result of my request for Florida orange juice, the crystals were delivered to NASA.

They were tested, found acceptable for spaceflight, and were to be aboard the *Challenger* when it flew in January. Dietitian Rita Rapp, who seemed embarrassed by the entire flap, promised to go to the grocery store and purchase enough grapefruit for me to share with the entire crew.

NASA decided they would do for me what they had done for Jake Garn during training, by assigning a member of the astronaut corps to help with questions I had. They assigned Jim Adamson, who prior to coming to NASA had been a teacher at West Point. Jim was a career Army helicopter pilot who had been working at NASA for a number of years before being accepted as an astronaut the previous year. It was worthwhile to have him spend time with me, answering a number of questions I was reluctant to ask Hoot and the rest of the crew because I did not want to interrupt their training schedule.

Each separate shuttle crew—in fact, all the crews, all the way back through the Apollo missions—had had their own crew badge. This embroidered patch was not only to be worn on the chest of all our outer uniforms, but it was the official signet of our flight. Our particular patch was designed by Hoot after input from the other NASA crew members. For some reason that escaped us all, George Abbey wanted a picture of a dragon to appear on the patch. None of the crew members felt a dragon was appropriate. Instead, the patch showed the *Columbia* in a nose-up position with shock waves coming off the nose as it reentered earth's atmosphere. In addition to the Stars and Stripes, the astronauts decided to include the constellation Draco in the background. Pinky Nelson, who has a doctorate in astronomy, joked "that's as close as we can come to George's dragon."

Shortly after Thanksgiving, I was presented with a personal flight patch from the artists at Disney World. During World War II, Walt Disney shut down his movie production company and made war training films for America. The one I remembered, in particular, was *Donald Duck Fights the Führer*. During

Gibson, me, and Astronaut Jim Adamson at KSC. [Photo courtesy Jim Adamson]

The STS-61C crew patch. [Photo courtesy Congressman Nelson]

My personal flight patch. [Photo courtesy Congressman Nelson]

that time, the commander of a U.S. Navy aircraft carrier asked
Disney if he would be willing to design a patch for the carrier's
aviators. News and pictures of the patch were widely publi-
cized, and Walt Disney wound up creating twelve hundred
aviator and unit patches during the war. It was in that spirit
that Disney World volunteered to create the red, white, blue,
and silver patch for *Columbia*'s mission *61-C*.

As we came down to the end of the training period and approached the quarantine phase, I scrambled to get my
congressional work to a place where I could step back for the
two weeks of absence. The traveling back and forth to Washington was beginning to get to me. On December 6 I got up
at 1:30 A.M., missed my connection in Atlanta, arrived in
Washington at 10:30 A.M. and just missed a vote on the floor
of the House. It was frustrating.

On Saturday night, December 7, when I tucked the children
into bed, the thought passed through my mind that this was
the last time I would see them until after the flight. That afternoon I had played football with Billy and had listened to the
songs Nan Ellen had prepared for me.

My family was very much a part of what I was doing. Early
on, Grace and I decided to make this an experience in which
the children and she would participate. Participate they did,
and in a big way.

I had been returning from Houston to Washington on the
weekends so that I could be with my family. Each visit gave
me a fresh opportunity to share the latest training experience
with them and to talk about what was next.

The children had watched in amusement as I ate a strange
concoction of raw oats, bran, wheat germ, and apple juice. They
had made frequent comments as I began running more—
sometimes in between the children's weekend soccer games.
They loved to point out that if the shuttle didn't take me into
space, I could always run there.

With my family at home in Florida: Billy, Grace, and Nan Ellen. [Photo courtesy Cecil Stoughton]

Grace, Nan Ellen, and Billy wait at home for news about Columbia's *next launch attempt. [Photo by Tim Mueller]*

It was hard to say goodbye for my last trip to Houston that Saturday night. For inevitably the thought occurred—What if?

Grace had doubts only once, when she heard about the claustrophobia bag—the bean bag used to transfer us from one space vehicle to another in case of an emergency. Then the reality hit her, and I know she did not sleep much that night. She is a person of deep resources, however, and as the launch date drew near she became rock steady.

Around 11:00 P.M. that last night in Washington, Billy came stumbling into our bedroom, half-awake, half-asleep, and mumbled the question "Where's Dad?" I assured him I was right there, and he returned to bed. I lay awake, well aware that even the children sensed the danger of the mission. I wondered if I was right to put them through this.

The next morning I was at Dulles Airport before dawn. As the plane taxied out to the runway, I gazed out of the window. There in the early morning sunlight was the space shuttle *Enterprise*—the first shuttle, built primarily for testing—sitting on the apron next to the taxiway. It was there awaiting the Smithsonian Institution's arrangement of an exhibit of historical aircraft of the United States. I craned my neck to watch it as long as I could until our plane turned and it disappeared from view.

Scrubs

Following our first scrub in December and our time off for Christmas, I reported back to Johnson Space Center in Houston on December 28. Aside from the weakness brought on by the mild virus, I was feeling fine—eager to resume training.

Immediately, we were placed back in quarantine, which meant no one except those who had been cleared by a NASA doctor was allowed within six feet of us. In reality, however, that proved to be an impossibility. For one thing, the people who had been cleared by the physicians could have been cleared months in advance. Unless they voluntarily withdrew if they had a virus or were not feeling well, they could easily have contaminated us. And even though the various training areas were always cleared of unauthorized and uninspected persons, as we walked to our assignments we were constantly passing people who were sniffing and coughing.

One morning, after a training session in the shuttle simulator, we were on our way back to the quarantine trailers where we lived. The simulator quarters were secured by a security airlock, meaning we had to open one door with a security card, step into a small room and lock the door behind us before opening the outside door. That morning all seven of us crowded into the little security room. Just as the inner door was closing, a young woman, a NASA secretary, shouted, "Hold the door!" and scooted in with us. The door shut behind her. There we were, seven astronauts supposed to be in strict quarantine, jammed into a little room with this strikingly beautiful, but uninspected young woman.

"Hold your breath," Charlie Bolden whispered out of the side of his mouth, trying to keep from laughing.

The outside door opened. "Bye, you all," the secretary said with a Texas twang and was on her way. Walking down the sidewalk, Hoot observed, "Anybody who smells that good can't be sick."

Actually, the quarantine had two purposes: to keep us away from germs, but also to get us away from the daily routine so we could concentrate on the mission and work with each other as a team. Fortunately, I was able to speak to my children several times by telephone and was promised I could see Grace when we returned to Florida—that is, if she was cleared by the doctors.

We were well aware that quarantine actually began our countdown, and we were eager and ready. Hoot and Charlie continued to sharpen their flying skills in the simulator, while I continued to review the procedures for my medical experiments with the NASA personnel who were not away on holiday leave. The time was especially valuable to me since it allowed me the opportunity to get to know my fellow crew members at a deeper, more personal level. We spent New Year's Eve just among ourselves, lingering over a delicious dinner with a lot of good-natured banter. Hoot, Pinky, and Franklin were guitar players, so we joined in a songfest that lasted until midnight.

We returned to the Cape shortly after New Year's and took over our old quarantine quarters at KSC. A traditional barbecue party was thrown two days before launch at the lonely beachhouse south of the pad. It was for the crew and close family members. Children were not allowed because of the quarantine rules, so I invited Grace's mother and father, Tillman and Ellen Cavert, as my substitute parents. It was too cold and windy to walk on the beach, so we spent the time visiting with the crew families and getting to know each other.

Franklin Chang-Diaz's widowed mother and younger brother from Costa Rica were there. It was obvious how happy and proud his mother was from the smile that never left her face. Her radiance was more eloquent than her broken English. "Everyone in Costa Rica," she said haltingly, "is proud of my *muchacho*."

I was honored to get to know Charlie Bolden's mother— also a widow. She had been the force driving Charlie to excel through education. Now she was about to see the culmination of a lifetime of praying and planning as her son flew into outer space. Although proud of him, she was reluctant to see him go. I stood to one side as Charlie hugged her goodbye. "Aw, Mama, don't worry. Everything is going to be all right."

In many ways Mrs. Bolden reminded me of my own mother, who had died in 1967, after a long struggle with Lou Gehrig's disease. I thought of her often, and, for a moment, as I watched Mrs. Bolden, I imagined she was there, bidding me on.

My thoughts turned to my father, who died when I was fourteen. I remembered his encouragement and was grateful.

So it was that day on the beach at Cape Canaveral, not far from the old family homestead—my parents touched my life again as I watched other parents with their astronaut children.

I was lonely . . . but only for a moment.

I glanced over at Grace, chatting easily with her parents. Like Grace, her mother, Ellen, is a woman of elegant bearing. Tillman, my father-in-law, is disciplined, hardworking, and a successful businessman. He had flown in World War II. He knew the risk of our mission, and when he put his arms around me to say goodbye, we both choked up.

Charlie's mother, Franklin's mother, and Grace's mother and

father had all ridden out to the space center clinic together to be cleared by the doctors before joining us at the party. One came from another country and did not speak our language. The others were descendants of the American South—one family white, the other black. It was an eloquent reminder of the sweeping changes that had taken place in our society over the years.

Our second try for launch was January 6, 1986. We all went to the pad with spirits high, confident that this was the day. I rode in the cab of the van so I could see everything—especially the shuttle, sitting out there in the predawn darkness on the pad, bathed in the powerful xenon lights. I knew from past experience the lights could be seen as far away as the front yard of my home on the Indian River south of Melbourne, almost thirty-five miles away.

Climbing out of the van, we were met by Troy Stewart, our suit technician. Incongruously, he was wearing a Scottish golf cap. I should note that the term "suit technician" is actually a holdover from the old days when astronauts had to wear space suits during a launch. Shuttle crews no longer have to wear such gear unless they are leaving the shuttle for a "space walk." Instead, they wear a helmet, body harness (in case an emergency egress becomes necessary), and emergency breathing gear. Though this gear can by no means be considered a "space suit," the people who help put it all on are still referred to as "suit technicians" or "suit techs," for short.

As we started toward the elevator that would take us up to Level 195, I noticed again the white cloud of vaporized hydrogen coming from the top of the fuel tank by the "beanie cap," as it was called, as well as from the nozzles of the engines. My own breath, too, was condensing as I exhaled—the frigid air was some fourteen degrees colder than the morning of our first launch attempt.

Again, we were early, and I had time to walk from one end of the launch tower to the other. I looked over at the other

pad where *Challenger* was poised, also bathed in xenon lights—
a proud kid sister to *Columbia*, silently waiting its turn to follow
into space. I felt a special kinship with my new friends who
would board *Challenger* in just a couple of weeks.

I walked around to the other side of the tower where I could
see the monstrous Vehicle Assembly Building—one of the
largest buildings in the world. The story is told that when it
was first built it was so big and cavernous that on hot, high-
humidity days clouds would sometimes form in the upper levels and it would rain inside the building. Maybe it was just
another of the fables that had grown up around the space industry.

I decided to make one last bathroom stop. I remembered
how uncomfortable I had gotten on the first launch attempt.
Lying on my back with my feet in the air for all that time had
forced the fluids in my legs down to my midsection, putting
tremendous pressure on my bladder—actually a significant pain.
I hated to think what would have happened once we lifted off
and the G force added to the discomfort.

Suddenly, I heard Franklin calling my name. The crew was
ready to enter the White Room and suit up.

I crawled into the hatch and took my now-familiar place in
my seat. After being strapped into that uncomfortable up-
ended position, I looked around. The suit techs were just leaving, closing the hatch behind them. I watched as the little latch
came down and noticed it had not fallen into place. Nice, I
thought. Now they leave the door ajar!

I could see the latch jiggling as the handle turned from the
outside; it kept snapping up and down but still did not catch.
Finally, Franklin unbuckled his seat harness and crawled over
to see if he could help. By the time he got to the door, it had
opened. The technicians gave us a "we're trying" smile and
closed it again. Franklin started to crawl back into his seat, but
once again the door had not latched. The technicians kept
twisting the outside handle, but the latch refused to fall into

place. I was beginning to worry. We'd already had one scrub. Could this kind of thing cause another?

Franklin crawled back to the door just in time to see it open again. "Ah, sorry, guys," the technician said as once again he closed the hatch—firmly. This time it caught. Franklin waited until they had finished on the outside, then he reached over and gave the latch a final push. It was secured and locked. Giving me a big grin and thumbs-up signal, he crawled back into his seat and perched there to stay in a more comfortable position until closer to takeoff. My neck was aching from looking around and over my shoulder at the door.

After an hour of waiting, I heard Fred Gregory's voice from Houston coming over the radio. Fred, the nation's first black pilot astronaut to fly, had been assigned as the CAPCOM at Mission Control in Houston. Right now he was sitting in the big Mission Control unit with all the TV monitors, running through the crew check. Fred said our emergency landing site had been changed to Morón, Spain, instead of Dakar, Senegal. Dakar was down to half a mile visibility, which would have made for a tough landing. None of us relished the thought of having to land at Dakar. We had all seen pictures of the landing strip there—and they left us shuddering. Trying to land a fully loaded spaceship chock full of satellites and experiments on a 10,000-foot landing strip that ended with a cliff dropping off into the Atlantic Ocean would test even Hoot's flying abilities. Then, there was that little matter of the brakes. . . .

Suddenly, the master alarm sounded, indicating the orbiter was coming to life. I could feel movement. We were at T-20 minutes and counting. There was a lot of conversation between Hoot and Charlie and the ground. I was able to catch most of it in my earphones, but my ear was not tuned to the highly technical language of the pilots. Once again, I was reminded I was an outsider.

The fact that I was a layman among professionals was constantly before me. I remembered—and was embarrassed as I thought of it—the first time I had walked into the White Room that surrounded the shuttle hatch door. It had been an especially windy day and my hair was tousled. Seeing what I believed was a mirror on the wall just inside the door, I walked over, bent down to get a good reflection, and started combing my hair. The other members of my crew chuckled, but none of them said anything. That afternoon when we walked back over to the Launch Control Center, the technicians were doubled up with laughter. I had been combing my hair in the lens of an active TV camera, one of those that monitors and tapes the activities in the White Room. The entire TV staff at the LCC—in fact, personnel all over KSC—had been watching me put my nose almost on the lens. They threatened to auction the footage off to one of the TV networks.

Ten minutes before launch time, Franklin crawled back into his seat and cinched up his seat belts. We all double-checked our own belts. I glanced up. There was a big sign hanging above the door to the flight deck that read: Steve Hawley—Big Foot—a standing joke about Steve's shoe size.

At T-9 we went into a hold for six and a half minutes before resuming the countdown. Several of the fellows said they wished they would hurry up and lift off; they needed to use the bathroom. I nodded soulfully in agreement.

But lift-off never came. The count proceeded all the way to thirty-one seconds and was abruptly halted. An alert operator monitoring his console had noticed that one of the oxygen propellant lines was getting too cold. He stopped the count, and we recycled back to T-20, with an hour's hold before starting the count again. Everyone unstrapped and took a potty break.

The Launch Control Center later discovered that a switch had mistakenly been thrown, allowing liquid oxygen to drain from the main fuel tank. That meant there was a possibility of *Columbia* running out of fuel before reaching orbit. There was a lot of debate later about what might have happened. If we had launched, some of the technicians said, we could have made it to orbit, since we had less than a full cargo load and were lighter than we might have been. Others doubted, saying we would have ended up trying to meet the emergency with a transatlantic abort.

It was hard to believe this was happening. We sat around, chatting, with our helmets off. It was breakfast time, but we had to settle for some Hall's Mentholated Cough Drops someone had stuck in his pocket. Franklin, Bob, and Pinky sat down on the floor (actually, it was the back wall, since the shuttle was sitting on its tail) and rested. At 7:38 A.M. we were told our launch window extended to 9:01 A.M., meaning we could launch as late as that and still get into our planned orbit. We all strapped back in, and shortly after 8:00 A.M. the countdown started again.

It was obvious from the chatter on the earphones that the engineers at RCA, whose satellite we were carrying, were not happy with the situation. They wanted a longer launch window. Finally, the word came to shut down the orbiter. We'd try it again the next day.

It was interesting that NASA's public explanation of what caused the delay was that a valve had failed to close, thereby allowing the liquid oxygen to drain out of the fuel tank. The truth is, however, that the valve did not close because it was not commanded to close. It was later that the Rogers Commission, investigating the series of mistakes that forced this second scrub, recognized that the problems were personnel-related, caused by fatigue from overwork:

One potentially catastrophic human error occurred 4 minutes, 55 seconds before the scheduled launch of mission 61-C on January 6, 1986. According to a Lockheed Space Operations Company Incident Report, 18,000 pounds of liquid oxygen were inadvertently drained from the Shuttle External Fuel Tank due to operator error. Fortunately, the liquid oxygen flow dropped the main engine inlet temperature below the acceptable limit causing a launch hold, but only 31 seconds before lift-off. As the report states, "Had the mission not been scrubbed, the ability of the Orbiter to reach defined orbit may have been significantly impacted" (Rogers Commission, page G-11).

Of far greater import, however, although not even noted at the time, was that the outside temperature that morning was forty-two degrees. Had our engines fired, it is possible the same fate would have awaited us that awaited the crew of *Challenger* three weeks later, on January 28. At thirty-six degrees, the rubberized O-rings in *Challenger*'s solid rocket booster joints stiffened so much that they failed to seat properly—leading to the shuttle's fiery destruction seventy-three seconds after lift-off.

Why them, and not us? There are no answers for some questions. As for us, we would yet fly.

On Tuesday, January 7, we tried again. The temperature was up to an almost pleasant fifty-six degrees, but the sky was overcast. This time we went no further than the nine-minute mark in the countdown. We were scrubbed again. First, the weather at our RTLS (return to launch site) landing strip was bad. Then, a small boat wandered into the area where the big solid rocket boosters would drop into the ocean. Finally, it was determined we should not go because the weather in Senegal and Spain, our two alternate emergency landing sites, was bad. We were in the orbiter a total of five hours before crawling out and heading back to our quarantine quarters.

Only later did we learn that a temperature probe had broken its weld in the ground-support equipment and had passed along the oxygen line to stick in a prevalve near the engine. This was discovered during the detanking procedure after the scrub. Had we launched that day, it is possible one engine would not have shut down on orbit and would have blown the aft section of the spaceship to bits.

NASA had never before scrubbed a shuttle launch three times in a row. Our crew had now been on their backs inside a loaded orbiter on the pad more than any other crew. Of course, not all our time was spent on our backs. Part of the time was spent sitting up on the backs of our reclining seats. During these breaks, if the two fellows up on the flight deck wanted to stretch, they had to crawl down to where we were because there was no place for them to stand in the cockpit—every wall was covered with switches. We were all beginning to feel a bit tired, though we were not disheartened.

Still, we couldn't help but wonder: If we didn't get off soon, would the entire mission have to be scrubbed to make way for the *Challenger*, which was sitting, ready, on the other pad?

We tried again on January 10. The forecast called for heavy showers throughout the region, with the possibility of clearing skies later in the morning. Despite some hesitation on the part of the crew and outspoken criticism of the decision to launch by senior astronaut John Young, we loaded into the van before dawn and rode to the pad in a driving rainstorm. Shielded by umbrellas and yellow rain slickers, each man dashed out of the van for the relative shelter of the metal elevator. Out over the ocean I could see lightning flashes.

By the time I was suited up and strapped in, it was obvious to all of us that unless there was a drastic change in the weather, there would be no flight that day. By 7:00 A.M. the rain was still hammering on the silica tiles of the shuttle and the lightning had become more fierce. We were sitting in the middle of an early morning thunderstorm—a real rarity along the east coast of Florida.

Launch Director Gene Thomas came on the radio to talk to us. He said they were going to continue the countdown to T-9 and hold for the remainder of the launch window. He said the weather across the entire state of Florida was bad.

On the flight deck I heard Hoot and Charlie give a yelp. They said something big had just flown through the xenon lights and across their windows. "Bigger than a bird," Charlie said. What mysterious force was out there? I knew better than to say anything.

Lying on my back, helpless to make suggestions, listening to my commander and pilot commenting about the lightning strikes, I began to get philosophical. I silently renewed my resolves concerning my relationship to my family, to my goals, to my God. Things come into clear focus when you are on top of a rocket loaded with millions of pounds of explosives, sticking up like a lighting rod in the middle of a thunderstorm.

About 8:45 A.M. the word came that there was no chance of a launch. They told us to sit tight.

As we waited for the hatch to open, I could see the worried looks on the faces of my crew mates each time the lightning flashed. It was obvious what lightning could do if it struck our spaceship loaded with liquid hydrogen and liquid oxygen. The lightning rod on the top of the launch tower had always worked in the past, drawing lightning away from the loaded rocket. But I knew of too many instances where lightning had not struck the tallest thing around, but had capriciously struck lower objects—especially if they were made of materials that would conduct electricity. It was like sitting on top of an open powder keg while fire rained from heaven.

It took thirty minutes for the suit techs to get to the pad, the rain was so violent. Everyone got sopping wet as we raced down the access arm. Driving away from the pad, we could barely see the orbiter through the drenching rain—except when it was momentarily illuminated by a brilliant lightning flash.

Afterward, I talked to John Young, America's daddy astronaut, who had been highly critical of NASA's decision to fill the shuttle with fuel when the weather forecast predicted severe thunderstorms. "I'm not a particularly religious man," he told me, "but I am convinced there was Someone taking care of you on this mission."

Fourteen months later, NASA and the U.S. Air Force weather advisors at Cape Canaveral had still not learned their lesson.

On March 26, 1987, in the midst of a thunderstorm with light-ning in the area, a decision was made to launch an unmanned Atlas Centaur rocket carrying a sophisticated military payload essential to our nation's defense. It had barely cleared the tower when it was struck by five lightning bolts, broke up, and plunged into the sea.

Desperate to get NASA to change the regulations, Hoot Gibson released a statement to the *Houston Post* citing the light-ning that had also scrambled the electronics of a moon-bound Apollo in 1969. "Maybe sometimes we have to learn lessons over," Gibson said. "Hopefully, we won't do that with the manned program."

Four scrubs! None of us could believe it. The joke going around the space center was that they were holding Bill Nel-son hostage to get more money from Congress. However, if I could promise them what they wanted, they'd hurry up and fix the problems and get me into space.

We were given one more shot at a launch two days later— probably our last chance. January 12, 1986, dawned as "severe clear": unlimited ceiling, unlimited visibility. We launched just before the sun peeked its golden head above the dark blue, mirror-smooth Atlantic Ocean. We were right on schedule for what turned out to be an almost flawless six-day mission.

Straight Up and Accelerating

There's a certain amount of desensitizing that occurs after four scrubs. In our case, after our four trips out to the pad and the four times we'd strapped in for lift-off, the fifth trip was almost routine. Except for the few days off at Christmas, we had been in quarantine thirty-three days. It was Sunday morning, January 12, 1986.

Riding in the van from our quarters to the pad, one of the fellows suggested we get the "old gang" back together again in March. We could meet in Vero Beach, just a few miles south of the Cape, and work out with the L.A. Dodgers for spring training. We all shouted approval.

Despite the horseplay and the now established routine, I still felt my heart begin to beat faster as we approached the rocket in the early morning darkness. I suspected this would be it. The weather was perfect. Patrick Air Force Base had reported the outside temperature at fifty-one degrees. The dark sky was cloudless, the wind calm. As the brilliant xenon lights reflected off the dazzling white wings and fuselage of the shuttle, I was struck by the remarkable contrast between the white back of the craft and the dull black of the underside, made up of heat-deflecting silica tiles. Once more that magnificent space creature was alive, waiting to be saddled, mounted, and given free rein to take off. I had been through this procedure four times already. Yet still, the sense of personal excitement, the sense of being on the cutting edge of exploration, the sense of making myself totally dependent on the grace of God—all combined to the extent that I actually gasped for breath as the door of the van opened and I stepped out, looking up at the miraculous ship.

I had just strapped in when Steve Hawley stuck his head in the hatch door. He was wearing a Groucho Marx mask, the kind with the black hornrimmed glasses, huge nose, and bushy mustache. He had stuck a piece of gray conduit tape over his name plate.

I burst out laughing. "Who *is* that!"

Hawley, who had the distinction of having had more scrubs than any other astronaut, said, "Shhhh! I'm trying to fool *Columbia* so she won't know who I am and scrub again!"

The suit tech finished cinching my harness. The harness had been prefitted and had my name tag on the Velcro. It consisted of a chest belt that went over my shoulders and strapped through my crotch on both sides. We wore it in case we had to use the emergency rope pulley from the escape hatch in the flight deck window. Built into the harness were two inflatable life preservers in case we came down in the ocean. I thought of a friend of mine who discovered, after he purchased his flame-resistant camping tent, that while it would not burn, neither was it waterproof. I wondered if my inflatable life preservers were flame-resistant as well as water-repellent—or was that a moot question? If there was a flash fire on lift-off, I'd certainly never live to find out.

Lying on my back with my feet elevated in lift-off position, I checked my pockets. Five times I had put the same things in them. I had my voice-activated tape recorder; my pocket Bible; the regular equipment pieces NASA had issued—scissors, knife, and small flashlight; and last, stowed carefully in my ankle pocket, Nan Ellen's tape. I had a NASA handkerchief but carried my own comb—the same one I had used to comb my hair in the active TV camera lens. I was also wearing my hard contact lenses. The doctors did not think I would have any trouble with them in space. They took care to remind me, however, that when you drop a contact lens on earth the only place you have to search for it is on the floor. If you drop it in space, there's no telling where it might float off to.

I smiled when I realized I had automatically reached back to check my left hip pocket. There was no need to carry a wallet into space. Even American Express cannot give you credit once you leave the state of Florida—that is, if you're traveling straight up. Nor was I wearing the ever-present plastic security badge all NASA personnel are required to display on their shirt, jacket, or blouse. There was a standing joke that the astronauts had better wear their badges when they climbed aboard the shuttle or the security guards would not let them on.

Bill Shepherd, our Cape crusader—the astronaut designated to make the final checks—talked us through the radio checks. Bill had been in the shuttle since midnight, checking all the switches to make certain they were in the right configuration. His final task before leaving the shuttle was to do a voice communication check to make sure we were all on the right channels. I reached down and touched a button on the black box clamped to one of the straps on my flight suit. It activated the microphone in my helmet so I could use the intercom.

"Okay, Steve, this is PS-Two. [That was my designation, short for Payload Specialist Two.] How do you read?"

"Loud and clear, PS-Two," Hawley answered.

Next, Bill Shepherd talked us through our communication checks with Fred Gregory, at Mission Control in Houston. Fred went through each crew member in turn, checking us out to make certain we could both hear and be heard.

"Good morning, Fred," I said. "This is PS-Two."

"Loud and clear, Congressman," he replied.

Bill was the last one to leave, climbing out of the hatch and waving goodbye. The hatch door closed. This time the latch caught the first time. I looked at my watch. It was 5:01 A.M. We had one hour and fifty-four minutes to wait.

The night before, as we had on most of the nights before our scrubbed launches, we had eaten together in the dining area next to the crew quarters. Then we headed for the sauna before taking a shower and going to bed early. As usual, the conversation turned to all the things that could go wrong. The possibilities were legion. Since our first launch, I had discovered that the number of moving parts on the rocket and shuttle that could malfunction and cause disaster on lift-off had increased from what I first thought was 750 to a more accurate figure of 1,192. If I were a gambling man, and the odds shifted like that just before the bell at the track, I would have changed horses.

But I was certain this was the steed I was to ride—despite the 1,192 things that could go wrong and destroy the mission.

Danger was not new to these men. Men like Hoot and Charlie knew that every time they strapped into one of those powerful military jets, they were taking on almost the same odds. Therefore, that Saturday night, sitting in the sauna, the same positive spirit prevailed that I had noticed before each of the other flight attempts, but this time even stronger. We knew the weather was going to be good. We'd gotten a report on the weather in Dakar, Senegal, and Morón, Spain—our emergency transatlantic landing sites. That looked good, too. Everything looked "go."

I knew we could make it if we lost one of the engines on lift-off. "But what happens if we lose two of the three engines?" I had once asked Hoot.

"We're in the water," he had replied matter-of-factly.

From previous conversations I had surmised that there was

little chance we would survive a water landing. Structurally, the men felt, it was very likely that the speed necessary to maintain a glide slope in landing—in excess of two hundred miles an hour—would cause us to break up the moment we hit the sea.

Nevertheless, Hoot went ahead to outline what we would do in such a case. Assuming we were in a normal glide as we came in for a crash landing in the sea, he would blow the top hatch just before hitting the water. He did not feel the shuttle would stay intact when it hit. That meant the frame around the internal crew compartment would probably bend, fouling up the alignment of the window we would need as an escape hatch in case the door did not open. Unless the hatch was opened before impact, there was a good chance it might not open at all.

The astronauts discussed their hopes that NASA would redesign some aspects of the shuttle—such as the door that could be accidentally opened in space—and make additional evaluations of how the shuttle would act in an emergency water landing.

The critical point, as far as the main engines were concerned, was seven and a half minutes after lift-off. Although the main engines cut off at eight minutes and thirty-six seconds into flight, if they worked through the seven-and-a-half-minute mark, the shuttle would still go on into orbit—or we could pick an emergency landing site. We would not drop back into the ocean. I made a mental note to check my stopwatch at seven and a half minutes after lift-off so I could breathe more easily.

Perhaps because this was the fifth launch eve I had gone through in less than a month, I didn't have any problem going to sleep. I had set my wrist alarm to go off at 2:20 A.M., a few minutes before the normal wake-up call on launch morning.

As soon as I was awake, I dashed for the bathroom down the hall. The crew quarters took up part of the third floor of the Operations and Checkout building. The *Columbia* crew had a corridor to themselves. The rest of the rooms were occupied by the Cape crusaders, the other astronauts who came over from Houston to go out to the orbiter and configure all the switches prior to our boarding. George Abbey, chief of the astronauts, also had a room there.

Bob Cenker always beat me to the bathroom. That morning our timing was perfect. Cenker showered while I shaved, allowing me to get into the shower by the time Franklin and Pinky arrived in the bathroom. We dressed casually, then gathered in the dining area for breakfast. A few other NASA people had arrived by that time, and the NASA TV cameras were in place, taking our pictures as we ate. After breakfast we put on our lightweight flight suits, then gathered for the morning weather briefing.

As usual, the briefing was extensive. The commander and pilot sat with their lap boards, writing down all the usable data. This was necessary to determine things like which runway to use at alternate landing sites, what to expect if we aborted on takeoff and had to do an RTLS (return to launch site), winds aloft, and ground wind speeds. I had to keep reminding myself that the shuttle was not an airplane. It did not have an engine to be used on landing. It was nothing more than a huge, heavy glider that had the aerodynamic ability of a large, flat rock.

Jet pilots, and especially astronauts, have a reputation for being daredevils. Even though Hoot was studied and deliberate in everything he did—actually supercautious—he had a daredevil streak in him as well. I found out during training that some fighter pilots consume a drink called a Flaming Hooker, which is a lighted Drambuie. The procedure is to pour the drink into a glass, set it on fire, swallow the entire contents while it is flaming, then set the glass back down—the fumes still burning. I had not seen this done, but everyone said Hoot could do it. Fighter pilots seem to be a special breed.

Back in the shuttle we went through the multitude of checks that are part of the lift-off procedure.

I could hear the air blowing in as they pressurized the cabin from the outside. We went through the initial cabin-pressure leak check, and everything was fine. Cabin pressure was a steady 14.7 psi.

During the next hour, as the checks continued, I spent a good bit of time dictating my thoughts into my handheld tape recorder. At the time I had no idea that those thoughts, and the details I was recording, would make up the core of this book.

All the while, the pilot and commander were running their checks. At T-20 I felt movement on the orbiter as they configured all the switches, checking the flight surfaces and gimballing the engines. Next, they checked the pneumatic helium valves. At T-9 the launch director, Gene Thomas, came on the air.

"It looks like it's a 'go.' Our best to the best flight crew we've had around here in a long time."

"That's because we've been around here a long time," Steve retorted.

A minute and a half later, I imagined a slight scraping outside the orbiter. By twisting my head to look outside the window, I could see the access arm retract. Now we were standing alone on the pad. I was reminded just how complicated the space machine was. We were, in pilots' lingo, going to "push the envelope."

At four minutes before launch we lowered our visors. I thought of Grace and the children on the roof of the Launch Control Center watching this spaceship poised to ignite toward the heavens. They and everyone else not directly involved were kept a good three and a half miles away, in case of explosion.

Thirty-one seconds before launch, we switched to the on-board computers. I pulled back my gloves to glance at my watch. We had been given a choice as to the type of gloves we wanted to wear for launch: a light tan doeskin glove, or the greenish-gray standard Air Force glove that is fire resistant. I was wearing the Air Force glove and pulled back the cuff so I could punch my stop watch at T-O.

The engines ignited at T-6.6 seconds. I felt a powerful surge of energy, even though there was no perceptible movement, since we were still bolted to the pad. I knew it was possible, still, for the automatic sequencer to shut down the engines. Steve Hawley had been on a previous flight that had gone into automatic sequencing, and the computer had shut off the engines at T-2 seconds—four and a half seconds after the engines had ignited.

I knew it could happen to us, but I didn't expect it. During this time, tens of thousands of gallons of water were being dumped on the exhaust in the huge concrete exhaust basin at the base of the rocket. Without this precautionary measure to suppress the acoustic shock wave, the shock would destroy the shuttle.

Now the entire ship was vibrating, and the roar of the rocket engines was almost deafening as the engines thrust against the restraints. Yet, *Columbia* was still strapped to the ground.

At T-O I punched my stopwatch. At the same instant there was a jolt and a huge roar. I pulled my hands back up against my chest and turned my head to the left so I could see out of the window. Everything was gray. It was the gray steel of the tower, and I could see it sliding by the window as we began our ascent.

I was astounded at how quickly we were moving, slow at first then faster with each second. It took only four seconds to clear the tower, the engines burning furiously. As we cleared the tower I could see the ground illuminated by the fire of the motors. The next view from the window was darkness, then the lights of Cape Canaveral.

Hoot Gibson was talking us through the lift-off. "There go the engines."

Suddenly, I felt a tremendous kick, a surge of energy as I was pinned on my back.

A launch of the space shuttle. [Photo by Michael R. Brown]

"Okay, the solid motors have ignited. We're climbing."

Ten seconds into launch, above the roar of the engines, I heard Charlie Bolden say, "We're starting our roll maneuver."

The launchpad, which had originally been used for the Apollo missions, had been refurbished for the shuttle launches. As a result, the orbiter's back was facing south as the rocket sat on the pad. In order to get into the proper flying attitude, the orbiter needed to change position. That meant as soon as we cleared the tower, the computers sent us into a ninety-degree roll maneuver that turned us so our back was facing east. Now we were climbing straight up, strapped to the huge rocket.

Suddenly, over my earphones, I heard the words that made my skin prickle.

"We have a malfunction."

It was Charlie Bolden's calm voice talking on the intercom.

"We have a helium leak."

He was talking to the crew, not the ground.

Even though I could not see Charlie, who was eight feet above me in the separate flight deck compartment, I knew what he was doing. There was no panic. He was efficiently reconfiguring the switch—going by the book.

During the next few seconds he calmly talked us through a potential crisis—a crisis I later discovered was sufficient to have shut down one of our three engines while we were ascending straight up. As this was going on, Hoot was talking to Mission Control in Houston, which had taken over from Launch Control at KSC the moment we had cleared the launch tower. Charlie, however, was too busy trying to stop the helium leak to talk to Mission Control. That was not done until the emergency was resolved, the apparent leak electronically blocked off, and the danger past. Then Charlie pushed the button that put him in touch with Mission Control and reported what had just happened.

A few seconds, I discovered, can seem like a lifetime when your safety hangs in the balance.

The emergency underscored that it was not the people on

the ground who flew the machine; it was the commander and pilot. They were at the controls. Even though everything was programmed by computer, when something went wrong, they had to know what to do. But after having spent hundreds of hours in the simulator, working through every possible type of emergency, both Hoot and Charlie knew exactly what to do when the gauge on the instrument panel went wild, showing helium was leaking in the spacecraft.

Thirty seconds into flight, we entered the stage of maximum dynamic pressure on the spaceship, or *Max Q* as NASA calls it. Even though there was no sensation other than the vibration and noise, it was at this point that we passed through the sound barrier, gaining speed at an incredible rate. However, since we were still in the thicker, lower atmosphere of the earth, full speed during Max Q could destroy the spaceship. It was impossible to control the thrust of the savage solid rocket boosters, which were burning violently on each side of the spaceship. But it was possible to control the thrust of the three main engines located in the tail of the orbiter. As we entered Max Q, the computer throttled the main engines back to 65 percent of their power. This condition of stress would last until we broke free from the dense lower atmosphere.

About sixty-five seconds into the flight, we passed through the tropopause, the limiting boundary of earth's lower troposphere, into the thinner atmosphere called the stratosphere. The stratosphere was first reached by Auguste Piccard in a balloon in 1931. Back then it took him many hours of ascent. We had just made it in less than one minute.

Coming up on forty thousand feet, we heard Hoot's calm voice.

"Throttle up and go."

We had left Max Q. The engines were being throttled up to 104 percent, or full power.

I was surprised how quickly time now began to go by. At two minutes and eight seconds into the flight, there was a loud thud as pyrotechnic charges blew the bolts and separated the solid rocket boosters from the external tank. I was startled by the huge jolt as they broke loose. Suddenly, it was quiet as the SRBs, still burning fiercely from their tails, slipped away. Later, the big parachutes opened, and they began their long fall back into the Atlantic Ocean, where they would be recovered and used again.

For a moment I was puzzled at the lack of noise; then I remembered we were flying faster than the speed of sound and the exhaust of the main rocket engines was behind us. Our speed was increasing toward our maximum of 17,795 miles per hour—which would be our orbiting speed around the earth.

At six and a half minutes, the G forces began putting powerful pressure on my body. I was aware that I was aboard a finely tuned racing machine. Everything was working perfectly. I glanced at my watch and saw the digits change as we passed the seven-and-a-half-minute mark. I felt a sense of relief. Now, even if two of the main engines cut off, we could make it to one of the emergency landing sites without having to ditch in the ocean. All three of our engines kept on humming.

The G forces on my body continued to increase until there were three Gs of pressure on my chest, back, and stomach. I strained against them by tightening my stomach. Although I had experienced G forces in the supersonic jets, these were stronger than I expected. Then I realized it was because I was on my back, and the force was sustained for almost two minutes through the chest. The sensations were much different from those I'd experienced in the backseat of an F-16 as it made tight fifteen-second turns, only momentarily ripping the oxygen mask off my face and causing my lips to pull away from my teeth.

As we reached orbital velocity, the main engines suddenly cut off. Instantly, the G forces disappeared, replaced just as suddenly by weightlessness.

Now in zero gravity, still strapped to my seat, I stared in wonderment as my arms started floating at chest level right in

Smoke trail of the Columbia *during launch ascent on January 12, 1986.*
[NASA photo]

front of my eyes. I glanced over at Franklin. His arms were floating, too. Debris on the cabin floor, which had shaken loose during the vibrations of the ascent, was starting to float up. The entire powered ascent had taken only eight minutes thirty-six seconds. I felt a mixture of gratitude and disbelief.

The huge external fuel tank, now empty of its liquid hydrogen and oxygen, suddenly separated with an audible bang. It blew away and fell, tumbling back into the atmosphere where it would burn up on reentry.

Fred Gregory, our CAPCOM at Mission Control back in Houston, greeted us enthusiastically: "Welcome to space, rookies!"

On Orbit

Life at zero gravity has its own peculiar laws, and I at once began to notice changes. Most immediately, my body fluids had started to shift out of my legs and into my upper torso. I looked around. Both Bob's and Franklin's face had become red and puffy. I could feel the pressure in my own cheeks and realized I was puffing up like a chipmunk with a mouthful of acorns. The sensation was like hanging upside down when all the blood rushes to your head—which is precisely what had happened. Well, actually, it hadn't all rushed to my head. It was simply being distributed evenly throughout my upper body, rather than heading for my feet, as it does on earth. I was somewhat uncomfortable, and I was thankful for the many warnings I'd received in training.

Suddenly, the quiet of orbit was broken by a huge clap of thunder. Startled, I shouted, "What's that?"

Almost at the same time, the first shock was followed by several smaller thuds, sending a tremor through the entire ship.

Franklin, who had already unbuckled and was floating over his seat, smiled. "That's the big jets firing."

These "burns" were caused by the mixing of the hypergolic fuels controlled by our on-board computers. The result was an instant explosion, or burn, in the nine-hundred-pound reaction-control thrusters. As these big rockets fired, usually for only a second or two, they adjusted the attitude of the orbiter.

After we achieved orbital velocity above the earth's atmosphere, our flight profile called for us to have two burns of the big, hydrazine OMS (orbiter maneuvering system) engines located in the rear of the spacecraft. The first burn raised us from our initial orbit altitude of 70 miles above earth's surface to 203 miles up, in an eliptical orbit. Thirty minutes later, the second OMS burn circularized our orbit at the higher altitude. The first burn produced only a light jolt, and I didn't feel any acceleration. When the engines cut off, there was another jolt. The engines then burned for two minutes for the second time, setting us in orbit at 17,795 miles an hour. This meant it would take us approximately ninety minutes to circle the earth. We were moving, if you were viewing us from the earth's surface, from west to east. Of course, in space, just as there is no up or down, neither is there any east or west, north or south.

I remembered the explanation Professor Pope gave to his class in James Michener's *Space:*

> You must break the habit, in your thought if not in your speech, of saying 'up to the moon' or 'back down to Earth' or 'up to the stars.' There is no 'up' or 'down,' no 'above' or 'below.' There is only 'out to' and 'back from' in reference to the center of the Earth. If you use the plane of the Galaxy as reference, we're clearly off the central axis, but whether we're up or down, who knows? I don't even like the phrase 'out to the edge of the universe.' We may be on the edge, so that everything we see exists between us and the opposite edge. More likely, the

edge is everywhere, for I think that space is without direction or definition. You can't express it in words. . . .

Unlike the millions of pounds of thrust it took to force us out of the earth's atmosphere, it only takes a gentle shove to move the 110-ton orbiter in any direction in space, because there is virtually no air resistance at all. In fact, a man could turn the orbiter over by himself—if he had anything to brace against. Therefore, we used the small rockets, called *verniers*, to push us into the desired position. These same rockets would fire automatically throughout our orbit, making course and attitude corrections. The jolts of the bigger jets—the nine-hundred-pound thrusters—were so pronounced in the absolute silence and virtual weightlessness of space that they sounded like one freight train car coupling to another.

I stuffed a stick of chewing gum into my mouth. I thought that might help me maintain a degree of normalcy. Franklin was chewing some also. What's good for the professional should be good for the amateur, I thought.

Still strapped in my seat, I kept watching my arms float in front of my face. My brain was so accustomed to Earth's gravity that operating at zero gravity would take special effort.

As I unhooked my restraints, I felt my body gently float away from my chair. I was hesitant at first. The sensations were similar to those I had experienced in the KC-135, but there was one profound difference. I felt a rush of elation: This was real!

Franklin and Bob had already started the cabin-unstow procedure. During this time the second lengthy OMS burn took place, putting us in proper orbit around the earth. It was a longer burn, and this time I was aware of a definite acceleration. The helmets and helmet bags that had previously been floating freely were now tugging gently against their cords like a helium balloon in a breeze.

I was eager to get to the window, but just as eager to test out my weightlessness in my new microgravity environment.

Remembering my mistake in the KC-135 when I pushed off too hard and bashed my head against the ceiling, I allowed myself to drift upward away from the seat, then grabbing hold of the wall, I gently pulled myself over to the window. I had seen the photographs of earth from space, of course, and had looked at the movies and videotapes. But nothing came close to matching what I saw as I pressed my face against the small aperture.

"It's unbelievable!" I exclaimed out loud, more to myself than to anyone else.

I could see quite clearly the curvature of the earth. At the edge was a bright blue band that faded into the pitch black darkness of space. The whole impression was one of azure blue and dazzling white—blue from the oceans and white from the clouds and the polar caps. Words tumbled through my mind: beautiful, fragile, magnificent. On the night side of the planet, the inky black was punctuated by brilliant stars. It seemed I could see forever.

Suddenly, I saw something right outside the window, floating along beside us. It was a shiny cylinder about one and a half inches long. I finally determined it was a piece of ice that had formed on the super-cold external fuel tank. Now it had broken off and was following us around, sparkling and flashing in the sun as it slowly rotated on its own parallel orbit— journeying forever in space.

Earth was quickly moving into darkness, although the sun was still reaching the shuttle window. Floating freely now, I felt myself rotating so that my feet were touching the ceiling of the orbiter. There was no sensation of being upside down. I watched as the bright blue of the earth quickly slid away, swallowed up in the inky blackness of night. All that remained was the brilliant blue strip of the horizon—then that disappeared, too. Nothing was left but pure black—and a million stars in space. I found myself chewing my gum furiously.

I kept having to steady myself in my floating position to keep from drifting away from the window. But I knew I could not stay. There was too much that needed to be done inside the spacecraft. I had removed my helmet and I now put it in my color-coded stowage bag, which I tied to a handle in front of my seat. Each crewman had such a bag, in which he placed his space helmet, flight boots, space harness, and the emergency supply of air that had been attached to the seat. Hoot's color was red; Charlie's, yellow; Steve's, green; Franklin's, orange; Pinky's, blue; Bob's, brown; and I was purple. A color-coded dot had been attached to every item of our personal possessions in case any of our stuff—such as my tape recorder—floated off into the cabin. These seven stowage bags, packed full of equipment, were stowed in any nook or cranny we could find. Most of the men stuffed theirs under the lockers.

Since we'd entered zero gravity, my nose had become stuffy, but my eyes, even with the hard contacts, seemed fine. I attributed my stuffy nose to the adjusting of the fluid levels in my body. The only problem I had was when a small piece of debris floating around in the cabin got in my eye.

We activated the space toilet and the galley. Then we detached the heavy seats from their fasteners on the floor, folded them down, and floated them over to a location under the lockers, where we taped them into position. They would not be used until reentry. The only seats that stayed were the pilot's and commander's seats. We opened the airlock door. Then we unclamped the treadmill that was to be used in one of my experiments from its position in front of the crew seats and moved it away from the lockers to its on-orbit position in front of the airlock.

It turned out to be a lot of work. At first, tasks took twice as long as on earth, in part because we were adapting to our new environment. Thus, the simple act of moving the treadmill—unlocking the clamps and locking it into its new position—required the joint efforts of Bob, Franklin, and myself, for a period of some five minutes.

While this was going on, the commander and pilot were going through their checks—aligning us by computer into the proper attitude and reconfiguring our position in inertial space so that the computers had the updated information on exactly where we were. The rest of us grabbed these spare moments to change from our flight clothes into the more comfortable short-sleeve shirt, space trousers and slipper-stockings.

Finished with my initial assignments, I floated up to the flight deck as the other crew members finished their tasks. We were just coming up on the west coast of Africa from the Atlantic. Ahead was the Indian Ocean. The clouds were brilliant white and puffy, and the air was so clear I could see the shadows they cast over the land below. I remembered hearing stories that had drifted back from the Russian cosmonauts—true or not, I did not know—that after a number of days in space their eyes had become so acclimated they could actually see submarines beneath the surface of the sea. Behind us, through the window that opened out over the cargo bay, I could see an unbelievable sunset, in hues of deep orange and red. Beyond that was a dark blue that faded into the black of space as the sun went down beyond the earth's horizon.

I reached down into my zippered pocket and pulled out my Bible. I remembered when, as a student at Yale, I had read the ancient words of the Nineteenth Psalm, written by a shepherd boy in Israel almost three thousand years ago. My college mind had wondered, What could David possibly know about space? As I read those words again, I was amazed that they could express my feelings so perfectly: "The heavens declare the glory of God. The firmament sheweth His handiwork."

Yury Gagarin, the first Russian cosmonaut, proudly proclaimed when he returned to earth that he had looked for God and had not found him. I looked, and could see nothing else.

Once on orbit, as the fluids shifted into my upper torso, my body's sensors began to tell me to eliminate the excess. I had been putting the matter off for as long as possible, for I still regarded the space toilet with some trepidation. While the familiar variety we use on earth works very well in gravity—

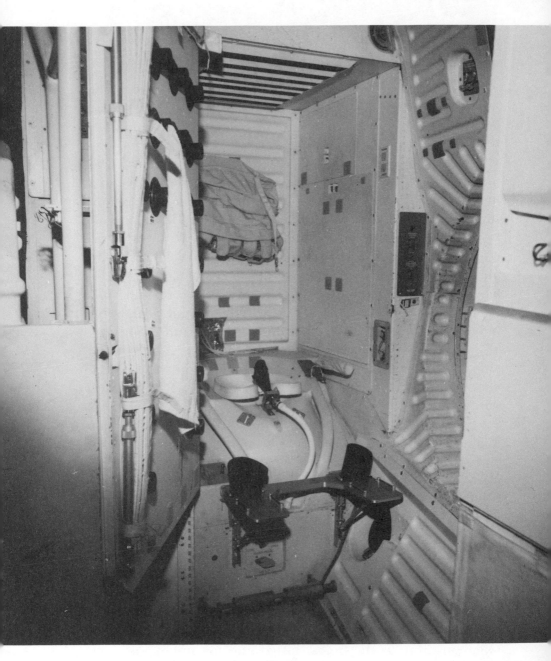

The space toilet aboard Columbia. *[NASA photo]*

where fluids flow downward—it goes without saying that the conditions of weightlessness require such facilities used in space to be of a highly unusual design.

Known in NASA language as the *waste collection system*, the toilet was affectionately referred to by the crew as the WCS. It was relatively easy to use as long as one followed the correct procedures of turning it on and turning it off. It was located in a recessed part of the middeck and came complete with a privacy curtain—a fixture mistakenly omitted from our flight. Each man had his own color-coded urine funnel which was custom-fitted and could be connected to a suction hose running to the holding tank. Had we had a woman on board, she would have used a similarly fitted attachment in essentially the same way. I was puzzled as to why NASA had included several of these latter items aboard *Columbia*, even though we had an all-male crew. I concluded the procedures called for a certain number of "his and her" devices, and if NASA doesn't do anything else, it goes by the book. The toilet itself also worked on suction. This device was a considerable improvement in man's adaptation to spaceflight from the days of the old "Apollo Bag," which was a rather rudimentary procedure for handling waste elimination. The WCS was certainly a great deal more convenient to use. The space toilet now developed for the shuttle surely will work well in the living habitat of the future space station.

One of the primary objectives of the mission was to deploy the RCA communications satellite, which had been carefully prepared and was now cradled in the cargo bay. Once the cargo bay doors were opened, a special sunshield was set in place to protect the satellite from any ultraviolet radiation before it was activated and launched.

Bob Cenker, known as PS-1 (Payload Specialist One), had been invited by NASA to accompany this flight because RCA was NASA's primary customer on the mission—paying NASA a fee of $17 million to launch its satellite. But although he had helped design the satellite, Bob was not responsible for any of the launching procedures. These would be handled by our mission specialists: Pinky Nelson, Steve Hawley, and Franklin Chang-Diaz.

After the cabin gear was unstowed and the orbiter configured in the proper attitude, the preparation and countdown began for the launch of the satellite, which was to occur about ten hours into the first flight day. There were elaborate procedures to be performed by the three mission specialists—procedures that had been practiced over and over in the simulators. Now, on orbit, they went like clockwork, with the three men exchanging verbal data crisply and concisely.

The satellite was deployed with a noticeable thump, and it spun out beautifully, twisting away from the shuttle in a slow rise. Hoot and Charlie, back in the drivers' seats, then moved *Columbia* some eight miles away by firing the small rockets. This kept our underside facing the satellite, to protect us when the engines of the payload-assist module ignited to carry the satellite to geosynchronous orbit 22,300 miles above the earth.

As the OMS hydrazine engines burned briefly to move us out of harm's way, I could once again see unattached items on the middeck floating back—letting me know we were in motion. On earth the awareness of movement is prompted largely by visual cues, as things move past the window of a vehicle, or by feel, as the vehicle moves over an uneven surface. But there was none of that in space, of course. There was no indication we were moving at 17,795 miles an hour. Nor were we aware we had accelerated or changed course except in the initial firing of the rockets, and the way the floating objects in the cabin responded to the acceleration.

We had been warned during training about excess fluids, and on the first flight day I did not take anything to drink. By the evening meal I was fairly hungry, but ate lightly—soup and whole wheat bread. By Flight Day Two, I was hungry as a horse and ate a full breakfast. Also, I had finally adapted to moving around by means of the footloops, which kept me from banging off the walls and ceiling.

Satellite deployment on our flight day one. [NASA photo]

I knew from training sessions that about half of all astronauts get sick in space. I had been told by the NASA doctors that when one turns his head on Earth, the human brain receives messages from eyesight, from neck sensors, and from the movement of the otolithic stones in the inner ear. However, in zero gravity different signals are sent to the brain, since the otolith stones, which respond to gravity, do not stimulate nerve endings in the same way when the head is moved. This "confused signal" is thought to be a cause of SMS—Space Motion Sickness—experienced by our astronauts.

These stones, called *otoliths,* normally detect the position of a person's head and his relationship to the ground. Without gravity, however, the otoliths send confusing signals to the brain. For instance, an astronaut's eyes might tell him he is floating sideways in the space shuttle cabin, but the otoliths send a different signal. Because the signals don't match, as they normally do on Earth, the astronauts get space sick, often throwing up their space food. The space traveler stays sick until his brain learns to ignore the otoliths and only pay attention to what his eyes are telling him.

In consequence, the doctors had warned us to avoid excessive movements on the first flight day so as not to provoke any intense sensations until the brain had adjusted. Although I appeared to be one of the lucky ones and felt no dizziness or nausea, I took care to move slowly and resisted the temptation to perform acrobatics.

On Flight Day Two, however, I began to experiment. I found that as long as I was not touching anything, I could float in zero gravity, make all kinds of movements, then stop—only to find that I was right where I started. Motions such as swimming and walking, while suspended in midair, had absolutely no effect, since there was no resistance.

One of the next things I tried when I was sufficiently acclimated was the fulfillment of a boyhood dream: to stretch out my arms and fly through the air like Superman. But my push off was too hard, and I sailed through the cabin and crashed headlong into the wall. I quickly learned that the slightest push against the wall was sufficient energy to translate me across the entire cabin. Since there was no gravitational resistance, I would continue to move until I bumped into something.

The one who seemed to enjoy zero gravity the most was Pinky Nelson. Pinky frequently amused himself with some acrobatic maneuver as he performed his duties. If there was something different that could be done in zero gravity, Pinky would try it. After lunch on Flight Day Two, he showed me how to play the M&M game. His lunch that day contained a packet of M&M candies. Opening the package, he pulled one out and left it floating in midair in front of his face. Then, by gently blowing against it, he set it in motion across the cabin. By pushing off quickly, he could sail across the cabin, pass the M&M in flight, turn, and catch it in his mouth as it approached.

Another trick was to release water in a big globule and then break it into little globules and catch them with one's mouth.

Later, Franklin showed me how a small magnet, suspended, would actually oscillate back and forth as it tried to align itself with the earth's magnetic field.

Zero gravity allowed me to do all kinds of maneuvers. Having grown up in the Chubby Checker era, I was curious to try to dance the twist in space. It worked terrifically in zero gravity because, with my feet off the ground, there was no restriction at all as I twisted back and forth. My arms would go one way while my body went another. Then, once I stopped, I was right back where I started. The other fellows, all younger, watched my performance with amusement.

Movement across the cabin was best achieved by pushing and pulling. Footloops had been placed at strategic points about the cabin so that we could control our direction with our feet, thus freeing our hands for other duties. That was one of the reasons we all removed our flight boots and spent most of the mission in our slipper-stockings.

I had seen pictures taken on other flights showing astro-

Eating a grapefruit section as it floats into my mouth. [NASA photos]

nauts as they slept. Being earthbound at the time, I found it difficult to comprehend how a person could sleep upside down, floating in the cabin, all without a mattress or a pillow. Therefore, the first night was something I awaited with curiosity. (Flight days were divided into sixteen-hour awake periods and eight-hour sleep periods, regardless of the constantly changing daylight and darkness as we circled the earth every ninety minutes.)

Each of us had been assigned a color-coded sleeping bag (called a *sleep restraint*), which we attached to something stationary, to keep the bag from floating about the cabin. Since up was down and down was up, it made no difference which way the sleep restraint was positioned. I attached mine vertically to the lockers. Others attached theirs to the walls or to the ceiling, while our commander and pilot slept in their seats so they could be at the controls in case of emergency. To sleep while floating was, to say the least, a new sensation. After floating into my sleeping bag, I quickly discovered I wanted something to rest my head against. I knew it was habit, but I felt the overwhelming desire for a pillow. In zero gravity, of course, even if one has a pillow, there is no way to use it. I wound up strapping my head to a foam rubber cushion that was a part of the sleep restraint, with a Velcro strap secured tightly across my face. This strap also served to keep the light out of my eyes during the recurring daylight periods. A couple of the men arranged their sleeping bags in a normal horizontal position, meaning they were level with the cabin floor, facing the ceiling of the orbiter. This was done simply as an aid to the brain so it would not have to deal with another surprise. That first sleep period I took the prescribed thirty milligrams of Dalmane. Although I slept vertically, I got a good eight hours' sleep, my arms tucked inside my sleep restraint for warmth.

After the final meal of one rigorous flight day, Bob Cenker fell asleep floating freely in the cabin. He was so exhausted that none of us wanted to wake him up to put him in his "bed." I was the last to turn in and noticed that Bob was floating close

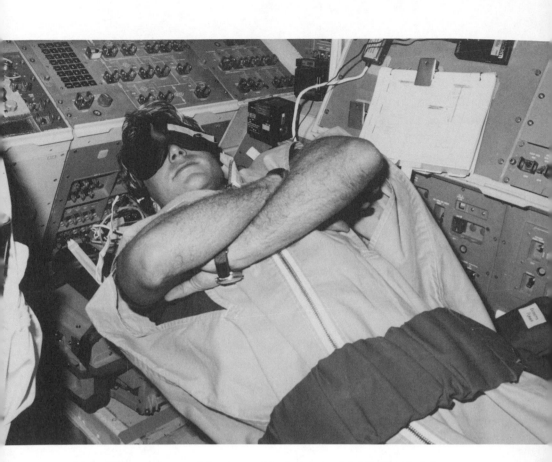

Pinky Nelson asleep and floating in his sleep restraint. [NASA photo]

to where I was strapped to the wall. I knew that sooner or later during the sleep period the air condition currents would drift him over to where I was. He would then bump into me and probably wake us both. Intent on fixing the problem, I tore off two feet of gray sticky tape, stuck one end to a wire coming out of Bob's flight suit, then floated him gently and quietly across the cabin. There I taped him to the wall. And there he remained, sleeping soundly for the rest of the eight-hour sleep time.

I looked forward to meal times. As I had discovered in training, space food was good. NASA had come a long way from the old days when meals were prepared in tubes and squeezed into your mouth.

Pinky Nelson and Steve Hawley showed me a system for preparing a meal that was quick and efficient. We took our food items out of our lockers one by one and stuck them to the food trays, either by using the little strips of Velcro, or by pressing the plastic containers into the flexible, rubberized sockets. We then attached the trays to the lockers by means of the Velcro strips on the back of each tray. The tray could also be stuck to our flight suits, since we had Velcro strips on the suits.

The items that needed to be reconstituted with water were put in the galley and prepared by Steve. Food that needed to be heated was put in the oven. When the food was ready in its individual packages, Steve then floated each one across the cabin to Pinky, who stuck them on the individual trays. It looked so odd, seeing the food arrayed all over the locker doors, or simply floating out in the middle of the cabin.

When dinner was ready, there would be seven trays located on the Velcro strips of the lockers, complete with all the items from the prearranged menus distributed according to the color code.

The two utensils most frequently used were a spoon and a pair of scissors. NASA provided a full set of utensils, including

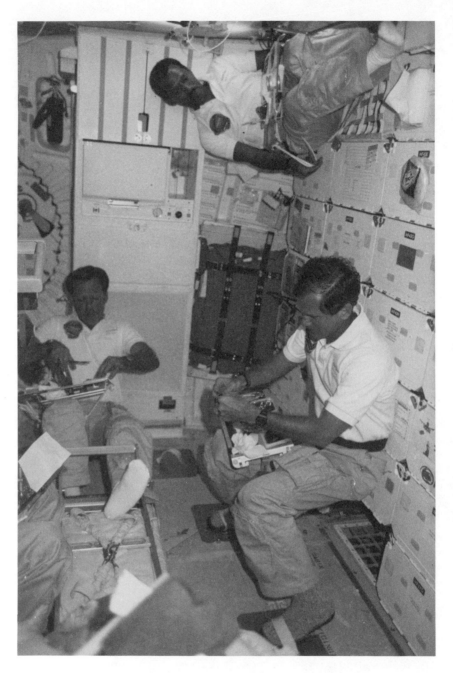

Mealtime for Columbia's *crew. [NASA photo]*

a knife and fork, a large and small spoon, and even a can opener. But like many campers, by the second day I had stowed the knife and fork. For the rest of the flight I ate everything, including my main courses, with my spoon. The only other tool I needed was my scissors, to clip open the package once it was prepared. The spoon was not only easier to clean but easier to eat with, because the food remained stuck to the surface by its own moisture. With the knife and fork, morsels would float away and I would have to go after them. I did learn early on, however, that flipping my spoon would cause the contents to go sailing across the cabin.

Getting into a space-food package was a delicate matter. We first had to clip a small hole in the top to allow air to enter. Then, we scissored off three sides of the plastic top so it stayed connected to the container. I found that the best position to eat in was with my feet in the footloops on the floor and my body taped to the treadmill so that I would be secured and not float away.

I particularly enjoyed the first meal of the day, which was usually granola, oatmeal, and grits. I experimented with a big spoonful of grits, letting them float away and then moving so they would float straight into my mouth.

The only time I thought I would have to use my knife was in trying to cut my space steak. The steaks had been irradiated, then packaged in plastic in their natural juices. Trying to eat one in zero gravity presented a messy problem—keeping the steak juice from floating away when the steak was pulled out of its plastic container. Franklin, the first Hispanic-American astronaut, solved this problem for us with a package of tortillas he had brought along. He just wrapped the steak and its juices in the tortilla. It could then be eaten easily as a steak sandwich without any mess.

While Franklin showed off his ethnic cuisine by bringing out his tortillas, I opened my locker and introduced America's spacemen to the first grapefruit in space. I peeled the grapefruit in its entirety and then pried apart the segments into manageable pieces. However, the first time I tried to open one of the segments, the juice squirted out, formed a ball, and floated off. I tried to go after it with my fingers, but the moment I touched it, it broke into countless little droplets. I was obliged to spend a while floating around the cabin with my mouth open, inhaling grapefruit juice globules before they floated up into the flight deck or disappeared behind the lockers.

While all this was going on—and unknown to me—the Great Grapefruit Controversy, as some of the newspapers were calling it, was gathering momentum on earth. Yet still, as far as I know, NASA was the only one to be overly sensitive about it, and at least one joker responded with good humor. When we finally landed at Edwards Air Force Base, California, the first thing I saw through the hatch window was a sign that had been placed on top of the mobile stairs as they were being rolled out to the shuttle for our disembarkation. It read, "Congressman Nelson: Welcome to California from the California Citrus Association!"

Every minute on orbit was planned in advance, carefully rehearsed, and detailed chronologically in the crew activity plan, according to the mission-elapsed time. The spacecraft was such a complicated machine that it was imperative for the crew to follow the written procedures exactly. With the endless repetition of tasks, there was always a tendency for astronauts to perform their activities by memory. To offset this, we had constantly to remind ourselves of the necessity of going by the checklist. There was a standing rule during training that anyone who carried out a procedure without going by the checklist had to buy beer for the rest of the crew. Throughout the many hours we spent in the simulator, the humdrum of the procedures often would be interrupted by Steve Hawley's mirthful yelp of "Beers!" whenever he thought he had caught someone going through a procedure without referring to the

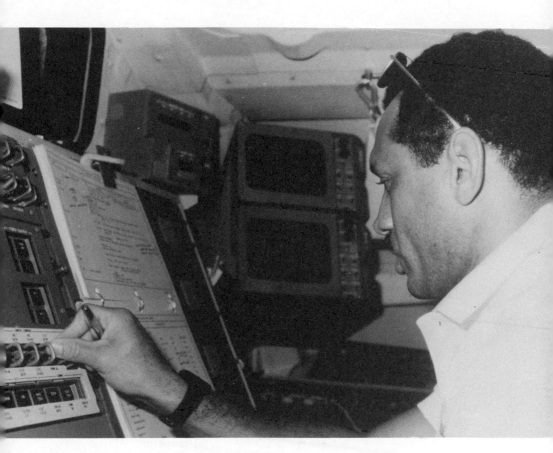

Charlie Bolden does his procedures by the checklist. [NASA photo]

ever-present checklist. So effective was this that on orbit, everyone went according to the book without exception.

During the first part of the mission, none of us really had much opportunity to gaze out of the window back at Planet Earth, because we were all extremely busy. As a result, most of our early views were snatched glimpses that, although short, were breathtaking. The sunrises and sunsets were brilliant and rapid, and when we came out of the shadow of the earth at 17,795 miles per hour, the sunlight would just flood the space-craft. From our perch two hundred and three miles up, we could see part of the earth blanketed by darkness and part lit by the sun's brilliant rays, and we could watch the transition from night to morning. The inky black of outer space was the same whether on the night or daytime side of the earth. That black sky of space was unbelievably black.

On Flight Day Two, I was sitting strapped in Hoot's seat on the flight deck. As I turned to look through the payload bay windows, I could see the tail of the orbiter sticking down toward earth as we flew along, our nose pointed out into space. I was suddenly aware that we were accompanied by a number of little pieces of tile that had come off the bottom of our orbiter. When we left earth there were thirty thousand heat tiles glued to the shuttle, each of which had a serial number. Some parts had obviously broken loose and were now following us around. They were our companions, flying along with us like tiny, glittering fireflies as they caught the light of the sun.

As the earth passed through night and back into the sunlight, I saw we were over Australia. A one-quarter moon, brilliant as could be against the completely black void of space, was moving right along with us. I thought of Vaughn Monroe's song of the late 1940s, "Racin' With The Moon." It was so beautiful I wanted to shout.

Earlier in the day I had been down on the middeck looking out of the hatch window when I saw a water dump. This excess water came from the electrical fuel cells, which combined hydrogen and oxygen. Occasionally we jettisoned water we did

Columbia's *vertical stabilizer points to the earth from 203 miles up. [NASA photo]*

not need out of the spacecraft. It was sprayed out from behind the side hatch, freezing immediately, and gathering in tens of thousands of clustered but individual droplets, looking for all the world like pink cotton candy against the blackness of space.

Everytime I opened my locker, I felt like a kid at summer camp. Carefully packed inside were the NASA-issued dark blue, short-sleeve shirts, my light blue sleep shorts, long flight trousers, enough T shirts and underwear and socks for the duration, handkerchiefs, a big pocket with Velcro strips that could be Velcroed onto any of the flight suits, a jacket, a cassette recorder, a sleep kit including blinders, an extra knife, pencils and pens, and an extra set of eyeglasses. To top it off, before we left earth some unknown Mother to the Astronauts had marked each piece of my clothing with my name. Each of us also had a personal hygiene kit filled with toiletries: toothbrush, toothpaste, comb, brush, skin cream, soap. NASA had even gone to the length of having a special toothpaste dispenser designed, when in fact just squeezing toothpaste out of a regular tube would have been entirely adequate—and a lot less expensive.

Bathing was easy. All I needed was a wet washcloth. The idea, I soon learned, was to bathe only one part of one's body at a time. Since we were manufacturing our own water in space, water was abundant. I would hold my washcloth over the nozzle of the small water hose, then squirt just enough water to dampen it. On one occasion the water shot past the cloth, yet— miraculous to behold—the surface tension of the liquid held it together in a sphere. I was able to trap it by just touching it with my already damp washcloth, whereupon it was quickly absorbed back into the fabric.

Franklin and Pinky even washed their hair with soap—which was a fascinating operation to watch. Since there was no gravity, there was no holding your head over a basin and letting the water rinse your hair clean. You had to continue to dampen your hair all over until the soap came out. After washing, Franklin used the air-conditioning vent—a four-inch-diameter hose from the airlock—as a blow-dryer. It was cold but effective.

Without gravity, the human spinal cord tends to stretch. I had been warned ahead of time this would happen. But after some initial lower back discomfort, there were no other sensations, so I gave it no more thought. Late in the mission, however, we all measured ourselves against the lockers. Each of us had grown. Over the four-day period I had stretched from my normal height of five feet ten and a half inches to six feet— an increase of an inch and a half. I thought of one of my friends back home, who even while I was orbiting in space was lying in traction in a hospital bed, his head encased in a painful harness and his feet dragged down by weights on what looked like a medieval torture device. What the orthopedic doctors were trying to do by stretching his neck and spine, nature was doing to us in space. My spine felt better and more relaxed than I could remember.

One sleep period, I was the last to get into my sleep restraint. The other men were already asleep. Fastening my head against the foam rubber pillow, I had just started thinking of Grace and the children—so far away on earth—when suddenly the silence was broken by the shrill warbling of the shuttle's master alarm. Hoot and Charlie were instantly alert and at once began checking the switches, dials and gauges. I heard Charlie say in a serious voice, "Nitrogen leak."

But after several minutes of intensive checks, they could find no trace of a malfunction that would result in a nitrogen leak in our two-billion-dollar orbiter. They were baffled. Then suddenly they remembered a possibility raised during training: that continuous use of the space toilet might cause such a nitrogen problem to show up on the instrument panel. To our relief, this was subsequently confirmed in a conversation with Mission Control in Houston. My pre-slumber reverie now thoroughly shattered, it was a long time before the adrenalin— which had started pumping furiously the instant I heard that dread alarm—began to subside.

The crew compartment was a cramped space for seven people, and I was beginning to understand why Dr. McGuire, the psychiatrist at JSC, had spent so much time questioning me about my love of people, my ability to give up all privacy for a period of time, and my feelings about taking orders and being part of a highly disciplined team. In such close confines a bad temper, over-sensitivity, a demand to have your own way, or an insistence on private space could cause as much of a crisis as a stuck valve or an immobilized computer. Let it be on record that I never heard one cross word from one crewman to another. Their sense of humor was part of the glue that bound us together. We not only respected one another, we genuinely enjoyed one another's company. But we never delved into the personal areas that could have caused anger or distrust on the mission.

I think astronauts instinctively hold deep feelings inside— simply to survive in space. While I was a people-oriented person, my companions aboard the *Columbia* were basically technicians—highly tuned, disciplined men who had little time to deal with emotions and feelings. As a result, I never felt I could, or should, force a discussion of things such as their religion or their political persuasions. Nor did I feel I was free to ask about their marital relationships, even though we were living in such close quarters. Those things—the emotions, feelings, and deep things of the heart—were much better left for earthlings to handle—rather than seven men locked in a spaceship with no place to hide.

Instead, I learned to confine the expressions of my feelings to frequent conversations with my dictating recorder. I kept it handy in my flight suit pocket, often just turning away from the other crew members to whisper detailed remarks into the machine—usually private observations or records of my feelings. At one point, I floated into the airlock, where I had complete privacy, and did my dictation next to the two spacewalk EVA (Extra-Vehicular Activity) suits. It was almost as if two additional human beings were in the airlock with me, staring back through the glass of their special helmets. We had not planned for a spacewalk on our mission, but the shuttle always carried two spacesuits in case an emergency would require an EVA to correct any problem that could occur outside the spaceship.

After the last meal of each flight day, we would go into the presleep period, which was a time for buttoning up the orbiter for the eight-hour interval. The crew configured all of the switches, established the proper attitude for the spaceship in relation to the earth, and got ready for bed. It was a good time for each of us to dwell in his own thoughts as we drifted off to sleep. Most of us used our tape players with individual earphones to listen to the cassette tapes we had brought along. Charlie had brought Handel's *Messiah,* because he had earlier thought we would be on orbit at Christmas. What more uplifting music to stimulate later explorers than that miraculous oratorio by George Frederic Handel. Sometimes I would glance over at Charlie, relaxed before sleep, his eyes closed, and note the slight smile on his face as he soared on the inspiration of the eighteenth-century music while orbiting earth at five miles a second.

Christopher Columbus wrote that the memory of the music of the monks at La Rabida singing the Gregorian chant "Te Deum" was one of his great inspirations and motivations as he sailed westward into the unknown. As for me, I would listen to the tape that my eight-year-old daughter had made for me. I never tired of listening to her songs over and over as I drifted off to sleep.

Whither Earth?

Gazing out of the window on the third flight day, I was amazed how those early mapmakers could have been so accurate. Looking at earth from space was so much like looking at the big globe in my office that I found myself searching for the lines that divided Georgia from Florida, California from Nevada, and Mozambique from Malawi. There was absolutely no difference between earth seen from two hundred and three miles away, and the outlines of maps I had studied. From where I was floating, I could see whole countries—almost entire continents.

There were no dividing lines, however. Seen from the perspective of space, political, racial, linguistic, and religious divisions all disappear. Looking at earth from high up I saw only one globe—a planet that is itself a fragile spaceship in the black void of space. Although common sense says that with many stars and planets out there, there must be others inhabited by life forms, at this writing the only solid evidence we have of life is life on earth. How sad, then, that those of us privileged to live on this beautiful planet should battle with each other over who owns what. From space it was abundantly clear that earth is very tiny and very precious. Contemplating what man has done to the planet that had been entrusted to him gave me a sad feeling.

Over the Amazon basin of South America, I could see where man had encroached on the jungle—mining, drilling for oil, cutting timber. Incredibly, I could pick out the areas that used to be rich, lush jungle and were now slowly being deforested, turning into desert wastelands. I could see, too, the mighty rivers of the world—the Mississippi, the Amazon, the Nile, the Congo—all producing huge sand deltas where they emptied into the sea as a result of man's misuse of the land along their banks.

It was impossible to look out at earth, from this extraordinary perspective and remain unchanged. That night, after gazing out from the flight deck for a long time, I floated down to the middeck to get into my sleep restraint. I slept for only four hours, then awoke so I could watch as we passed over Egypt and Israel. I was cold, and pulled on my long pants and jacket. I floated over to the window just in time to see the River Nile passing below. It was dark in that hemisphere. The sun had already set across the desert in Libya and both sides of the Nile were lined with what seemed to be millions of tiny Christmas tree lights. I could imagine the Bedouin tents pitched on the banks, with small campfires burning. To the north, twinkling in the sunset, was ancient Alexandria. Beyond it the delta of the Nile extended into the Mediterranean like a huge fan. Directly below me was Cairo, brilliantly lit in the desert like a huge diamond in the sparkling Nile necklace.

Down there, in the rapidly darkening desert, was the place of the extraordinary parting of the Red Sea enabling the Israelites to flee Egypt approximately three thousand years ago. I was intrigued by that miracle as I viewed the earth from my new perspective.

Then, we were over the Sinai. Nine years before, with twelve

The Sinai Peninsula as it looks from space. [NASA photo]

other men, all from different parts of the United States, I had gone on a research trip into the desert. We had spent nine days following the legendary footsteps of Moses, camping out at night under the stars, drinking water from the wells, making friends with the nomadic Bedouins who live in that harsh, hostile land. We had spent one night at the base of Mount Sinai, called by the Bedouins "Jebel Musa"—the Mountain of Moses. That day we had visited the ancient Saint Catherine's Monastery, the oldest inhabited monastery in the world. I had talked to the Greek monks who bury their dead in the sand and later reclaim their bones in order to put them in a charnel house awaiting the return of Christ. That night we had camped in the sand of a deep *wadi*—or canyon—with steep, granite sides. We had gone to bed at dark, knowing we would rise long before dawn to begin the ascent up Mount Sinai. I had stretched out on my back in my sleeping bag, gazing at the incredible array of stars that blinked overhead in the clear night air of the desert.

As I lay there, a hundred thoughts raced through my mind. In just a few hours the thirteen of us, along with our Israeli guide, would rise and start the long, rugged trek up Mount Sinai to reach the summit before dawn. I had been excited— the same kind of excitement I had felt the night before we blasted into space.

Then I saw it: a tiny star moving steadily across the sky from west to east. At first I thought it was a meteor, but it was going too slowly. It was smaller than Mars but as bright as most of the stars in the sky. With sudden recognition, I understood that it was a manmade satellite. I watched it cross the sky until it disappeared behind the dark stone mass of Mount Sinai. What a magnificent irony I had thought—viewing spaceflight from that great symbol of antiquity.

Now, from my perch in front of the window in *Columbia*, the earth darkened in its spin away from the sun, and I could see the Sinai and the nation of Israel. The lights of Tel Aviv and Jerusalem blinked up. Beyond were the lights of Amman, Jordan. To the north and east were Lebanon and Syria, with the lights of Damascus clearly in view. The irony of what I was seeing was clear—from my window the view was so peaceful—a marked contrast to the reality of human hatred on the face of the earth below.

The thought kept running through my mind: if only all people could see earth as I could see it! Here, floating in the midst of an airless blackness that stretches for billions of light years, is flung this fragile ecosystem of a globe we call Earth.

It occurred to me that someday, perhaps in the next century when spaceflight is more routine and less risky, it would be of tremendous value for political leaders to venture into space simply to witness earth from a truly global point of view. Maybe in the next century a summit meeting will be held in space, where the leaders of the superpowers, meeting to decide matters of war and peace, would experience for themselves the fragile unity of the earth in its lone journey.

My perspective was changed because I have seen the earth without political and cultural boundaries. I was awed to see our planet flung out into the black darkness. "Up there" I realized afresh the need for men to come and reason together for understanding and peace.

I floated back to my sleeping bag, praying the message of the angels would yet be heard: "Peace on Earth to men of good will."

Depending on the attitude of the orbiter in space, I always got a different picture of the earth. When the orbiter stayed in a fixed position in relation to a star, its attitude to the earth's surface would change as we orbited the planet. At one point, *Columbia*'s nose would be pointing straight out into space and the tail would be pointing toward earth. Half a revolution later, with the nose straight down, I could be seated in the commander's seat with the Earth filling our windshield.

Sometimes our program called for us to maintain a fixed

attitude to earth, however. After one eight-hour sleep period, we woke up and everyone was cold. We checked the temperature: It was fifty-eight degrees, even though the temperature control had remained constant. The explanation was that during that sleep period the cargo bay had been facing the earth, and the belly of the orbiter had been facing out toward space. That meant that as we circled the earth, the sun only shone on the orbiter's heat-reflecting silica tiles rather than coming through the windows. Normally, when we were in what Hoot called the "barbecue configuration," we were moving sideways around the earth, always turning over and over, which allowed the sun to come in the windows and warm things up.

We carried with us two miniaturized computers, officially called the *shuttle portable on-board computer*. We referred to them as "SPOC." By viewing the screen, we could see the ground-track and location of the spacecraft. Mr. SPOC even alerted us with a beep when a photographic opportunity arose.

When we looked directly at a land mass, the color appeared dull brown. But when we looked out over the whole earth, the impression was of blue and white. I was struck by how prominent certain geographical features appeared from space. Tampa Bay, on Florida's west coast, and Cape Canaveral, on the east coast were the easiest Florida features to identify. The Andes, in South America, rose unmistakably. The Himalayas, near the horizon, seemed to reach out almost through the atmosphere.

The coastal regions were clear and distinct. The browns, reds, and oranges of Somalia contrasted sharply with the bright blue water of the Indian Ocean. The land masses nearly always had clouds over them because the sun warms the earth more quickly than the water, causing the moisture to rise over the land and condense into clouds.

Orbiting earth at 17,795 miles an hour, we passed over continents within a matter of minutes. I no sooner was able to spot the Horn of Africa than we were over India, then China, and out over the Pacific Ocean. Yet it was amazing how much detail I could spot. Crossing the isthmus of Panama, it was

The mission started from there—Cape Canaveral and the Kennedy Space Center, as they appear from orbit. [NASA photo]

easy to see the plume of an erupting volcano, Masaya, in Nicaragua. The wind from the east was blowing the plume of smoke hundreds of miles out to sea. Lake Maracaibo in Venezuela was clearly visible. Passing over the Persian Gulf at night, I could see the bright flares of the oil wells in the desert as they burned off excess gas. Looking down on the jungle-covered mountains of the Philippines, I could almost imagine the thatched huts in the Filipino villages. I spotted the Soviet submarine base in Ethiopia, sitting at the narrow opening where the Red Sea joins the Indian Ocean, and realized how strategically situated it was. The cotton fields of Egypt, Lake Okeechobee in Florida, the contrail of a jet airplane over Malaysia—all were vividly clear. Hanging upside down with Pinky Nelson, sipping hot coffee through a straw, I saw the brilliant night lights of Rio de Janeiro and wondered if any sightseers on top of Pão de Açúcar—Sugarloaf Mountain—were sipping Brazilian coffee and looking up at us as we emerged from the Southern Cross constellation and streaked across the night sky.

On one night pass across the United States, I could see the extensive lights of the west coast of California, with the Los Angeles area brilliantly distinct. But the brightest lights at night in the U.S. were from the city of Las Vegas. Across the Sun Belt, from an orbit near twenty-eight degrees inclination, the lights of Houston, New Orleans, and the east coast of Florida—from Miami to Jacksonville—were the most plainly visible. On one pass across the East Coast, I could see the lights all the way from the tip of Florida up the Eastern seaboard to Washington, D.C.

The lightning storms were most spectacular. They were easy to spot, and one night the entire eastern half of America was lit up by brilliant lightning that lasted as long as we maintained visibility. On the night side of the earth, during times of intense thunderstorm activity, thousands of square miles would light up with each flash. In one massive storm over the continent of Africa, the lightning seemed to flash in syncopated impulses, as though it were huge strobe lights hundreds of miles apart.

Surely, I thought, if some extraterrestrial being ever does look down on us from outer space and sees those magnificant electrical flashes from cloud to cloud, cloud to surface, he will know without a doubt that there is a special energy and vitality on the planet below.

The sunrises, appearing at their ninety-minute intervals, were equally gorgeous. The brilliant blue of the dawn sky would start to glow a pale orange, then bright orange, and finally red orange. The colors were always brilliant—nothing like we see on earth.

I spent as little time sleeping as I could, preferring to float at the windows looking out over earth while the others slept. I figured I could sleep when I got home. I did not want to miss a single detail of this unrepeatable experience.

One daylight period during Flight Day Three, while the others were in their sleep restraints, I floated up to the flight deck and held on to the windowsill. We were crossing southern Mali, in the Sahel region of Africa. I could see the effect of the hot, dry wind over the centuries as the sand had been swept in a huge pattern from north to south. Here and there the sand was interrupted by a river. At Khartoum, Sudan, I spotted the junction of two Nile tributaries. Khartoum looked like a patchwork of little fields from space.

After the Sudan, I could see the grim wastes of Ethiopia, where starvation has repeatedly caught the world's attention. Indeed, the entire Sahel region of Africa was desolate and barren, the expanding desertification painfully obvious from space. Almost directly below me was the parched land where Grace had taken forty tons of food to be distributed to starving children exactly one year ago.

The "Flight of Mercy" had been Grace's own idea. In Mali in 1984, she had held a starving child in her arms. She had not been able to forget it. She talked with friends in Washington and Florida and with the editor of the *Florida Times Union* in Jacksonville. He suggested that although people wanted to help, they had no direction. They needed a clear and concrete project to contribute to—one that could be tracked to a successful conclusion.

A DC-8 was chartered and loaded with forty tons of food, medicine, and blankets. WCPX-TV in Orlando collected over eighty thousand dollars and two truckloads of blankets. World Vision, a Christian humanitarian organization, provided the organizational network for obtaining the two tons of medicine and thirty-eight tons of fortified food—eleven tons of which was donated by a former Ethiopian official in Indiana. The food was a mixture of oats, powdered milk, and honey—the ingredients of *atmit*, a dish eaten throughout Ethiopia. Another 120,000 dollars were raised from churches, civic clubs, private industry, and individuals before the flight departed from Chicago on January 12, 1985. The late Mayor Harold Washington of Chicago saw us off.

The plane was so long, we wore ourselves out walking from one end of the cargo bay to the other. During the twenty-four-hour journey, our group of "food shepherds" slept on top of the pallets of provisions, using some of the donated blankets for warmth. Our arrival was the first time a stretch DC-8 had landed on the Addis Ababa runway, but TransAmerican Cargo Airlines and World Vision soon had the cargo unloaded.

We ran into immediate problems, however. Food was being delayed on its way to the feeding centers because rebel activity in the region was interrupting the overland supply route. When we finally were cleared to have an old DC-3 fly us to the camps, we found the centers dangerously low on food. Our supplies had arrived just in time.

Ethiopia had now slid past the shuttle, replaced by an earth shrouded in darkness. I settled back in Hoot's seat and remembered. I thought of the suffering children with their spindly arms and legs, stomachs bloated from malnutrition. If mankind could only see the world from outside, as a tiny planet, he would know that they are all our children.

With Grace and a throng of Ethiopian children in one of the feeding centers during 1985. [Photo courtesy Florida Today*]*

I remembered walking through one of the parched fields far north of Addis Ababa and being appalled at the primitive agricultural techniques. January was considered the rainy season, but it virtually had stopped raining years ago. If it did rain, it fell in such torrents that it washed away what little crops a family might have nursed to the surface. The next day the fierce sun would reappear, drying up all the surface water— and the drought would return.

I thought of Grace's experience in Nior, a remote village in Mali. Soon after she arrived with the care packages, one of the tribal women had placed a dying child in her arms. The little girl's mother had died during the birth of another child just weeks before. I remembered her tears as she told me the story.

"I could hardly feel her breathing and thought she would die in my arms. Village customs said a woman could not wet nurse another woman's baby unless she was part of the family. The dead woman's sister had no milk so it was up to the baby's grandmother.

"As I stood there, holding the child, the old woman took one of her breasts and began to pull on it. She pulled and pulled and finally held it up so I could see. A very small drop of milk, not even enough to fall off, had appeared. That's all she had for the baby."

Grace had never forgotten that experience.

Yet, as I orbited through the ultimate blackness of space, with Earth on one side of the shuttle and an endless universe on the other, the problems of Earth—including our own problems at home—seemed removed. I had read the figures on Earth, but out in space they seemed even more incomprehensible. Our galaxy contains, astronomers tell us, close to four hundred billion stars. I let the zeros flash across the screen of my mind like digits appearing on the screen of a computer: 400,000,000,000 stars. In addition to that, there are as many as one hundred billion other galaxies besides our own. The figures were staggering: 40,000,000,000,000,000,000,000. And those were just stars. If each star had nine planets, each the

size of Earth, and each planet a dozen or more moons like
Jupiter and Saturn have . . . the zeros were more than I could
even imagine. The thought that was even more staggering,
however, was that with this almost infinite number of land
masses out there, the chances of life on some planet other than
Earth seemed almost certain. The question arose: should we
and will we care about them as well?

Coming Home

For three days we tried to get back to earth.

The weather did not cooperate at KSC. Each day we would get right up to the moment of the deorbit burn, ready for reentry, and Mission Control would wave us off for another twenty-four hours because of bad weather at the space center.

The procedure for deorbit preparation was extensive. It meant getting the shuttle ready for another dangerous phase of the mission—reentry into earth's atmosphere and the landing of a one-hundred-ton spaceship without the benefit of engines. By the time of the deorbit burn, therefore, everything had to be just right. The deorbit preparation was carried out according to extensive instructions. This procedure took close to eight hours and consisted of a "backing out" of all the operations we'd performed to get the shuttle ready for its on-orbit activities.

The Ku-Band antenna for high-frequency communication was pulled back into the cargo bay; the sun shield that housed the satellite was opened for structural strength; and the payload bay doors were closed. If the huge doors failed to close, or if other parts failed to position properly, Pinky and Franklin would have had to don their space suits, lock out of the shuttle airlock for a spacewalk, and perform the operations manually with special space tools.

The commander and pilot had an entire sequence of computer instructions to go through. The big and little jets had to be ready to fire to bring us down at precisely the right attitude. Before reentry, the attitude of the orbiter was controlled by the verniers. As we got ready for the deorbit burn, we changed from these little jets to the big nine-hundred-pound thrusters.

Besides configuring the shuttle's instruments, we had to put the seats back in place, take down the treadmill and stow it in the right position, get out all our gear—putting on boots, G suits and harnesses—plus get everything packed away in our pockets. That was followed by putting on our helmets, strapping ourselves into our seats, and waiting for the go or no-go from Mission Control. Once we got the go-ahead for deorbit burn, we were to drink thirty-two ounces of water and take eight salt tablets so our bodies would retain fluid as we reentered gravity. Early in the space shuttle program, the doctors learned that twenty percent of an astronaut's bodily fluids were lost during space travel. During reentry, as gravity caused more blood to flow back into the legs and out of the head, a loss of consciousness could occur. Thus, as an extra precaution, additional fluid was consumed, along with salt tablets. The less blood that flowed out of the brain, the less chance there was we would black out or "gray out."

An additional precaution was the use of an inflated G suit to apply pressure against our leg and abdominal muscles to help keep the blood from rushing into the lower torso. These precautions were essential because the crew needed to be in peak mental condition for reentry.

The reconfiguration of the cabin had to be completed prior to our last sleep period so that when we woke up we'd be pretty much ready to go.

A space walk with the manned maneuvering unit. [NASA photo]

As I lay awake on what was to be the last night in space, I looked over at the other men sleeping in their odd positions, their hands floating in front of their faces. In preparation for our final drink before reorbit, Pinky had Velcroed water containers all over the wall next to the galley. He had also taped our flight suits to the wall beside the lockers so they would be ready in the morning. Like me, he had already stuffed his pockets with his personal belongings.

Upon waking, we had breakfast and finished the last of the cleanup chores, one of which was to wipe down all the open faces of the shuttle interior, where dust and debris had floated up and stuck to the walls and doors of the lockers. We locked the seats into place and secured all loose items. It took several hours before we were ready.

Our expected last pass over the United States was beautiful. It was nighttime, and I could see all the major cities from the west coast to Phoenix, Denver, St. Louis, Houston, New Orleans, then Atlanta, and the east coast all the way from Florida to Washington, D.C. An hour later we were over the Pacific Ocean, approaching the west coast of the United States again, when our CAPCOM, Fred Gregory, told us that the weather at the Cape was a no-go. The clouds were at 3,300 feet and broken at both ends of the runway. Since the commander needed complete visibility of the alignment lights and the runway, it was an unacceptable condition. Houston waved us off for twenty-four hours.

There was an immediate emotional and physical letdown. We had been up for eight hours with little sleep the night before, and everybody was pretty tired. We decided to leave the seats up and keep the airlock closed to minimize the changes in the cabin. Nevertheless, I had to admit that part of me was pleased to have another day in space: I had enjoyed it so much and was in no hurry for it to end.

Some of us drifted in and out of naps. I slept with my hands to the floor, my feet up toward the ceiling. I dozed for about forty-five minutes, then got up and fixed a cup of coffee, mixing the hot water with the dried coffee, sugar, and cream in the little plastic bowl and then drinking it with a straw in the way that had become so familiar. I took my scissors and clipped open a pack of peanuts. Emptying them out in the cabin, I separated them with my finger in front of my face. One by one, I drifted them to me and into my mouth. It was a skill I would have little use for back on earth.

The day before, we had been using the IR (infrared) camera to look at volcanoes. I drifted to the window. I was now able to pick out several volcanoes with my naked eye, aware just how "alive" Earth was beneath that beautiful brown, blue, and white surface. This too, I reflected somewhat sadly, was a skill I'd have little further chance to practice.

Eventually, I went back to work on my medical experiments. This additional day would be more relaxed, and I could carry on with my work at a less feverish pace. The original plan called for me to do all of the experiments during five flight days; then, at the decision of NASA, the mission had been shortened to four. This meant I had had to combine all my experiments planned for Flight Days Four and Five into a single day. Now that we had been waved off, I could continue gathering additional data. In particular, I wanted to spend more time on tests to estimate the blood pressure in my heart. In another experiment, I had experienced a lot of trouble early in the flight with an apparatus that, although stable on Earth, proved to be most unstable in zero gravity. This had been especially true of the cameras I used in photographing my experiments.

My only disappointment was that I had been forced to deactivate the protein crystal growth experiment a day early. The additional time would have meant a day's extra crystal growth. Once deactivated, unfortunately, the experiment could not be restarted.

Even after Mission Control had told us it was a no-go for the deorbit burn, there was actually little additional work time. Much of the day had already been consumed preparing the orbiter for another twenty-four hours in space. Once that task was complete, it was practically time for the evening meal and then bed. At dinnertime, I told everybody that I was going to treat them to supper. Steve and I prepared the meal amidst good-natured banter. There was a lot of camaraderie and a lot of joking about the weather.

The next flight day we went back through the deorbit prep a second time. We were all prepared for the deorbit burn when the CAPCOM once again said it was a no-go for Kennedy. We were to go around the earth one more time and come into Edwards Air Force Base in California.

This time I felt a deep pang of disappointment. I knew Grace and the children were waiting at KSC. In fact, they had been waiting two days for us to return. Now we were going to land in California instead of Florida. It took us only nine minutes in the shuttle to cross from California to Florida, but for those on earth it meant an enormous journey—obviously impractical at such short notice.

Just after we passed the point where we would have burned to deorbit to Kennedy, Mission Control changed our orders again. They told us to go back out of the burn configuration and hold off for another twenty-four hours. We would try one last time to get into Kennedy the next day.

NASA management really wanted to get the orbiter back to Kennedy so it could be prepared as fast as possible for the next flight. If we landed in California, it would mean losing a week as they transported the shuttle back to Florida atop a Boeing 747.

After the second wave-off, the big nine-hundred-pound thruster jets were getting low on fuel. But we had to use them for attitude control until the small vernier jets warmed up. The instrumentation was showing the verniers were not warming quickly because our attitude had kept them from being exposed to the sun's rays.

Again, as during the previous day, the stress of the deorbit prep tired each of us. I took a nap with my feet and legs wedged between two sleep restraints and my head wedged behind the lockers against the wall. Next to the orbiter frame, I could feel the vibration of the big thruster jets as they boomed on and off at the commands of the computer.

By the sixth flight day we were running out of food and clean clothes. Hoot took note of this fact as he penned the lyrics for a song he and Charlie sang to Mission Control to the tune of "Where or When."

> It seems that we have talked like this before,
> The deorbit pad that we copied then,
> But we can't remember where or when.
>
> The clothes we're wearing are the clothes we've worn,
> The food that we're eating's getting hard to find
> Since we can't remember where or when.
>
> Some things that happened for the first time
> Seem to be happening again.
> And so it seems we will deorbit burn,
> Return to earth,
> And land somewhere,
> But who knows where or when?

Mission Control gave them a standing ovation.

NASA had planned a new experiment for *Columbia,* one that had not been attempted on previous missions. During reentry, Hoot was to fire both the forward and aft reaction control system (RCS) jets. Normally, only the aft RCS jets were fired during reentry, when they played the crucial role of keeping the shuttle in the right attitude for its high-speed descent through the atmosphere. If the attitude is incorrect, the three-thousand-degree-Fahrenheit heat would not be properly distributed over the thermal protection system engineered to withstand it, and the orbiter would simply burn and break up. The military lingo is "crash and burn"; the astronauts speak of "vehicle loss of control." Either way, it means instant death.

The reason for this experimental firing of the forward

thrusters during reentry was simple: to burn up fuel. Previously, they had been used only for positioning the shuttle on orbit; for if they fired during the high-speed descent, their position on either side of the shuttle nose meant they had to fire at exactly the same moment or they would cause the craft to tumble out of control. Not firing them, however, meant the shuttle had to land with its nose at least partly filled with fuel—and it was this the experiment was designed to avoid.

Hypergolic propellant, despite its highly explosive nature, has proved to be the best way to control the shuttle while in space. It consists of two components, a fuel and an oxidizer, which, when squirted together, cause an instant burn. When the supply to the nozzles is cut off, the flame is immediately dead. There is no warm-up, no burn-down, it is instant on and instant off. Thus, by regulating the amount of fuel mixed in the combustion chamber, it is possible to determine the length of a burn. The problem, as we have seen, is that this fuel remains on board, and if there is any kind of rupture allowing the components to mix, it would mean a massive explosion.

Before we got to the deorbit burn, the engineers at JSC had huddled and decided the experiment was too risky. They canceled the test. They did not say why, but I was relieved, even though we had too much hypergolic propellant in front of us for the landing.

What we did not know was that the forward RCS jets on *Columbia* were the old type that worked fine in the vacuum of space but were not built to withstand the pressure of the atmosphere. *Columbia*, in its refurbishment, had not been outfitted with the new thrusters. If the test had been conducted as planned, the old nose thrusters would have exploded from the atmospheric pressure of reentry and *Columbia* would likely have become a giant fireball, evaporating into nothing.

In the early morning of Flight Day Seven, I awoke about three hours before the end of the eight-hour sleep period. Again, it was cold. I went into my locker and found my jacket and trousers to keep warm. Since I was awake, I checked the flight deck and found Hoot up staring silently at Vietnam and Cam Ranh Bay, where, years before, he had flown missions from a navy aircraft carrier.

As we flew over Cape Canaveral three hours and fifteen minutes before our scheduled landing, I could see the entire state of Florida. There was a little haze on the eastern coastline and some big thunderstorms out in the Gulf of Mexico, but they were far from KSC. I was so sure that we were going to land in Florida that on the next pass over the Cape, I forced myself to walk up and down the ladder to tune up my leg muscles and get ready for gravity.

Then came the final no-go from Houston. The NASA minimum landing requirement was broken clouds at 7,000 feet. With scattered clouds at 2,000 feet and broken clouds at 3,500 feet, the weather was just not clear enough. Finally, Mission Control gave the word: We were cleared for deorbit burn for Edwards Air Force Base in California.

I was heartsick. I would miss the thrill of having my family with me when I stepped out of the shuttle. The last several days had been an emotional roller coaster for us. It had begun with five attempts to launch; now it was ending with four wave-offs before final landing. All of us were concerned about our families, knowing that they had been waiting for us to return for three days. We knew they would be more disappointed than we were.

We approached the U.S. for one more pass and expected the deorbit burn to begin over the island of Madagascar. The lights of Los Angeles were spread out far and wide. We passed quickly over Phoenix, and I saw the lights of Denver on the horizon. By the time we passed Houston, it was daybreak. If we had been landing at Kennedy, we would have been descending on this orbit as a fiery streak in the night sky. Instead, we made another crossing of the U.S., the entire journey accomplished in nine minutes.

The last of the water and salt tablets were consumed. I felt bloated—like a blimp full of water. Everyone was ready for the burn. This was one of the procedures in which the crew wanted to be well ahead of the schedule so there would be no surprises. Hoot and Charlie were on the flight deck, strapped into their seats, relaxed, with their arms floating and hands clasped. The rest of us were strapped in the same seats we had arrived in. All were expectant.

The deorbit burn began with only a small jolt. It lasted for four minutes, putting a slight pressure on our bodies as we felt the G forces. Hoot's voice came through the intercom speakers in my helmet: "Everything looks good."

I held up my last water container, and it floated back toward me because of the deceleration. It was amazing how just that little bit of slowing would bring us back to earth.

Now the big jets, our reaction control system, started firing frequently, positioning us as we started to free-fall through space, gently pulled by earth's gravity. For the next thirty minutes we descended from over one million feet above the earth to 400,000 feet, traveling one third of the distance around the world at the same time.

As we got closer to the earth's atmosphere, the big jets were firing almost constantly, adjusting the shuttle so that we would not hit the atmosphere at the wrong angle of attack.

The NASA term for this critical part of the reentry is *entry interface*. At 400,000 feet, still at Mach twenty-four (twenty-four times the speed of sound), we lost radio contact with the ground because the atmosphere heated up as we reentered, producing an ionized shield that radio signals cannot penetrate. We had fallen about 127 miles in thirty minutes and were now forty minutes from touchdown at Edwards AFB.

As we started down through the thin air, I could see the effects of gravity reappearing. When I placed my tape recorder in front of me, it began to fall ever so slightly. Pinky, still unstrapped, was relearning to walk on the locker wall.

The dark of night outside the window started to give way to what appeared to be early morning dawn. It was a pinkish glow that got brighter and brighter and turned to a tangerine-peach color.

The tape recorder was dropping more quickly now, and my helmet was starting to grow heavy. So were my feet. I had a feeling I was going to have a harder time readjusting to earth's gravity than I had had adjusting to weightlessness. Hoot's calm voice in my helmet said we were on a smooth trajectory—right on the money.

Gradually, I realized the red-and-orange glow outside the window was not dawn. It was the reflection of the searing heat of reentry. Those thirty thousand silica tiles protecting the aluminum skin on the underbelly of the shuttle were now glowing at three thousand degrees Fahrenheit. We were shining like a meteor in the night sky over the Pacific. Pinky reported that he could see sparks flying past the overhead windows from his position on the flight deck. I could also see flashes of white light from the thrusts of the big RCS jets.

Gravity was becoming increasingly apparent. I felt the shuttle roll to the left and right as the computers created maneuvers to bleed off the speed in order to get us exactly where we needed to be over the runway.

At 230,000 feet I felt turbulence. My recorder would no longer stay in the air. I could feel the blood draining out of my head and my helmet beginning to get loose as the puffiness in my face disappeared. I was also starting to become lightheaded, and my feet were hard to move off the floor. I turned the G-suit knob up to its maximum pressure.

From Hoot's conversations with Charlie, I could tell they were working hard with the brake pedals to try to get some sensitivity back into their legs and feet. I was amazed how well they were flying the ship as they readjusted to gravity.

Suddenly, there was a loud bang. I thought something had exploded. Several men at once shouted into the intercom, "What's that?"

I looked over. It was the same kind of thing that happens on an airliner when it comes in for a landing and the flight attendant has not fastened the door to the galley or the bathroom. The toilet door on the WCS was loose, swinging back and forth. Pinky used this as an excuse to practice his earth walk. He climbed down from the flight deck and slammed it shut.

At Mach eighteen, we were definitely feeling heavy. The atmosphere was tearing at the shuttle as we plunged back to earth. At 200,000 feet, the colors outside the window gradually changed from red and orange to white, which faded into a dark gray. At Mach fourteen the drag was up to thirty-two, meaning we were pulling about one G. Charlie said he could literally see a shock wave outside his pilot's window.

After having lived in space for six days, weighing zero pounds, the reintroduction of gravity was dramatic. I felt like I weighed two tons.

Meanwhile, our families were huddled together in the crew quarters at Kennedy, awaiting our radio signal. It was a tense time for them, as we were later to learn.

At precisely the moment the radio blackout ended, I heard Hoot on the radio. "Houston, this is *Columbia*." I knew that Grace, the children, and all the other astronauts' families were smiling and cheering at the sound of his voice.

Below Mach seven we started hearing wind noise. Pinky reported he could see Bakersfield, California, through the hatch window. I could feel a strange pressure on my back until suddenly I hiccuped, then gave a healthy burp. I felt better.

Now we were no longer a spaceship, we were a glider. It was up to our commander to fly and land just as he was trained. Hoot had practiced landing over and over in the STA—the shuttle training aircraft. But if there was a miscue in practice, he always had an engine to fall back on. There was no such engine on the shuttle. To come in short now, or to overshoot the runway, would mean a hard landing in the desert mountains.

Columbia was not terrifically aerodynamic. It had the glide ratio of a one-hundred-ton flat rock. Hoot took manual control of the spaceplane at forty-eight thousand feet over Edwards AFB. During this period of adjustment to earth's gravity, he had to be careful not to lower his head for fear of getting dizzy. All the vital instruments in the cockpit were projected on his front windshield in what was known as a *heads up display* (HUD). When Charlie, sitting in the right seat, said he had the runway in sight through the left window, Hoot refused to look, knowing that even the slightest tilt of his head could cause debilitating dizziness at what was an extremely crucial moment.

The wind noise was now very loud, and there was some buffeting. Otherwise, the sensation was just what we had experienced in the practice runs on the STA. *Columbia* was approaching nose down at an angle of seventeen to twenty-two degrees. It looked and felt as if we were plunging straight for the earth. Actually, we were just in a steep glide, maintaining enough speed to stay airborne. To have slowed down any further would have meant stalling out and tumbling to earth.

Charlie Bolden was chattering feverishly as he read off all the data and talked Hoot down. As the final numbers were given, he gave him constant encouragement.

"Nice, Hooter, you're right on the money!"

Hoot was aiming his plunge at a set of bright lights called *PAPI*s, which were seven thousand five hundred feet in front of the runway's threshold. If he was on the proper glide slope, the lights would look white. If not, the colors would indicate whether he was high or low. This was another means of corroborating what he was seeing through the window with the data he was reading on the HUD, including the lock on the microwave landing system.

On the ground below, it was early morning darkness. We had planned to land in daylight in Florida. This was to be the second shuttle night landing.

"Twenty thousand feet," Charlie's voice intoned.

I could hear the air noise as our unstreamlined spaceship plummeted to earth.

"Ten thousand feet. Surface winds calm."

"Five thousand. Radar altimeters checking well."

"Two thousand feet." I felt Hoot pull the nose up as we flared out of our steep descent.

"One thousand feet." He pulled the nose up a bit more.

"Five hundred feet." Charlie dropped the landing gear. I could feel the shuttle slow with the added resistance as it howled through the air at more than three hundred miles per hour.

Charlie continued to read off the altitude from the digital display on the instrument panel.

"Two hundred feet."

"One hundred feet."

"Fifty feet."

"Twenty feet."

"Ten feet."

"Nice, Hooter! Touchdown at one hundred and ninety knots [about 228 mph]. Nose is coming down right on the center line. Touchdown! Nose is down!"

It was rough on the brakes. Hoot was holding a constant eight feet per second deceleration.

Charlie continued to read off the ground speed.

"One hundred knots."

"Eighty knots."

"Sixty knots."

Hoot began to ease off on the brakes as we slowed to thirty, twenty, then ten knots before finally braking to a stop. We were home. Thank you, Lord.

Our crew cheered and cheered for Hoot as the radio reported there was a convoy coming our way. *Columbia* was back on earth.

Postscript

NASA flew all the astronauts from Edwards AFB directly to Houston. I decided to remain there for Grace and the children to join me. Jack Waite, a long-time NASA employee, drove me over to the Nassau Bay Hilton to check in before Grace's arrival late that night. Still dressed in my NASA flight suit, I approached the front desk and asked for the room NASA had reserved earlier that day. The reception manager nodded and asked if I would by paying with cash or credit card.

I explained to the lady that my wallet and credit cards were at the Kennedy Space Center where I had left them six days earlier. She was unmoved.

"Ma'am, I just came back from space. I don't have any credit cards with me."

"I'm sorry, sir," she shrugged. "You cannot check in unless you have cash or a credit card."

I had been up for twenty-two hours and didn't know whether to laugh or cry. Luckily Jack pulled out his personal Master-Card and offered it to the receptionist. I thanked him and stumbled up to my room and flopped on the bed. Exhausted.

PART TWO
THE CHALLENGE

The *Challenger* Is Down

It was only ten days since we had landed the *Columbia*. I had returned to Washington because Congress was in session that day and would hear the President's State of the Union speech scheduled that evening.

The morning the *Challenger* was to lift off, January 28, 1986, I gathered my Washington staff in front of the TV in my inner office in the Cannon House Office Building. We were going to watch the launch on the NASA channel, and I wanted to point out the details of the spaceflight as I now knew them. It was well past 11:00 A.M. as the countdown proceeded from T-20 minutes and counting.

I felt very close to the crew as I relived the experience. They had already been through two delays and had scrubbed the launch two days before. The previous day I had called the crew quarters in sympathy to suggest that champagne would be "on me" upon their return. Unknown to me, that morning Commander Dick Scobee had penned a note of thanks for the gesture and had asked Nancy Gunter to send it to me. As it sat on the launchpad, *Challenger* was a beautiful sight. The solid rocket boosters—only two feet shorter than the Statue of Liberty—rose like gleaming spires in the morning air. It was a perfect day. The sky was clear blue, cloudless. As we watched *Challenger*'s engines ignite and the solid rocket boosters push the shuttle heavenward, I explained the various actions that the crew were performing and the accompanying sensations during the ascent.

The bright morning sun reflected off the glistening white spaceship as it cleared the tower in the incredible burst of fire and smoke that accompanies a lift-off. The two SRBs were generating a combined thrust of 5.3 million pounds, equivalent to 44 million horsepower, and consuming eleven thousand pounds of fuel per second.

I remembered how Ed White had thrilled American television viewers in June 1965 when he became the first American to walk in space. With Brigadier General James McDivitt at the helm of the Gemini 4 orbiter, White had spent twenty-one minutes at the end of a tether outside the capsule. When asked how he felt after he had come back from outer space, he said, "I feel red, white and blue all over."

That's how I felt, sitting in my congressional office that morning, watching *Challenger* lift off into the sparkling clear Florida sky. As the takeoff got underway, I was talking my office staff through the experience, explaining exactly what was happening in the shuttle and what could be expected next. Then, seventy-three seconds after lift-off, there was a puff of smoke, just barely visible. I knew that something was terribly wrong because it was too early for the SRBs to separate from the rocket.

Then, from the blurred television picture, reality started to sink in as the two condensation trails of the solid rockets gone awry started to tell the story. I felt a deep, sinking feeling in the pit of my stomach. I tried to keep from gasping, but it was as though all the air had been sucked from my lungs. My eyes were glued to the TV screen. When I saw the smoke trails, the solid rocket boosters veering off wildly into space, I knew the worst had happened.

"There's been an explosion!" I told the staff.

My mind did not want to accept what my eyes were seeing. I kept waiting to see the *Challenger* emerge out of the smoke. I thought of the possibility of an RTLS (return to launch site) emergency landing. I strained to see the orbiter coming back to the runway at Kennedy. After all, that was the accepted emergency procedure we had practiced so many times. But I also knew that any explosion that happened while the SRBs were in place, prior to the two-minute-eight-second separation, would inevitably be disastrous.

Suddenly I was no longer in Washington. I was with them— those seven souls I had grown to know and love. I was strapped in my seat in the shuttle, my back to the earth and my face toward heaven. I could feel the vibrations, the roar, the surge of incredible energy as we lifted off the pad. I could see them, sitting there in their sky-blue flight suits, sturdy black boots, helmets on, visors down and locked into place. I fought back the tears.

In those confusing moments I flashed back, finding it difficult to separate this flight from my own. Watching the pieces of the rocket flying off in all directions, I realized, "There, but for the grace of God, go I."

I had always known it was possible. We had come uncomfortably close to a potential emergency, seconds after lift-off when Charlie Bolden had discovered the indication of a helium leak. But this was something a million times worse. This was something the commander and pilot had no control over.

Numb, I watched the pieces of the rocket spiraling down into the Atlantic Ocean, leaving white contrails against the blue sky. The television caught a picture of a parachute trailing above a piece of metal. The commentator speculated it was an escape mechanism on the shuttle. Even though I knew the shuttle had no parachute, I was confused and for a moment felt a pang of hope. Of course, it turned out to be a piece from the SRB, which is deployed by parachute when it breaks off and falls to the ocean.

Later, as I struggled to make sense of the catastrophe, more words from Ed White came to mind. "As we fly more and more spacecraft, we're going to have one come down, and we're probably going to lose somebody. I wouldn't want it to hold up the space program. Just think what would have happened if the first time somebody got hurt in an airplane we'd stopped fooling around with airplanes. We'd be the most backward country in the world." A year and a half later, the deeply religious White, along with Gus Grissom and Roger Chaffee, died in the service of the space cause when they lost their lives in a fire on the launchpad inside *Apollo 1*.

Now, there were seven more: Dick Scobee, Mike Smith, Judy Resnik, El Onizuka, Ron McNair, Greg Jarvis, and Christa McAuliffe.

While each crew's training is separate, there had been considerable overlap in the training schedules of *Columbia* and *Challenger*. Christa and I had trained together on the KC-135, when we performed our weightlessness experiments. Greg Jarvis had been on the same zero-G flight and had worked diligently on his experiment in fluid dynamics.

I had also gotten to know Judy Resnik (some called her J.R.). I had spent an hour with her at lunch one day in the Johnson Space Center cafeteria. She was a brilliant as well as beautiful woman who seemed to enjoy answering my questions about NASA and the astronaut office. She wore a beautiful gold star around her neck. When I inquired about it, she had winked mysteriously. "Given to me by a friend," she said.

Judy was sensitive to the public image of the spaceflights. In our lunch together I asked when she was scheduled to fly. She mentioned she was scheduled aboard the *Challenger*. I said, "Oh

The **Challenger** *crew, mission STS-51L. Left to right are El Onizuka, Mike Smith, Christa McAuliffe, Dick Scobee, Greg Jarvis, Judy Resnik, and Ron McNair. [Nasa photo]*

yes, the teacher's flight." She laughed and said, "Yes, I guess that's my designation now. I'm on the 'teacher's flight.'"

Ron McNair was a karate expert. I had watched him working out in the gymnasium at the crew quarters. After their crew had finished their final training at the Cape and returned to Houston, Ron and Ellison Onizuka had stayed on at the Cape to finish some additional tests they were going to run in space. They had been with us through the evening of January 9, staying in the crew quarters. I was impressed by Ron's discipline as he worked out. He did not have the heavy musculature of some of the superb athletes I had met in the astronaut corps, but Ron was constantly working with his karate motions. The night before we finally launched, I had gone out to run, and when I returned to the gym, Ron was still there, working on his karate.

Ellison Onizuka had been especially kind to me. He would go out of his way to come over to say hello, carry on idle chitchat, and just be friendly. That was unusual; most of the astronauts were all business.

Dick Scobee's wife, June, had been a real inspiration to Grace. It was traditional for the wives of the next shuttle flight to have a party for the wives of the shuttle flight about to take off. June Scobee hosted the party in December for the spouses of our crew. Grace and June had a long visit in the kitchen, and Grace felt June had been extraordinarily kind, especially since she was the newcomer and the outsider.

I knew of Mike Smith through Jake Garn. Mike had been assigned to Senator Garn to answer questions when Jake was in training in Houston, just as Jim Adamson had been assigned to me. Over time, a real friendship had developed between them, and those of us who know Jake know that he was devastated by Mike's death.

Within an hour of the disaster, the phones in my office were ringing wildly. The press wanted my immediate response. However, I knew better than to speak off the top of my head—

at least, until I had tried to compose myself and was able to comprehend what had happened. It was essential that I speak objectively rather than emotionally. I agreed to a press conference later that afternoon.

In desperation to talk to someone, I tried to reach Grace by telephone. She was not at home. I put in a call to Jake Garn and could not get him. I finally reached Congressman Don Fuqua, the chairman of our committee. I had to talk to someone with a knowledge of the space program, who would understand my feelings.

My mind had been seared by the image of the astronauts' families as they witnessed the spectacle. I thought of the schoolchildren of America who had been watching because Christa McAuliffe was aboard. What would this do to them?

I was concerned, too, about the possibility of emotional scarring in my own children. When the news broke, Nan Ellen's and Billy's teachers took them alone outside their classrooms to explain what had happened before it was announced to the class. Billy's friends told him they were glad his dad wasn't on the *Challenger*, and Billy said he was glad, too, but confused as to why the *Challenger* had exploded, since Christa McAuliffe, the schoolteacher, had been on board. What Billy was feeling was the perplexity felt by schoolchildren all across America.

At about 2:00 P.M. Congressman Tony Coelho called to tell me that they wanted the House majority leader, the minority leader, and me to speak on the House resolution commemorating the crew, to be offered on the floor of Congress. By the time I got to the floor, however, that number had vastly expanded.

A call came in from the Vice President's office inviting me to go with Vice President Bush and Senators Glenn and Garn to see the families at KSC. I insisted Grace be allowed to accompany me, since she had just been with the spouses at the party hosted by the crew's wives. The Vice President's staff balked, saying it would need to be approved. Grace met me at my office, and we started walking over to the Vice President's office in the Capitol to meet them for the drive to Andrews Air Force Base. When we arrived, a secretary for Bush said that Chief of Staff Craig Fuller had decided they could not wait for me and the party had left. I contacted Fuller by car telephone. Even though they knew I was on my way, they had had to leave, he said. I asked him to wait at Andrews Air Force Base while I got the Capitol police to rush me to the airplane. He said they could not wait.

I tried to reach Senator Garn in the car with the Vice President, who was on his way to Andrews, but my call was blocked. Frustrated and disappointed, Grace and I walked from the Senate side of the Capitol to the Science and Technology Committee room to find my 3:00 P.M. press conference already in progress and conducted by the full Science and Technology Committee. For the next half hour I answered questions from a press corps that was all too plainly unprepared for a space disaster.

It was after midnight when I finally crawled into bed, but I couldn't get to sleep. I was stung by the realization that throughout the day, while wanting to say the right thing, I had been thinking about myself—the slights, the politics, the disappointments—rather than about the real tragedy that had occurred in the lives of seven astronauts. I was disgusted with myself.

I arose at 5:00 A.M. and throughout the day there were more press inquiries. They consistently asked questions about the funding of NASA, an additional orbiter, and the place of civilians in space. Throughout the interviews I was aware that the tight discipline on my emotions might tend to make me appear insensitive and overly analytical. That was not what I was feeling; I was hurting. Not since the assassination of President Kennedy had we been faced with such a national tragedy. The pain and grief I was feeling was part of it. As the red eye of the camera clicked on, I struggled to offer words that might be helpful to a nation searching painfully for answers. Yet I tried also to direct my remarks to the future of the country's space program.

During the day I called Hoot Gibson and talked to Steve Hawley. Later, Hoot's wife, Rhea, called me back. Hoot had been sent to KSC to help with the investigation of the solid rocket boosters.

The cataclysmic explosion that engulfed *Challenger* could just as easily have struck *Columbia* sixteen days earlier. Naturally, I had thought about the possibility of an accident before my flight. But I thought the greatest danger was that we might be stranded in space by the failure of the OMS engines to ignite when the time came to deorbit for reentry. Yet even that was a minor fear, since our flight was the first in America's space shuttle program when there was another space shuttle waiting on the second pad. Had we become stranded, there would have been a real opportunity to attempt a rescue mission.

I had also thought about a crash landing and how I would try to get out of the shuttle, either through the side hatch or by blowing out the top left window and coming through over the top and the side on a rope pulley. I had thought ahead of wanting to be mentally alert so that I could help out my crewmates if they were in need.

If an emergency had occurred after landing, however, I was so dizzy from the medical experiment, which had me rolling and shaking my head, that I would have had difficulty making an emergency egress. I would have been the one the crew would have had to help out.

In the aftermath of the catastrophe, a refreshing suggestion came from an attorney in my hometown that seven of the new moons just discovered by the American spacecraft *Voyager* around the planet Uranus be named as a permanent memorial for the seven lost astronauts. The idea was appropriate, sensitive, and a comforting way to memorialize seven courageous Americans. It was important not only for the nation, but timely for the families and friends to have an immediate, tangible gesture that their loved ones were important and appreciated. Although the International Astronomical Society has continued to this day with its tradition of naming newly discovered heavenly bodies only after Greek mythological figures, this congressional recommendation later became part of our NASA authorization bill.

Had I, or any member of the crew of my flight, been prepared to respond to such an event as befell the *Challenger*? The answer is obviously no. We knew such malfunctions could happen. That risk is understood by every member of every crew that climbs into a loaded spaceship. "If you have a dream," Christa McAuliffe said, "don't let anything dim it."

Frank Borman, who later went on to run Eastern Airlines after commanding *Apollo 8* around the moon in December 1968, said he estimated he and his companions—James Lovell and William Anders—had about eight chances in ten of returning to Earth. Before the mission, Borman compared the risk to a combat tour in Vietnam. But he said the venture was worth the risk. "What risks we have are well compensated by the gains we will get from the mission," he said.

Gus Grissom, who almost lost his life when the *Liberty Bell 7* capsule sank after splashdown, and who was killed later in the fire aboard the *Apollo 1*, knew the dangers of space travel. Commenting on what it would be like to return from the moon in the Apollo, he remarked that the capsule would enter earth's atmosphere at a speed of approximately thirty-six thousand miles per hour. "This will require the pilot to skip his ship like a stone over water," he wrote in a special article for *Today* newspaper in 1967. "He'll have to dip into the upper layers of the atmosphere just deep enough to slow him down to earth-orbital speed and then climb out briefly and dip back again so he reenters at speeds and gravity forces the spacecraft can withstand . . . and it will have to work exactly right the first time. If the pilot skips out too far after that first dip into the atmosphere, it's '*Sayonara*, pals, we'll never see you again.'"

Grissom, by the way, is buried in Arlington National Cemetery just outside Washington, D.C., near where Lieutenant Thomas Selfridge is buried. Selfridge is considered the first aviation casualty. He was killed while flying the Wright brothers' plane near Fort Myer, Virginia, in December 1908.

One of my own crew members, Pinky Nelson, later commented on the risk of manned spaceflight. He said even though it was difficult to watch the lift-offs—including the videotapes of his own flights—because he keeps waiting for an explosion, and even though his daughters had asked him to give up the space program, he had made up his mind to press ahead. "I've come to believe it's more important than ever," he told me. "The huge public support evidenced after the *Challenger*—the tons of mail—gave me a feeling it's very important to the public. I guess I've picked up some of that feeling. I've become even more of the evangelist."

The afternoon the astronauts were killed, I spoke to the Congress from the well of the House of Representatives on the dangers inherent to all adventure. I recalled the remarks made by another adventurer, a gallant lady named Helen Keller, who broke through the barriers of sightlessness, deafness, and dumbness to become a national hero. "Security," Miss Keller said, "is mostly a superstition. It does not exist in nature, nor do the children of man as a whole experience it. Avoiding the danger is no safer in the long run than outright exposure. Life is either a daring adventure, or it is nothing."

Space Research

In early July 1985, I had gone to Huntsville, Alabama to visit the Marshall Space Flight Center, where I learned of a new experiment proposed by the University of Alabama Medical School. University researchers wanted to grow protein crystals in the zero gravity of space as part of their cancer research program. The moment I heard about it I made up my mind this would be my primary experiment in space.

Most of us have a personal interest in the battle against cancer. Over the last several years, some of my dearest friends had been stricken, including the wives of two fellow congressmen. In 1983 one of my best friends, Becky Beatty of Tallahassee, Florida, who had been like a sister to me, died after a five-year battle with the disease. The husband of my executive assistant had been hit. The beautiful college-age daughter of one of my neighbors in Florida was a cancer victim, as was the son of two of my closest friends in Washington. I hoped I could make some contribution through my crystal growth experiments and hasten the assault on this diabolical disease.

At the suggestion of Dr. Bill Smith of the subcommittee staff, I visited Dr. Charles Bugg at the University of Alabama at Birmingham in the Comprehensive Cancer Center. Doctor Bugg, head of the protein crystallography department at the medical school, explained the experiment. Later, I spent time with Dr. Larry DeLucas, one of Bugg's principal research assistants, practicing my experiments during those many twenty-five-second weightless periods aboard the KC-135.

As I was to learn during my background studies for this experiment, protein chemistry is at the foundation of all biological cellular processes, including cancer cures and treatment.

Doctor Bugg had spent the past several years developing ways to grow larger and more uniform crystals from liquid protein. With better crystals, researchers hoped to improve their understanding of the molecular structure of proteins linked to cancer growth and cancer treatment. Once the architecture of the protein was known, scientists could gain insight into exactly how the molecule accelerated or inhibited cancer growth. Moreover, in a kind of molecular warfare, some proteins could be designed to battle other cancer-causing proteins. Such diverse fields as genetic engineering, X-ray diffraction, and neutron diffraction had already made a contribution to this in recent years. Visionary researchers such as Bugg and DeLucas were holding out high hopes for successful solutions to cancer. Space research was vital to their program.

Growing crystals on earth is a tedious and imperfect art, partly because the liquid-phase molecules are disturbed by gravity. Rather than lining up in an orderly fashion to form perfect crystals, molecules are skewed by convection currents in the liquid, caused by gravity. But in the near-zero gravity experienced aboard the space shuttle, researchers hoped to improve the crystal formation of proteins that had proved to be particularly difficult to work with on earth.

Doctor Bugg, an energetic and articulate scientist, had already flown one protein crystal experiment on the shuttle when I met him in September 1985. He encouraged my participation. I made my request, and the protein crystal growth research was soon approved by NASA as my primary experiment.

While I worked with a variety of proteins during the flight, I was most interested in the successful growth of purine nucleoside phosphorylase protein crystals, called *PNP*. Researchers didn't know why, but PNP proteins inhibited the chemotherapeutic agents used to attack cancer cells. If a medicine could be developed to block the PNP's action, the chemotherapy could better treat the cancer. My experiments built on those first conducted by Charlie Walker, a payload specialist from McDonnell Douglas aboard the November 1985 flight of *Atlantis*. He had tried out a new method of "seeding" liquid protein by injecting a minute crystal into it. I expanded on that experiment with the aim of producing as many crystals as would survive reentry and landing.

I had expected to use an hour and a half to activate the experiment on Flight Day One. However, because of the tedious process of exposing the precipitating agents to the proteins, followed by taking detailed pictures of each of the forty-eight crystal growth chambers, the actual activation procedure took me closer to four hours to complete. On Flight Day Four, when we were told to prepare for reentry, I deactivated the experiment. However, in a marvelous but unexpected way, the crystals continued to grow for the full six days in space—giving the researchers some excellent samples to study after we got back to Earth.

Even though the experiment was prematurely brought to a close, crystals were grown of all the proteins tested, including hen egg, white lysozyme, human serum albumin, human C-reactive protein, bacterial purine nucleoside phosphorylase, canavalin, and concanavalin B. Despite the fact the protein solutions had not had time to mature, relatively large, X-ray quality crystals were obtained for all the proteins except lysozyme. In fact, the crystals of at least two proteins, canavalin and concanavalin, were of sufficient size and clarity that through X-ray diffraction, researchers were able to determine their molecular structure at a high resolution. Throughout the experiment, I documented and recorded the crystallization process, providing a detailed report for future experimenters.

The experiments I performed on this flight were an important step in developing the techniques future scientists will use on a space station. Each space mission points the way toward needed improvements for the next mission. For example, detailed comparisons between space-grown and earth-grown crystals will be made more accurately in the future by controlling other variables, such as temperature. I expect that an automated, temperature-controlled apparatus will be the follow-up to our protein crystal growth experiment. In fact, an improved procedure of this kind was considered so important that NASA selected it as one of the experiments to be flown on the first flight following the *Challenger* accident—and chose Pinky Nelson to do the work.

In addition to my primary experiment, I was requested to perform nine additional experiments sponsored by NASA's department of space adaptation research. These were called, in NASAese, DSOs—detailed secondary objectives. While working on the DSOs, I was constantly reminded that all experiments were secondary to the primary objectives of the mission: to launch the SATCOM satellite; to detect and measure ultraviolet radiation coming from deep space; and several other experiments, including the observation of Halley's Comet. Since the beginning of the space shuttle program, more than fifty biomedical DSOs have now been flown, primarily under the direction of one of the world's foremost medical researchers, Dr. Michael W. Bungo, director of the Space Biomedical Research Institute for NASA.

Data from the Apollo and Skylab missions had pointed to a number of health problems that could take place in zero gravity. NASA doctors were at that time primarily concerned with space adaptation syndrome (SAS), cardiovascular problems, and the problems associated with delivering adequate health care in the remoteness of the space environment.

These canavelin protein crystals were grown under identical conditions, except the crystals above were grown on Earth and those below were grown in my experiment in space. The enhanced quality of the cyrstals grown in space is apparent. [Photo courtesy Dr. Charles Bugg]

Space adaptation syndrome was the object of intense study because potentially it could wipe out an entire crew, not only making them ineffective but perhaps endangering the mission altogether. Some of the crew members on earlier flights had fainted on reentry, and others were so dizzy after getting to the ground they would have been unable to exit the spacecraft had there been an emergency. Others, including those who had spent thousands of hours flying jet airplanes on earth, were debilitated early in the mission with repeated vomiting. Frequently, the sudden, brief bouts of vomiting were quite severe, although, curiously, there was no accompanying nausea. There were even one or two reports of vomiting the first time the astronauts saw the earth inverted.

The Soviet cosmonauts had also complained of disorientation, delusions, malaise, nausea, and vomiting early in their space program. Later, when similar problems appeared in our astronauts aboard the Apollo spacecrafts, NASA doctors assumed this was the same kind of motion sickness that occurred on earth and treated it accordingly. However, it soon became apparent that the medications effective on earth didn't work in space. Further research revealed that space motion sickness was vastly different from earth's motion sickness. There was virtually no sweating, flushing was more common than pallor, and vomiting often happened suddenly without the forewarning of nausea.

On top of this, several of the astronauts who had been sick in space immediately climbed into their T-38 jets on return to earth and repeated every maneuver possible without experiencing nausea. One astronaut went so far as to repeat all the maneuvers for nineteen consecutive days after his first flight into space. But he could do nothing to make himself sick. Strangely enough, some of the astronauts most resistant to motion sickness on earth suffered most from SAS in space.

It was obvious the doctors were dealing with two kinds of sickness. In fact, one astronaut who had experienced both motion sickness and space sickness moaned from space, following a bout of vomiting, "I don't know what this is, but it isn't sea-sickness." As a result, the Astronaut Office and the flight med-icine people began a thorough investigation to determine the difference. Astronaut Dr. Bill Thornton was the principal in-vestigator for the project, doing extensive testing on a total of nineteen astronauts over a five-year period. It was through this research that SAS began to be understood in terms of a con-flict between signals sent to the brain by the eye and signals sent by the otolith stones in the inner ear under weightless conditions.

My experiment aboard the *Columbia,* undertaken in weight-lessness, was designed to teach me to rely on my eyes for judg-ing the position of my body, thus helping my brain learn to ignore the confusing signals from my otolith stones more quickly. It required me to stand on a swing-like structure with sensors attached to my cheeks and a blackout hood over my head. The sensors measured the movement of my eyes. When the structure gently swung to and fro in about a twenty-degree arc, I was asked to keep my eyes fixed on an imaginary boat sailing on the horizon. These data were added to data already recorded by NASA's doctors. The hope is that, in the near future, either an apparatus can be built to preadapt astronauts to zero gravity, or drugs can be developed that will not only eliminate SAS but will alleviate all travel sickness.

The near-weightless conditions of orbit offer a unique en-vironment in which to study any process affected by gravity. Space was the perfect environment, for example, for another experiment designed to find out why human blood deterio-rates when it is stored in blood banks.

Stored blood deteriorates for a number of reasons, among them, cell damage occurring when gravity pulls heavier ele-ments of the blood to the bottom of its storage bag. It also deteriorates when it is mixed with an anticoagulant, when it interacts with its container, and when it ages and absorbs non-toxic materials. By putting blood in space, researchers can eliminate the effects of gravity and more easily isolate the other factors leading to its deterioration.

In an experiment directed by Dr. Douglas Surgenor, president of the Center for Blood Research, in Boston, blood was stored in three different types of polymer bags to determine what chemical reactions occurred between the blood and the bag. It was also separated into its three major elements—white and red cells and platelets—so each portion could be studied independently. During the six-day flight, Pinky Nelson carefully monitored the temperatures of the two storage units used in the experiment, making certain that the storage environment varied by no more than two degrees.

Timing was critical to the success of the experiment. Blood had to be collected by the Central Florida Blood Bank in Orlando and flown by helicopter to the Kennedy Space Center. The blood, which was stored in two specially developed temperature-control units, had to be loaded aboard the shuttle at the last possible moment—approximately nine hours before lift-off. Since we were scrubbed four times before we finally launched, many central Floridians had to roll up their sleeves to donate the quantities of blood needed. The Orlando mayor and other community leaders were among the first forty donors who provided blood for the experiment.

When we were diverted from KSC to Edwards Air Force Base, the Center for Blood Research had to rush the blood by Lear jet from California back to Florida where a total of forty-two different blood experiments were performed as soon as the blood was unloaded.

The experiment had been five years in the making, and its special apparatus, designed by blood experts to fly the stored blood in one of the lockers of the space shuttle, represented a breakthrough in ground storage techniques. Researchers had found that blood platelets are the part of blood that deteriorates the most rapidly in stored conditions. Miraculously, the shelf life of platelets was doubled by the new apparatus, which stores the platelets vertically in a thin column. A rectangular piece of plastic strapped on each side of the storage bag kept it from bulging and kept the platelets from settling. Since the platelets didn't bunch at the bottom of the bag, the toxins they gave off when stored were evenly distributed and less likely to damage the valuable blood cells. It was a remarkable breakthrough that will reap great benefits. In particular, it will greatly enhance the ability of doctors to support a patient undergoing therapy that requires frequent blood transfusions, such as chemotherapy and radiation therapy in the treatment of cancer. In addition, it will help scientists understand the action of blood platelets in coagulation and could lead to a breakthrough in the treatment of heart disease and stroke.

By far the most grueling of my medical experiments was the one carried out on the treadmill. In Moscow, while leading a delegation of the congressional Space Subcommittee, I talked with the scientists at the Soviet Space Medicine Institute. Although we had some knowledge of the stress tests the Soviets had performed to determine the effects of long-duration spaceflight upon the heart, we all suspected they had not been entirely open in sharing everything they had learned. However, one of the things I discovered while I was there was that the cosmonauts in the Soviet space station were subjected to a stress test every ten days to monitor their heart condition at seventy percent of maximum heart rate—we even saw films of the Russian tests.

I offered to do a stress test for NASA and proposed to the Russians that we exchange the data from my test for Soviet data on long-duration spaceflight. It is imperative for scientists to have a broad data base in order to draw conclusions. Thus, when it comes to understanding how cardiovascular functions are affected by spaceflight, it would be helpful to have the information compiled by the Russians, whose experiences in space were under very different conditions from ours. This exchange of information is now taking place, according to Dr. Arnold Nicogosian, NASA Chief of Medical Research.

Medical researchers have evidence that spaceflight causes occasional abnormal heartbeats. These have been observed in our astronauts both during rest and during the high exertion of a spacewalk.

Prior to the flight, NASA doctors recorded my heart activity extensively during both rest and exertion. Our plan was to record my heart's activity for the last twenty-four hours in flight, including a thirty-minute run on the treadmill at 70 to 85 percent of my maximum heart rate. I was to continue to wear the recording devices through reentry and landing.

Exercise in space is absolutely necessary, since there is no gravity pulling against the muscles. Without exercise, the muscles slowly begin to atrophy. Treadmill exercise seems best, since it forces one muscle group to pull against another and causes overall exertion. Muscles that are not exercised wither quickly.

The on-board treadmill made a lot of noise. Bill Thorton, who had flown twice, was the sponsor of this experiment and warned me not to run in my socks because the machine would chew them up—along with my feet. I found a sports store in Houston and bought a new pair of running shoes to be used for "running around the world." But NASA canned the shoes as "unapproved," so I ran in my onboard slipper-socks and did fine.

Originally, the recordings of my heart's electrical activity were to be beamed directly to Houston via a data link on the TDRSS satellite. This procedure, requested by Drs. Mike Bungo, Pat Santy, and Jeff Davis, was turned down, however. It was decided that an inflight recorder would do just fine. But at the end of a twenty-five-minute treadmill run, I discovered to my horror that the tape recorder was not functioning. I was able to recycle and get it started again, and I ran for another fifteen minutes. At the end of forty minutes of running I was totally exhausted, but stopped only because Steve Hawley insisted—saying I was throwing sweat droplets all over the cabin and they were floating in his face. Besides, none of the others could stand the noise of the treadmill accompanied by my panting.

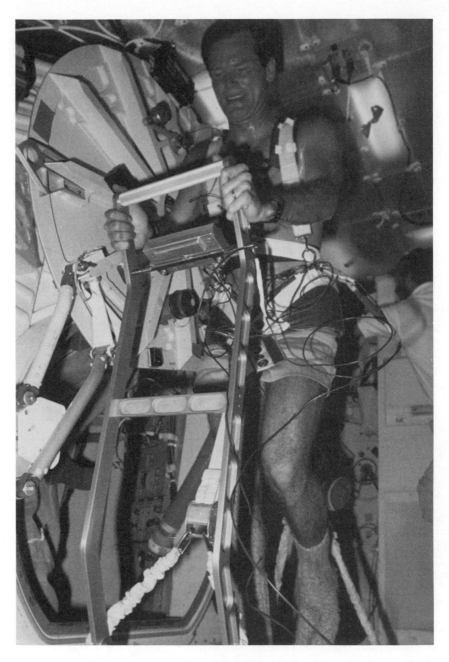

*The first American stress test in space being performed on the shuttle's treadmill.
[NASA photo]*

Halfway through the run, I noticed the monitor on the treadmill was showing that my heart rate was slowing down, rather than speeding up. I increased my speed and was shocked to see that the harder I ran, the more my heart rate dropped. It wasn't until afterward I learned the monitor was malfunctioning and was picking up electrical stimuli from the other muscles in my body, particularly my arms, which were straining as I struggled to keep myself centered on the treadmill in the weightlessness of space. But the fact I had to really "haul buggy" kept my heartbeat at 85 percent of the maximum rate, providing data not gathered by the Russians.

To make matters worse, however, another tape recorder jammed, eating the tape and scrambling it. I quickly activated a back-up monitor and recorded my heart's activity for the remainder of the flight. All of this confusion could have been avoided if the data had been directly sent to Houston as was originally requested by the doctors. In all, twenty-two hours of recording were obtained on the inflight Holter Monitor.

Another innovative experiment was a test to determine the changes in blood pressure in the right ventricle of my heart during spaceflight. This was monitored by Drs. Bungo and John Charles back at JSC in Houston. As we have seen, in the microgravity of space the bodily fluids (mostly the blood) are redistributed out of the legs and into the upper torso because gravity is no longer pulling them down. This redistribution is believed by doctors to change normal hydrostatic pressure in the blood vessels. Consequently, the body interprets it as a fluid "overload," and counters it by decreasing thirst and increasing urine production. I measured the blood pressure changes in my heart (central venous pressure, or CVP) by listening to the blood flowing through my jugular vein with a special Doppler listening device. I interpreted the flow by blowing into a specially designed pressure gauge, which estimated my CVP. Interestingly, results of this noninvasive technique paralleled data from two astronauts in a previous spacelab flight when their blood-flow measurements were taken by a needle inserted into a vein. From the results of our flight, this new technique appears to be a more convenient, quick, and accurate way of estimating blood flow in future astronauts.

In another experiment, I had to swallow a substance containing a special isotope of oxygen that would enable researchers to measure the changes in total body water that occur during spaceflight. There was also a project designed to identify factors that contribute to an increased risk of forming kidney stones during spaceflight. It is known by scientists that there is a loss of calcium, phosphorous, potassium, and uric acid from the bones and tissues during a space mission. Once these enter the bloodstream, they may increase the risk of renal stones.

Another way researchers are trying to understand how the body adapts to zero gravity is by measuring the fluid shift with a specially fitted stocking to determine the amount of shrinking in the circumference of the legs. I took measurements at various times throughout our days in space, from my ankles up to my upper thighs. The tape measures were built into the stocking, and the measurement could be recorded right on the tape measure with the use of a different colored marker for each day. What I found was that the volume of my leg shrank rapidly during the first flight day as the fluids shifted out of my legs into my upper torso. Overall, there was a volume change of one liter per leg, and most of that change occurred during the first ten hours of flight.

Incredibly, after I had recorded extensive measurements before and during the six-day flight, plus more measurements after landing, NASA lost my leg stocking, along with all the data! Despite my affection for the space program, I cannot help but feel that the taxpayer deserves more than this. Such data is not only expensive to obtain, its scientific value will be of great significance to future space travelers.

While the shuttle is currently America's sole manned space vehicle, in the future it will have a supporting role in space for a permanently manned space station. The twenty-five-billion-

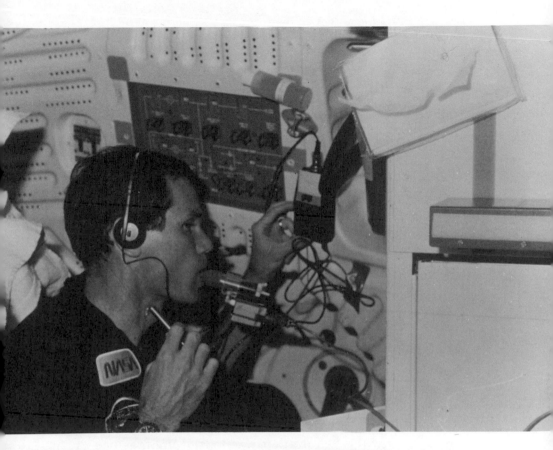

Performing an experiment to estimate the pressure of the blood as it flows into the heart. [NASA photo]

dollar structure is to begin in 1994, and the "vacancy" sign will go up in 1995. Completion is scheduled for 1997. Once the space station is in place, research will receive a primary, rather than a secondary, designation. Initially the space station will house eight people. That number might grow to twenty within ten years.

Ever since Alan Shepard's suborbital flight in May 1961, the U.S. has been in a race with the Soviet Union. This was given its greatest emphasis when President Kennedy called for an American on the moon by the end of that decade, a mandate that was accomplished when Neil Armstrong took his "one small step." After that, military objectives received increased attention—only in the era of the shuttle did we again begin focusing on scientific research.

That emphasis continues to grow. Of course, America does have essential military objectives, and the surveillance satellites are certainly one of them. But from here on, one of the primary thrusts of space research will be technology with commercial applications, including the manufacture in orbit of rare medicines and crystals by American pharmaceutical companies and university research labs.

Ironically, the one thing nobody seemed to feel was important—in fact, the feature that was looked upon as one of the liabilities of space, zero gravity—has turned out to be one of the greatest assets to research and development. In fact, one of the most important design criteria for the space station is to minimize the gravitational forces. Some of the pharmaceutical products currently being developed in space will be worth 22 million dollars a pound. That means space manufacturing is likely to be a profitable business for a long time, in spite of its expense.

The technical problem of separating a pure product from surrounding impurities and keeping it pure remains the prime objective for researchers using zero gravity. One current technique—called electrophoresis—can be carried out much more efficiently in space than on earth, as the astronauts on Skylab

An artist's sketch of a U.S. space station. [NASA photo]

discovered. On the ground, such separation can never be as effective, since the force of gravity tends to mix the molecules.

The experiments I carried out aboard the *Columbia,* and similar experiments done by Charlie Walker in an earlier flight, have shown that pharmaceuticals made in space can achieve five times the purity of the same products on earth. Not only that, they can be produced up to four hundred times as fast. This means that when the space station is finally operational, we could manufacture in one month a quantity of drugs that would take thirty years to manufacture on earth. This could benefit the man in the street by providing cheaper medicines.

Among the many medical experiments being carried out in space, one of the most exotic has to do with testing saliva. Preliminary studies in NASA's laboratories have verified the feasibility of using salivary drug levels for predicting blood concentrations of various medicines. In the near future we may use samples of saliva to test most aspects of body chemistry, rather than resorting to the uncomfortable and complicated method of drawing blood—and who wouldn't rather spit in a test tube than have a needle stuck in a vein?

Cardiologists and researchers working with heart disease cite urokinase—a medicine used to treat victims of pulmonary embolism and heart attacks caused by blood clots—as a prime candidate for manufacture in space. Last year almost fifty thousand Americans died of heart disease, and more than one million others suffer from it. Urokinase is produced by a specialized cell in the kidneys. Tests in the shuttle have proved that by using a process like electrophoresis, scientists can separate the productive cells from other cells, vastly increasing the yield of the medicine. Experts say this one development could save the lives of thousands of people who cannot afford treatment at today's prices.

Many other rare and expensive medicines, such as the beta cell, which produces insulin, and factor 8, used in treating hemophiliacs, may be ready for space manufacture. Transplanting beta cells developed in space into humans could mean a permanent cure of diabetes—currently the third largest killer in America and responsible for blindness, heart failure, and kidney failure. If beta cells become widely available, the result will not only save millions of lives, but billions of dollars now being spent to fight these diseases.

McDonnell Douglas, although better known as an aerospace firm, has already spent approximately $50 million of its own money for electrophoresis research. As a result it was able to announce the development of a new drug, erithropoiten, which could be a cure for some forms of anemia. The company manufactured large quantities on the ground using electrophoresis, with the aim that when the shuttle flew again the drug could be highly purified in zero gravity. Although it now appears this process has been overtaken by new genetic engineering techniques on earth, the learning curve is real, and there will be other products in the future.

Space People

A Candid Look at Some Behind-the-Scenes Personalities—and Politics—at NASA

South of Houston, in the college-campus atmosphere of Johnson Space Center, some of the most intricate engineering puzzles of spaceflight are solved. The men and women who perform this work are dedicated to placing man in space and getting him back safely. Their dedication goes beyond paychecks and retirement funds: Most of the employees could make more money by leaving NASA and joining a private aerospace company, and many do. But a core of seasoned veterans have stayed with the agency. They stay because NASA gives them the opportunity to serve national goals with a unique kind of research. They are a very special, technical, dedicated breed of people.

Relatively few humans have flown in outer space so far. To date, after twenty-five years of manned spaceflight, only 129 have been into space in the U.S. program and 73 in the Soviet one. The higher American number reflects the larger crews of up to seven or eight carried aboard the space shuttle. Before the shuttle program, only forty-four Americans had blasted into space.

To the general public, NASA is made up of two elements: the spaceships and the astronauts. Actually, the astronauts make up only a small portion of NASA's space team. From the Original Seven who were chosen, the ones who had the "right stuff," that number has now grown to an active astronaut corps of one hundred members. This superbly trained, singularly dedicated elite group of men and women are selected to perform the front-line task of actually going into space. None are paid extravagant sums. None have plush offices. Charlie Bolden, for instance, who was the pilot aboard our flight, is a lieutenant colonel in the Marine Corps assigned to NASA. As such, he draws the same pay as any comparable lieutenant colonel in the USMC on flight duty.

The far-larger space team is made up of several thousand dedicated workers whose names are mostly unknown to the public. It was my privilege to get to know a few of these men and women during my tenure as a member of the astronaut team. What follows is my candid, off-the-cuff impressions of some of the key people, a few astronauts, and some of the unsung heroes who are responsible for America's space program. This is not, in any way, a complete list—I don't intend it to be. These are simply some of the people who touched my life during my brief stint as a temporary astronaut.

Jay Greene. When the *Apollo 13 Saturn V* rocket blasted away from the Kennedy Space Center on a sunny afternoon in April 1970, Jay Greene was a member of the Mission Control team. His title: flight dynamics officer. A little more than two hours after launch, as the three astronauts were starting their journey toward the moon, one of the rocket's engines shut down prematurely. Plans to proceed to the moon were put on hold until Jay and other NASA officials determined whether the spacecraft had enough fuel to make it. Meanwhile, the capsule, with its moon orbiters aboard, went into a hold position in orbit around the earth.

Two days later, as the mission was moving more than 24,000 miles an hour away from earth, an oxygen tank in the Apollo capsule exploded. Astronaut James Lovell said, "We were losing everything at the same time—fuel, electricity, oxygen. Then I looked out the window and could see gas escaping. I knew we were in deep trouble."

The only way to get back home was for the three-man crew to crawl into the lunar module called the *Aquarius* and rely on its oxygen to support them for their ninety-hour return to earth. They never got to the moon's surface, but the crew and the spaceship did splash down in the Pacific with one of the most accurate landings of the Apollo program.

Jay was in agony throughout reentry and landing. "When they opened up that capsule, I was sure all they would find would be three dead bodies," he told me. "I honestly didn't see how we could get them home."

Jay was not only on the Apollo team, he was the lead flight director for the space shuttle launches of flight *61-C* (my flight) and flight *51-L,* which was the official title of the ill-fated *Challenger* mission. With all our scrubs and the disaster that befell the *Challenger,* Jay has dealt with more than his share of NASA's problems.

Jay is a fortyish, no-nonsense type of man, who shows the tension of his job by constantly dragging on a cigarette. Being ultimately responsible for every major decision made between launch and landing keeps him on edge—but also in love with his job. Like many others who work long hours and have an almost unbelievable responsibility—including responsibility over men's lives—Jay is underpaid and overworked. Along with the others, he grumbles about salary, but acknowledges it is too late for him to leave NASA and go to work for a private contractor where the pay is often twice or three times as high.

On the other hand, Jay gave me the distinct impression he

is not working just for money, nor would he leave just because bigger bucks are offered. He is a man dedicated to his job—he just wishes the government paid more. Born in Brooklyn, New York, he stayed there until he finished his degree in electrical engineering at Brooklyn Polytechnic Institute. He began at NASA in 1965 and was appointed flight director in 1982.

Jay is one of the few flight directors within NASA. The directors call the shots during a mission as soon as the rocket leaves the pad. Up until then, responsibility rests with the Launch Control Center at Kennedy Space Center. Upon launch, however, responsibility shifts to Mission Control in Houston—where Jay is in command. The flight director remains on the hot seat throughout the mission. Tension, of course, is at its highest during launch and reentry—and during any kind of emergency.

I had a long talk with Jay one evening when he joined me for dinner at a Mexican restaurant near the space center.

Jay was working in Mission Control in Houston when the first man landed on the moon. "After my shift," he told me, "I went home and grabbed a bottle of whiskey and walked out to a hill near my apartment. I sat on that hill and stared at the moon for hours. I just couldn't believe we had actually done it, placed a man on the moon."

He stares intently at his companions when he talks, almost as if he were an interrogator. He smokes and inhales deeply. His sentences are liberally peppered with curse words when the conversation moves to the pressure of his job; yet he freely admits he could not imagine doing anything else. It takes a strong will to shoulder responsibilities like Jay Greene's—not least because of their demands on free time and family.

In fact, flight director is the top job on the ground within NASA. The flight director must have an in-depth understanding of every major system in the shuttle and, in earlier days, in the Apollo rockets. If something goes wrong—and it often does—Greene or one of the several other flight directors is the person who weighs the options brought to him by his support team and decides what to do next. His decision is then passed on to the CAPCOM, who communicates it to the orbiting crew.

Jay is of medium height, with a growing waistline and graying temples. His eyes look strained, as if they have stared at computer screens a few hundred hours too many. Yet behind those tired eyes are, in the Hollywood vernacular, "nerves of steel." That's the kind of man it takes to be director of Mission Control.

Nancy Gunter. Nancy is the self-professed "mother" of the astronauts after they arrive at Kennedy Space Center. Her basic job is to run the astronaut office and crew quarters at KSC. She sees to the astronauts' personal needs and makes sure they wake up on time to get to their training sessions. Laughing, she told me her goal was to ensure that the astronauts ate everything on their plates and never went home with dirty clothes.

Nancy is one of those midlevel people who have a high profile with the press during launches, but she is basically a behind-the-scenes person. She played an important role in my life during all those scrubs, as well as when I was in quarantine.

To Nancy, all people are equal. The astronauts' quarters are her kingdom and she reigns as queen. She has a refreshing I-don't-take-any-guff-from-anyone attitude, and although she laughs a lot, she falls into the category of "tough." Outsiders sometimes see her as a she-bear. The astronauts, however, welcome the no-nonsense way she handles the press and others who might disrupt their finely tuned lifestyle. Her job is to make sure our nation's hero-status astronauts do their last bit of repetitious training before launch. To accomplish this, she often steps between them and the press, especially at launch time, using her limited authority to the full to protect her cubs.

Well known because of her high visibility during the pre-launch time, Nancy is a middle-aged woman with long hair that she pulls gently back from her forehead. She walks and talks quickly, and loves to hear the latest about NASA and its top people. She has stuck with the NASA program for decades, even though on several occasions she has been passed over for promotions and pay raises. "It's because they think I'm a bossy woman," she laughs. Indeed, she is. Her bossiness shows. Yet, despite it all, she has stuck with her children, the astronauts, with a dedication that has earned their trust.

Bob Crippen. He's an astronaut; he's famous; he smiles a lot; and he looks like he always has a tan. Bob "Crip" Crippen, along with John Young, flew the *Columbia* on her maiden voyage, departing earth on April 12, 1981 for two and a quarter days in space. While John Young is a quiet, matter-of-fact, intense person, Crippen is almost the exact opposite.

Weighing in at 160 pounds, five-foot-ten Crippen looks as comfortable in a space suit as he does in a pair of loafers. He has dark brown, close-cropped hair and is beginning to show some mature wrinkles. Despite his fifty years, this native Texan remains physically fit, with the smooth, springy walk of an athlete. When I first met him, I thought he looked more like a polished salesman than one of America's best and most recognized astronauts. He clips the ends of his words in quick, military delivery, sounding like the pilot he is. Like all the other astronauts (and like most technical personnel), he speaks NASAese better than he speaks English, punctuating his sentences with acronyms and technical words known only to his elite companions.

He has three grown daughters, by a previous marriage.

Crip joined the astronaut corps in 1969 and was a crew member on the highly successful Skylab Medical Experiments Altitude Test—a fifty-six-day simulation of the Skylab mission. He completed his first spaceflight as pilot aboard the first shuttle in 1981. In 1983, he flew as commander in mission STS-7, along with Sally Ride. When Crip commanded mission STS-41C in 1984, Dick Scobee, commander of the ill-fated *Challenger,* was his pilot. His last mission was to command the

Jay Greene. [NASA photo]

Nancy Gunter. [NASA photo]

Bob Crippen. [NASA photo]

John Young. [NASA photo]

Challenger in 1984, again with Sally Ride, as well as Kathy Sullivan, Jon McBride (pilot), Dave Leestma, and two payload specialists—Marc Garneau from Canada and Paul Scully-Power. Bob Crippen was, up until that time, the only astronaut to fly the shuttle four times. In early 1987 he moved from his status as an active astronaut to the management level of NASA in Washington, D.C.

John Young. The shyness of John Young can be disarming. He knows he is the top astronaut in NASA; his former job title told him so. He uses his top-flight reputation as a shield when he is more than a little blunt. He knows people don't like to cross living heroes who have logged more than 11,000 hours flying time, including 835 hours in six spaceflights—it is bad P.R.

Young has a peculiar habit. After he describes a close call in space, he spreads his lips into a smile-like grimace—and waits. It is smile-like because it bares his top row of teeth, but no emotion shows through. And the "smile" is quite obviously switched off once the point is made. Perhaps it is because he has told the stories one too many times. Maybe it's because he doesn't want to show the emotion that must have followed the close call. After all, he is a test pilot extraordinaire who has been trained to handle the diciest situations with a laconic phrase and emotionless voice.

John's primary recreational interest is running, and at fifty-seven years old, he remains in top condition.

As commander of the first shuttle mission, John performed perhaps the world's most famous test flight. Previously, all manned rocket systems had been flown and tested before a manned flight actually occurred. That was not possible with the shuttle, however. *Columbia* became not only the first manned spaceship to be flown into orbit without benefit of previous unmanned orbital testing, it was, quite literally, the first real manned spaceship. It was the first winged craft to launch using solid rocket boosters, and the first winged reentry vehicle to return to a conventional runway landing.

John is almost as well known for his criticism of NASA procedures as he is for his flight exploits. Some of these criticisms played a major role during the *Challenger* investigation.

Critical as Young is of NASA procedures, he was unfazed by the remarks of another acid-tongued astronaut, Buzz Aldrin, who when he first saw the plans of the new shuttle Young was going to fly, said in amazement, "You're not serious! You don't really mean this stack of three things with an airplane on it!"

NASA was serious, however, and so was NASA's top astronaut, John Young.

A native of Orlando, Florida, Young was one of the nation's top test pilots when he joined NASA in 1962. He flew aboard the first manned Gemini mission in March 1965 with Gus Grissom and later completed a dual rendezvous with two separate Agena target vehicles on *Gemini 10*. He then flew aboard two Apollo missions. On his last one, he and Charlie Duke explored the lunar highlands, collected two hundred pounds of rocks, and drove the lunar rover twenty-seven kilometers over the moon's surface. His last flight was as command pilot aboard mission *STS-9* in 1983. In preparation for his prime and backup crew positions on ten spaceflights, he has put more than 11,300 hours into training so far—mostly in simulations and simulators.

John's rasping voice and his half-rim glasses hint at the length of his tenure at NASA. He pulls no punches and is famous for writing some of the toughest memorandums ever to sport a NASA logo. While now part of management, as chief astronaut he often lashed management as the source of many of NASA's problems. His scathing notes and his confrontational style often give outsiders (and a few insiders) the impression John is crabby. I prefer to attribute his severity to the intensity of his purpose and his professional rigor—the very things that have made him one of the nation's top (living) test pilots and, without question, America's top astronaut.

When, following the *Challenger* explosion, Young's now-famous memo criticizing NASA for abandoning its safety-first principle was leaked to the press, its inflammatory tone caused Air Force Colonel Richard Griffin, commander of the USAF Space Command at Falcoln Air Force Station and brother of former JSC director Gerry Griffin, to write John. His reply was as acrid as John's memo—revealing the intensity these highly trained experts bring to their jobs:

> It is indeed difficult to decide to take on a titular national hero in print, even when he is dead wrong. A lot of us in this business have been reading your poisoned pen memos for years, and we understand the thrust of them—the great good parts and the totally bad. But to the "outside," your tone and style of writing make it sound as if you have a total corner on concern for flight safety. I resent your impugning the integrity and human sensitivity of a totally dedicated group of supertalented government and contractor people.

Regardless, John remains a highly respected man and is viewed as "the best of the best" by his peers. However, many in NASA, as well as a number of qualified space technicians and scientists who work with NASA, view John's concern for safety as overconcern. Because John had been head of the astronaut office since 1974, some thought he had been chief long enough and it was time to let some of the younger astronauts start moving up.

After the management changes at NASA following the *Challenger* explosion, John was moved laterally to a position of special assistant to the director at JSC for engineering, operations, and safety. NASA management assured John that he was not being shoved aside—just being used in a new way. But the potential perception was another problem for NASA: At a time when the agency needed frank discussion more than ever in order to correct its severe safety problems, it appeared NASA was ditching its most credible internal critic.

One astronaut loyal to John Young likened Young's lateral transfer to the story of a banana republic airliner that aborted a takeoff and returned to the terminal. After a long wait the airliner took off again. One of the passengers asked the flight attendant about the problem.

"Oh, it was nothing," she reassured him. "The pilot did not like the way one of the engines sounded as he was taking off, so he aborted the takeoff and brought the plane back to the terminal."

"I see," the passenger said, relaxing a bit. "And did you change the engine?"

"Oh, no, sir," the hostess said sweetly. "That would have taken time, and we have important people aboard. We changed the pilot."

The debate still rages as to whether John Young is right in many of his blunt criticisms, many of which I agree with. However, he remains an integral part of the NASA team, and his voice, although muted, is still heard.

One of John's duties is to do the final weather checks in the shuttle training aircraft before each KSC lift-off. While he is no longer responsible for internal safety, he remains the man who makes the go/no-go recommendation to the launch director, based on how the clouds look.

George Abbey. As the director of flight crew operations, George Abbey had the final say on who joined the astronaut corps, and, once they belonged, who flew and who didn't. Therefore, he is the one person the astronauts wanted to please more than anyone else.

Abbey oversaw a herd of some of the most confident self-starters ever assembled. The astronauts seemed to court his favor by performing only at their best. No one in the astronaut corps knew exactly how Abbey selected members of upcoming crews. It is best that the astronauts don't know, Hoot Gibson told me, because that lack of knowledge frees them to simply concentrate on their work. Obviously, Abbey shares my respect for Gibson, for he chose him to be the commander of the second shuttle flight following the *Challenger* explosion. On the shuttle *Atlantis* Hoot will fly a secret mission for the Department of Defense.

A heavyset, barrel-shaped man with dark hair and a crew cut, Abbey seldom smiles. It seemed to me he tries hard to avoid smiling. When a smile does come to his lips, it takes over his entire face. But then it quickly disappears, and he regains his staff-sergeant expression.

Abbey is not a staff sergeant, however. A graduate of the U. S. Naval Academy, he also holds a master of science degree from the Air Force Institute of Technology. He has four thousand hours as a pilot, a long list of technical and management accomplishments, and has been a member of the NASA team for twenty years.

George has a characteristic growl, and when I showed up for training, he made it plain to me that he did not like the idea of civilians being included in a crew of astronauts. However, Abbey is a good company man, and he did his best to go along with the orders he was given. The tension was always there, however, even though we both worked reasonably hard to keep it down.

Despite his somewhat shuffling gait, Abbey retains an air of authority and maintains an erect military posture. His large frame and growing waistline seem to fit that form of movement.

Abbey is single, and although sometimes gruff and forbidding during working hours, he can often be found on Fridays at a local watering hole during Happy Hour, knocking down a beer and keeping a close eye on the movement on the dance floor.

He has been accused of playing favorites when it came to picking crews. But with one hundred astronauts all wanting to fly the next mission, some disgruntled comments can be expected. I concluded he was probably the right man for the job—a man who had other priorities in life besides making friends, and as a result, able to be objective in his selections.

"I call them as I see them," is his only response to such criticism.

When asked how he began his career at JSC, George says simply, "I was assigned by the Air Force to come here."

Obviously, he is a man of few words to outsiders.

In late 1987 in a NASA shakeup, Abbey was relieved of his job and named special assistant to JSC Director Aaron Cohen. It was billed as a promotion.

Carolyn Huntoon. Doctor Huntoon was associate director of JSC while I was in training. The simple fact that she was the number-three person at JSC, where almost all the top people are men, speaks volumes.

A Ph.D. from Baylor University College of Medicine, she came to JSC in 1970 as a senior physiologist, heading up the development programs in the areas of endocrinology and biochemistry. She is one of the nation's outstanding women in science and has been so recognized by more than a dozen professional groups. She holds the Exceptional Scientific Achievement Medal, the highest honor that NASA gives to a scientist.

Carolyn is an extremely competent administrator with a good sense of humor about ironic or difficult situations. When my assistant stretched NASA's rules a little too much, or when it seemed my congressional duties might conflict with some of my duties as an astronaut, it was Carolyn Huntoon who let us know—but always with humor and grace, made more charming by a Louisiana accent. Dr. Huntoon is married to Harrison Huntoon of Houston.

Doug Ward. Chief of the Media Services branch at JSC, Doug is constantly writing and talking about others, preferring to keep out of the picture himself—as any good newspaperman should. Naturally, I had a lot of contact with Doug. As a congressman getting ready to fly into space, I was sought by the press. A lot of that activity came through, or was referred to, Doug's office. I quickly discovered that he lived by one primary rule: Keep your mouth shut until your mind is engaged.

Unlike many of the media people I was accustomed to in Washington, Doug's forte was not public relations. He knew the media were always eager to approach him and he did not feel he had to waste his time trying to sell them on anything. He almost never offered glib remarks, partly as a habit of his Idaho upbringing and partly as the result of twenty years' dealing with the press as a NASA spokesman. He knew that anything he said, even in jest, could cause national rumblings. Therefore he seldom jested, preferring to answer only the questions that were asked, and with as much accuracy—and generalization—as possible.

Thin, with a deep voice and dark hair, Doug oversees the NASA "news room" in Houston. Here, reporters hang out during missions to get the latest information, and news releases are distributed throughout the year.

Sonny Carter. Captain Manley Lanier Carter is the epitome of the image most Americans have of the astronauts. No man in the astronaut corps fits the bill better. A forty-year-old superachiever, Carter was born in Macon, Georgia, but considers nearby Warner Robbins his home. He graduated from Lanier High School in Macon and holds a B.A. in chemistry from Emory University, as well as a doctorate in medicine. He is an expert wrestler, golfer, tennis player, and baseball player. He played professional soccer for the Atlanta Chiefs of the NASL from 1970 until 1973—while he was completing an internship in internal medicine at Grady Memorial Hospital in Atlanta. After serving as a flight surgeon with the Marines, he returned to flight school and earned his wings in 1978. He served as senior medical officer on the aircraft carrier USS *Forrestal,* then

George Abbey. [NASA photo]

Carolyn Huntoon. [NASA photo]

Doug Ward. [NASA photo]

Sonny Carter. [NASA photo]

Bill Shepherd. [NASA photo]

Jim Beggs. [NASA photo]

graduated from the U.S. Navy Fighter Weapons School. A Navy captain, he's made 160 carrier landings in jet aircraft. In June 1984 he became a U.S. Navy test pilot and in June 1985 qualified for assignment as a mission specialist for the astronaut corps.

Sonny's thick Southern accent and his laid-back, happy-go-lucky attitude have earned him the nickname Billy-Bob. He was the Astronaut Support Person (ASP), otherwise called the Cape crusader for the ill-fated *Challenger*. He went out early on the morning of the launch, arriving shortly after midnight, to configure and check all the switches and systems in the shuttle. He was the last man to help the astronauts into their seats and cinch their straps before closing the hatch. He personally helped oversee the recovery of debris from his friends' fiery coffin.

A devoted father of two girls, he is a delightful person, with a humble, helping attitude. When we ran together, his long, skinny legs easily took one step to my two.

It was Sonny who convinced me to start chin-ups in my exercise routine. I realized I would probably never be able to do what he does every day— fifty chin-ups with a forty-five-pound weight tied to him—but he did encourage me. When I started, I was barely able to do ten chin-ups (without weights!), but it's amazing what you can accomplish when a superachiever is standing by saying, "You can do it!" By the end of my training, I was able to pump my body twenty times up to the chinning bar.

Even though he is a high-ranking naval officer and an extraordinary achiever among the astronaut corps, Carter's real appeal is that of an all-American boy who grew up loving baseball cards and still loves sports, his wife, his children, and his dreams. His dreams will continue to come true because, in addition to his drive, he loves people—even intruders like myself who invade the sacred realm of the astronauts on a temporary basis.

Bill Shepherd. Shepherd, blond haired and blue eyed, came out of the desert in Arizona to enter the U.S. Naval Academy, winding up with a master's degree in ocean engineering from MIT. He is listed here because he was our Cape crusader for the scrubs and final launch of the *Columbia*.

The U.S. Navy trained Commander Shepherd as a Navy Seal, a skilled diver who works not only with demolitions, but is trained to kill in underwater stealth missions. He had never flown, but was willing to take the chance that a frogman could become an astronaut. He was right.

During our long quarantine, I became impressed by Shep's love of a challenge. Ignoring his well-developed upper torso (the result of pumping iron for years—his biceps are almost as big as my legs), with reckless abandon I challenged him to an arm wrestle. Hoot immediately expressed surprise and voiced concern for my safety. I explained I could now do twenty chin-ups and was ready for anything. Hoot said no one in his right mind had ever challenged Shep. I snarled, sat down with Shep, and was able to hold out in the match for three and a half seconds before Shep almost splintered the table with the back of my hand. I decided I should stick to chin-ups.

Despite his physical prowess, Shep has a tender heart. He volunteered to help Sonny Carter in the recovery of *Challenger*'s debris and used his underwater skills to assist the Navy divers in recovering the astronauts' remains. He will be making his first spaceflight with Hoot Gibson aboard the *Atlantis*, the second flight after the long delay following the *Challenger* disaster.

Jim Beggs is a good man who got a raw deal from the United States Attorney for the Southern District of California. This nation has suffered because of the injustice.

Beggs was nominated by President Reagan on June 1, 1981, to become administrator of NASA. He was the sixth man to head the nation's civilian space agency. Before that, he had been executive vice president and a director of General Dynamics Corporation, St. Louis, Missouri, heading up the F-16 program.

A 1947 graduate of the U.S. Naval Academy, Beggs also holds an MBA from Harvard. Born in 1926, he is a devoted family man. He and his wife, Mary, have five children. He was considered to be an effective leader at NASA. He was politically well connected and had enough clout to get into the White House to see President Reagan on behalf of the civilian space agency. He presided over the success of the shuttle program.

Jim thought the shuttle could do everything. Preceding administrations had felt the same, and the shuttle was officially named the Space Transportation System (STS). It was to be the United States' way to and from space for all users—commercial, scientific, and military. Beggs and the under secretary of the Air Force, Edward Aldridge, used to go at each other because the Air Force did not want to be dependent on a NASA vehicle and have to pay to ride on it.

In the long run it became apparent the Air Force was right. America needed to diversify her launch vehicles to have assured access to space.

Beggs has a suspicion of the number thirteen. So after the successful mission of *STS-9*, with *STS-13* just a few flights away, Beggs insisted on a new numbering system. Henceforth, *STS-13* became *STS 41-C*, and *Columbia*'s mission, the twenty-fourth flight of the shuttle, was designated *STS 61-C*.

Beggs had able assistance in the job of running NASA. The Reagan administration had agreed on a Democratic former secretary of the Air Force, Dr. Hans Mark, as his deputy. Beggs and Mark were effective on Capitol Hill and with the administration. But then Mark decided to take a job as chancellor of the Texas university system, and Beggs's problems started.

Some political types on the White House staff wanted their candidate, Dr. Bill Graham, to be Beggs's deputy. Beggs would have none of it. He insisted that he needed someone qualified, with aerospace experience, to be the deputy administrator to run the day-to-day activities of NASA. Bill Graham, he thought, was a pleasant person but one who, despite his Ph.D. in electrical engineering, did not have the necessary experience. Beggs told the White House staff he would not take him.

What then occurred was a Mexican standoff. The White House staff eventually won. Beggs, however, resisted and stalled the process for nine months. In the meantime, he and Graham started to distrust—and dislike—each other.

Finally, according to Beggs, when he saw that White House politics was not going to produce another recommendation to his liking, he went to see Don Regan, the White House chief of staff. He told Regan that if, upon examination, Regan concluded that Graham was qualified, then he would not publicly oppose the nomination. Later, when he called Regan for his decision, the chief of staff admitted to Beggs that he did not think Graham, although talented, was qualified for the NASA post. But it was too late. Regan confided that the support for Graham was too strong with other staff members and White House friends. Beggs had no choice but to concede.

Two weeks after Graham started work, the United States District Attorney for Southern California brought charges against Beggs to a federal grand jury. Beggs was indicted for unlawfully charging the government for services while he was at General Dynamics. The timing was incredible. A number of people openly wondered what was going on. Beggs adamantly insisted on his innocence but had to step down as NASA chief. Doctor Bill Graham, the deputy, became acting administrator.

I had just arrived at KSC on Monday, December 2, 1985, when I was told Beggs had been indicted. I was shocked—and disappointed. Beggs had been a good administrator. I knew this would not only cripple his leadership, but the shock waves would be felt throughout NASA. I also had no doubts about his innocence, since I knew he was a man of integrity. At the same time, I knew he had no choice but to step down until the case was settled.

When the press asked me what I thought, all I could say was that I knew Jim was an honorable man.

It was not until Thursday of that week, on the platform outside the crew compartment trainer at JSC, that I was able to reach him by telephone. I told him I had been thinking of him. I wished him well and encouraged him. He indicated that a lot of congressional leaders had let him know they were behind him.

Bill Graham had a tough job as the new boss at NASA. He knew that Beggs was popular and that he would have difficulty getting cooperation from the staff and the contractors. He also knew he was very inexperienced in civilian space operations.

As part of his agreement to step down, Beggs had insisted that one of his most trusted NASA career men, Phil Culbertson, be named to a newly created position of general manager to run NASA's daily activities. Meanwhile, Graham plunged into his new job with vigor and determination. He actively solicited friends in the administration and Congress. He traveled extensively to the NASA centers. He impressed many NASA people by actually mingling among them and seeing firsthand what they were doing. He impressed some in the astronaut office by talking to them about their work and training. Although he was not an experienced NASA man, he knew management and was dedicated to a vision of space exploration and NASA's role in it.

Graham had only been on the job two months when the decision to launch *Challenger* was made. He broke tradition by not being at the Cape for the launch, preferring instead to meet his previously set appointments in Washington. Graham had made every effort to be present for our launch, even having launch breakfast with us on several mornings that turned out to be scrubs. But because of previous commitments, he missed the lift-off of *Columbia* as well.

Many people wondered, had Beggs been chief, would he have allowed *Challenger* to go? I doubt it. Later, Beggs said he would have been concerned about the ice and icicles on the launch tower, which could break off and damage the delicate silicon tiles at launch. This, by the way, was the concern also

Talking with NASA Associate Administrator Jesse Moore and Acting NASA Administrator Dr. Bill Graham at a prelaunch breakfast, December 19, 1985, at the crew quarters. [Nasa photo]

voiced by Rocco Petrone, head of the shuttle program for Rockwell, the company that developed the orbiter.

George Abbey was in the Launch Control Center at Kennedy Space Center the morning *Challenger* lifted off. He was agitated and worried. Final decision for the launch rested with Jesse Moore, associate administrator for spaceflight at KSC. Moore, who later said he was unaware of the objections raised by Morton Thiokol engineers and the phone conversations with Marshall Space Center in Huntsville, gave the order to proceed with the launch countdown. George Abbey asked what Rocco's recommendation was. He was told that Rocco said go. Petrone explained later, however, that he had expressed concern while stating he could not give the mission a no-go.

Beggs was in the NASA headquarters in Washington, D.C., at the time, since he had refused to vacate his office. He expected that the charges against him would soon be cleared and he would resume as head of NASA. He cried in anguish when he later told the story of his doubts about *Challenger*'s launch and how he should have tried to stop it—but had no authority.

As a result, *Challenger* launched.

At once, more heads rolled. Jim Fletcher, former NASA administrator, was recalled by the President to replace Beggs and Acting Administrator Bill Graham. Doctor Graham stayed on for a short while as deputy director. His friends in the administration then arranged for him to return to the White House as Reagan's science advisor. Jesse Moore, who had earlier been appointed to head up the Johnson Space Center, moved to Texas. It was quickly apparent, however, that the JSC people had lost confidence in Moore. After taking a sabbatical, he retired from NASA.

Nearly one and a half years later, late on a Friday night, the U.S. Department of Justice admitted publicly that it had made a mistake by not uncovering all the evidence in Beggs's indictment, thereby delaying Beggs in his search for the documentation that would have exonorated him much earlier. Beggs

was cleared of all charges, but massive damage had been done
to him personally—and to America's entire space program.

The deleterious consequences of the act of a federal prose-
cutor and a federal grand jury upon the U.S. space program
will never fully be grasped.

International Cooperation
in Space

Cooperation with our political enemies unsettles a lot of Americans. We don't seem to mind working with people like the Germans and Japanese—once our worst opponents—but cooperation with the Russians or Chinese is still looked upon by many as dangerous folly. Yet, nothing provides as much opportunity for global peace as the challenge of learning how to cooperate. The alternatives are too devastating to consider.

In his novel *Space*, James Michener captures the attitudes that prevent humankind from moving beyond exploration to cooperation. At the close of the book, old Senator Grant's wife says in a frail voice,

> "I wish we could retreat from all this unpleasantness about . . . people who want to take away our guns. I wish we could erase it all and go back to the simpler life I knew in this house with my father. . . ."

[Stanley] Mott reflected that this good woman had seen space and been repelled by it. As the wonder-machines leaped into the air at Canaveral, probing ever outward, extending the dimensions of the comprehensible universe, she had intentionally contracted the perimeters of her world, making it ever smaller and easier to control. And he concluded that all persons are obligated to wrestle with the universe as they perceive it, and those who are terrified by the prospect retreat to little corners from which they seek to destroy the machines doing the outward probing and the men who manage them.

Space exploration, like all pioneer work, demands more than physical courage and finances. It calls for a willingness to stretch the limits of one's horizons beyond the little worlds of comfort and fear in which we all live—to include the broader spectrum of life. This means we explore not only space, but the possibilities of working with all those who share a common goal for the grander purpose of "peace on earth to men of good will."

I knew, when I first got involved with the space program, that I wanted to give attention to the possibilities of international cooperation in space.

In early October 1985, I found myself jogging not along the side streets in Houston, before reporting in at JSC; instead, I was jogging along the Moscow River in an icy rain as passing cars splashed me with cold water.

I was in the Soviet Union leading a thirty-nine-member delegation in open discussions with the Soviets on future cooperative space exploration efforts between our two countries.

This exchange grew from an invitation I had extended to two Soviet cosmonauts, Alexi Leonov and Valery Kubasov, to attend a reception in Washington in July 1985, commemorating the tenth anniversary of the *Apollo/Soyuz* mission. The American astronauts involved in that mission—Tom Stafford, Deke Slayton, and Vance Brand—also attended the American reception. Tom and Deke were also able to join us for the follow-up activities in the Soviet Union.

Doctor Tom Paine, the chairman of the President's National

Commission on Space, and Jesse Moore, then associate administrator at NASA, also were members of the American delegation in Moscow.

During the trip I was careful about what I ate. The Soviet meals were usually unappetizing to me, so I mostly ate dried fruit, cereal, and natural peanut butter that I had brought with me. I continued my regime of jogging and exercise. For my four-mile run in the cold, damp Moscow weather, I bundled in a sweatsuit covered by a running suit, heavy gloves, and a ski cap. Actually, I enjoyed the runs because they were the only chance I had to sightsee in downtown Moscow. As I ran around the brick walls of the Kremlin early one morning, I was preparing mentally for later that day when I would be within the palatial surrounds of the Supreme Soviet for two and a half hours of heated discussion with Soviet President Andrei Gromyko.

Joggers are an unusual sight in Moscow, and as I ran through Red Square, people would often stop and stare at me. Running is, however, part of the daily regime of the cosmonauts at Star City, the cosmonaut training center forty miles north of Moscow. It is officially named the Yuri Gagarin Training Center, after the first person to orbit the earth. Gagarin died in a jet plane crash seven years after his April 1961 inaugural spaceflight. He is considered a national Soviet hero.

Tom Stafford, Deke Slayton, and I laid a bouquet of flowers at Gagarin's statue, which depicts him casually strolling in informal attire. It overlooks woods the cosmonauts often stroll and train in. The place was thought to be Gagarin's favorite spot.

General Alexi Leonov, the Soviet commander of the *Apollo/Soyuz* mission, is now the deputy commandant of the Star City training center. He was our personal tour guide as we inspected facilities that Americans had not seen since our astronauts trained with the Russian cosmonauts ten years before.

I was able to go inside the mock-up trainer of the Soviet space station *Salyut 7,* and Leonov explained its detailed inte-

rior. He openly told our committee that within a year the Soviets would launch a new, larger, and more sophisticated space
station. He was right. *Mir* (meaning "peace" in Russian) was
launched early in 1986. In Star City I sat in the cramped seats
of the Soviet transport spacecraft *Soyuz*, connected with a control room that created different simulation scenarios for the
cosmonauts in training.

The cosmonauts still use a huge centrifuge to train because
their spacecraft exert strong G forces on lift-off and reentry.
NASA long ago dismantled its centrifuge, since shuttle ascents
cause only a relatively benign three-Gs.

Star City contains a huge underwater training facility, similar to the U.S. facility at the Marshall Space Flight Center in
Huntsville. Five cosmonauts were simulating changing solar
panels on their space station while we were there.

As our delegation watched the reunion between the Soviet
cosmonauts and the American astronauts and their families, it
was apparent that theirs was a genuinely personal friendship—a bond that had developed during the two years of shared
experience as the Americans and Russians trained together.
The departure from the Moscow Airport was a tearful one for
both of the teams and their wives. They had not seen each
other since the 1975 *Apollo/Soyuz* mission, and they realized it
might be a long time before they got together again.

It is fitting and appropriate that the future of America's space
program should involve other nations. America is a space-
faring nation. But as the technology explosion continues, it
will become advantageous to all concerned that others be involved in the action. Of course, as Michener's Professor Mott
rightly surmised, in order for this to happen, the American
people—and their elected representatives in government—must
expand their horizons. For it must be admitted that cooperation in space projects means we are not as much "in control."
But it also means we begin to share the greater benefits of
working with people who have, whether we're willing to believe it or not, the same scientific goals.

The cost of space exploration is tremendous—yet no greater, relatively speaking, than the sum provided by Queen Isabella of Spain to finance the trips of Christopher Columbus in 1492 and following. The American space station will cost between 15 billion and 25 billion dollars. But in the context of a trillion-dollar annual national budget, those figures are less intimidating.

Most thoughtful Americans understand this, and are willing to help foot the bill. In late 1987 the National Research Council offered some sensible advice to Congress and the administration: Don't try to explore space on a shoestring budget. It specifically stated, "If the United States intends to pursue an aggressive manned space program, a space station is essential."

It is an inescapable reality, therefore, that the more we explore, the greater the cost will be—and the more desirable the sharing of expenses and efforts with other nations. But cooperation will not only help participating nations realize their goals in space sooner and less expensively, it will also create a more constructive international political environment. Aside from the military use of space, it is quite possible that in fifty years America's space program will be a part of Planet Earth's space program. For space offers a unique environment in which adversaries on Earth can come together peacefully. Certainly, that was true in 1975 when, after three years of cooperative training between the astronauts and cosmonauts, an American space vehicle rendezvoused and docked with a Soviet spacecraft.

During the visit, our hosts, the Soviet Academy of Sciences, seriously discussed far-ranging joint ventures in space, and showed us Soviet space facilities that had been hidden from the Western world since the 1975 mission. In addition to Star City, the cosmonaut training center, they took us to the Space Research Institute and the Flight Control Center in Kaliningrad. At their mission control, I spoke with cosmonauts circling the earth in the *Salyut* 7 space station. The exchange was generally lighthearted.

After discussing the possibility with NASA officials, I planned to continue the conversation later, during our flight in *Columbia*. It would have called for direct communication between an American space shuttle and a Soviet space crew. Unfortunately, the Soviet commander became ill, and the Soviet crew had to return to earth prior to our launch. But there will be other opportunities for symbolic gestures of cooperation.

Our Soviet hosts were evidently interested in resuming the formal cooperative agreement between our two countries that expired in 1982. But their optimism was clouded by recent political differences between the United States and the U.S.S.R. Nevertheless, it was made clear throughout our discussions that the Soviets wanted to exchange information about space, and there was general agreement between us that both countries would benefit from such cooperation.

Our delegation's intense meeting with Gromyko confirmed this interest. We met in the elegant treaty room built by the czars within the Kremlin walls. At times Gromyko's rhetoric became bombastic, for our meeting occurred only a month before President Reagan and Soviet General Secretary Gorbachev were due to hold their summit meetings in Geneva. The official Soviet line was to denigrate Reagan's Strategic Defense Initiative (SDI, or "Star Wars"), and Gromyko was a master at holding to the party line. Nevertheless, the fact that I was scheduled to fly in space was not lost on Gromyko. His welcome was enthusiastic; he heartily shook my hand and listened intently to my encouragement of future cooperative missions in space.

But SDI was his topic of the day. He said through an interpreter, in speeches that sometimes lasted twenty minutes, that as long as the U.S. insisted on being the first to militarize space, there was no sense in talking of peaceful, cooperative missions. I knew this was official propaganda, and I was well aware of the compartmentalization of the Soviet bureaucracy. Probably, many of the functionaries flanking Gromyko that day didn't know as much about Soviet activities in space as I did. So I said, "Your aides may not know it, but you and I know that the Soviet Union was the first to begin military activities in space. So, we should not talk about the U.S. being the first."

Gromyko did not try to refute this argument, but quickly moved on, wondering, perhaps, if I knew things that he did not. The Russian system of not letting the left hand know what the right hand is doing (or has done) works effectively in a nation that does not allow freedom of the press and penalizes even top leaders with prison terms if they try to find out too much about what may be going on in the next office.

For it is a fact that some Western observers—including former U.S. Defense Secretary Caspar Weinberger—believe the Soviets have a working satellite-killer system in place at this moment. While the Russian space station *Mir* may not be manufacturing a satellite-killer system, Soviet space expert James Oberg states: "The microchips they make in space don't go into video arcades in Moscow. They go into missile guidance." He points out that the Soviets "have been pursuing a space weapons program for twenty years and lying about it. We have to adjust to the fact that they do pretty nasty things in space weapons."

Time magazine, in an October 5, 1987 article, quotes U.S. intelligence authorities as saying, "At any one time the U.S.S.R. is operating some 150 satellites, and perhaps as many as 120 are believed to be performing military missions. For hours each day, say intelligence analysts, Soviet Cosmos military satellites drift over the U.S., photographing missile silos and naval deployments. Other Soviet spacecraft lurk with sensitive electronic ears that can pick up telephone conversations in Washington, while Meteor weather satellites monitor conditions over key U.S. targets. Soviet infrared satellites watch for the telltale heat signaling a launch of U.S. ICBMs. At the military launch site in Plesetsk, 500 miles northeast of Moscow, crews stand ready to launch additional intelligence satellites at a moment's notice."

Naturally, the United States uses satellites for the same military purposes.

Protection from other nations is also a major goal for the future. Now we know—and our adversaries know—what the other is doing nearly all the time. Our defense satellites are constantly photographing and sending back signals to home base. This sophisticated snooping actually stabilizes geopolitics and lessens tensions between the superpowers by providing information vital to the enforcement of treaties that otherwise would be mere political hypocrisy. Now, when we demand that atomic tests be restricted or missiles removed, we can monitor the agreements firsthand.

Yet despite the mutual and growing distrust between political leaders of the United States and the U.S.S.R., Roald Sagdeyev, the director of the Soviet Space Research Institute, has made a serious plea for joint cooperation on the Mars Sample Return mission. "If we start progress in this area," the Russian scientist said, "it could create a much better political climate." In my extensive meetings with Sagdeyev in Moscow and later in Washington, he clearly signaled his desire to foster coordinated efforts. He knew that only politics stood in the way.

Sagdeyev is one of the new breed of Russian scientists who believe it is impossible to go any further without global cooperation. His first introduction to scientific work outside the Soviet Union came in 1958 when he was working on nuclear fission control at the Soviet Institute of Atomic Energy. He relates what happened with a degree of wonder: "For the first time I met foreign scientists, Americans, doing the same job and reporting their results. It was like meeting extraterrestrials—extraterrestrials working with the same laws of physics. It was exemplary proof that science has no borders."

I, too, believe it is possible to forge new scientific relationships, despite the differences between our two nations. Underneath President Gromyko's gruff rhetoric, we detected both his and his country's desire for teamwork. Civilian space collaboration has its own identity and need not be linked with our arms control negotiations. Under Soviet leader Mikhail Gorbachev's new governmental policy of openness, or *glasnost,* the political climate has shifted so that space cooperation may be accelerated.

Gromyko was interested in my suggestion that 1992 be designated as International Space Year. Our committee included this concept—which would create a forum for international projects related to space exploration—within the NASA funding bill for 1986. As a result, discussions have already begun in its planning. We also urged the continuation of informal information exchanges and joint research projects by both scientific communities until a new research agreement could be signed. It took another year after we left, but that agreement was finally signed by our government and theirs in 1987.

In the Washington Summit of December, 1987 an agreement was reached on a space initiative to continue cooperation to understand our changing environment. This joint endeavor is called the Global Climate and Environmental Change Initiative.

More missions could be coordinated as parallel missions rather than joint ones, designed so as to avoid any valuable technology transfer. The Russians are several years behind us in microelectronics and computers. Their satellites sometimes break down in a matter of weeks. Some Russian photo-reconaissance satellites literally drop their film to earth for processing, rather than using the sophisticated process of electronic imaging developed by U.S. scientists years ago.

In other areas, the Soviets are clearly ahead of us. In the sheer number of launches, the Soviets are far in front. Cosmonauts have logged fourteen man-years in space, against less than five for U.S. astronauts. Their research in the medical and psychological fields is far ahead of ours. Their *Mir* space station is already deployed and is designed for permanent occupation. In early 1987 they successfully fired off Energia, a rocket that can lift one-hundred-ton payloads, while our shuttles have a limit of thirty tons. If all goes according to plan,

The USSR space station, MIR. [Photo courtesy Congressman Nelson]

their Phobos probes will take off in 1988 for Mars, arriving two hundred days later to photograph the surface of Mars's moon from an altitude of ninety-eight feet.

Thus, there is much we can learn from the Russians. For years the Soviets have shared their knowledge about long-term spaceflight with their counterparts in NASA. This has been done informally, however, since the political climate makes it difficult to exchange technical data. We have their diets and know details of certain physical disorders caused by long stays aboard their space station.

Vladimir Solovyov, the Soviet cosmonaut who had previously spent the longest time in space—237 days—told me that he was able to readapt to gravity and start walking again after three days back on Earth. Other reports, however, have suggested it took him weeks before he could walk properly. Much of this problem of readaptation, we know, was caused by a loss of calcium and a lessening of muscle tone. Both Russians and Americans need to be sharing this kind of information for the benefit of humankind.

On the other hand, basic questions about the direction of the U.S. space program and its relationship with other nations—especially the U.S.S.R.—remain unanswered. In fact, some of the programs that are necessary to continue space exploration, and which might lead to international partnership in space, seem to have been filed in White House limbo.

NASA asked Sally Ride to make a major study of the space program before she left the space agency to become a consultant for a Stanford University disarmament think tank. Her recommendations included the exploration of the solar system; a program to study earth from space; an outpost on the moon; and, eventually, a colony on Mars. Her proposal received little publicity and even less attention from the White House.

The same was true of a report made by former NASA administrator Thomas O. Paine, who had been assigned by the White House to assess America's space programs. Paine's 1986 report stated: "The inner solar system is the future home of mankind. In the next century, we expect to see permanent settlements on the moon and on Mars. NASA should take the lead in new technologies—robotics, supercomputers, tele-operators—all technologies terribly important to the next century."

Such programs cost money, however. With major funds being necessarily allocated to defend ourselves against our enemies, there is not enough left to fund all the programs that would not only better mankind, but just might be the means of helping turn our enemies into friends.

After we left Moscow, the working groups did maintain contact and exchanged information. Further impetus was given by the harmonious relations among the many nations participating in the flyby of Halley's Comet in 1986 by a Soviet spacecraft. Two American scientists had experiments on board. The Russians reaped a lot of goodwill from this mission during the international Halley's watch.

There are many possibilities for cooperative missions ranging from symbolic gestures to formidable technological challenges. For example, one possible mission that could recreate images of the historic *Apollo-Soyuz* linkup is for a cosmonaut to fly with an American space shuttle crew, rendezvous with a Soviet spaceship carrying a U.S. astronaut, and then have the two exchange places on orbit.

Another possibility is a robotic exploration of the planet Mars. The Soviets' 1988 mission to the Martian moons, Phobos and Deimos, will include some international cooperation. America was planning a 1990 Mars polar orbiting mission, now delayed to 1992. Exchange of data gathered during these two missions could be mutually beneficial.

In fact, the 1987 U.S.-U.S.S.R. Space Cooperation Pact is producing fresh agreements to exchange data and cooperate on these missions. Joint studies will be conducted to determine the best landing sites. And the Soviets will give us data from their past Jupiter missions before our *Magellan* spacecraft travels to that planet.

I am also hopeful we can work together on a joint unmanned mission to Mars to bring back soil samples. America could send a robotic surface rover to pick up several Martian samples and then rendezvous with a Soviet lander to deposit the soil. The Soviet spacecraft could then return the Mars samples to earth. If any parts of the mission failed, or if either nation withdrew, the other nation would still have a worthwhile project. In such an endeavor, each nation could protect against the technology transfer to the other. A successful U.S.-U.S.S.R. project would multiply the scientific and political rewards many times as we prepare for the next century and the possibility of a manned international venture to Mars.

The Soviet Union put the first satellite in space. Most Americans greeted the October 4, 1957 news of *Sputnik* with surprise and alarm. At the time other things were going on in the U.S. which were quite important. A week earlier President Eisenhower had ordered the National Guard into Little Rock, Arkansas to enforce his order to racially integrate Central High School. That same week, Jimmy Hoffa was elected president of the Teamsters union. We had more problems at home than we could handle, but we also worried about a twenty-two-inch steel ball weighing 190 pounds that was circling the earth.

Sputnik received a lot of attention in the Pentagon, for to the military it was a nightmare come true. If the Russians could orbit a satellite, they could also orbit nuclear warheads. It was the beginning of a new era—not just for war, but for peace.

The Soviets also launched the first animal, the first man, and the first woman into space. The Soviet space station was a first. They were the first to return pictures from the far side of the moon and the first to show pictures of the surface of another planet (Venus). It is now obvious they intend to send a manned mission to Mars early in the next century and will possibly settle a base on the moon.

Space scientists believe Mars is a storehouse of scientific information—information important in its own right, but important also because of what it will reveal to us about the environment of our own planet. There is evidence that Mars once had abundant liquid water. What went wrong? How did its earthlike environment become so frigid, parched, and virtually devoid of oxygen? Answers to these questions might help us save our own world.

For that reason and others, I am a strong advocate of coordinated efforts in space. It's difficult, as Michener's fictitious Professor Mott correctly pointed out, to keep an open mind when we seem to be fighting for the survival of our cherished traditions. But imagine a different sort of space program, one in which cooperation was an objective, because the leaders of the U.S. and the U.S.S.R. had come to a new understanding. Imagine space exploration as a conquest that would eradicate such things as disease, poverty, overcrowding, and ignorance—rather than just a race between superpowers to fill the sky with weapons and spy satellites.

The military space program is means at hand to protect ourselves, one of the highest priorities of our national government. However, we are in another race. Not a race against any other nation, but a race against time. People on this planet are dying by the millions—dying of disease, hunger, ignorance. What we conquer in space can help us win these battles on earth. But America cannot do it alone. Imagine our planetary leaders deciding to do something not just for their nations but also for their species, something that would capture the imaginations of people everywhere and would lay the groundwork for a major advance in human history. This would be not just the eventual settlement of another planet but, through exploration and research, the improvement and better stewardship of the planet we now occupy.

It really can be done. Satellites have already revolutionized the communications industry, replacing clumsy land-based wires and undersea cables with marvels in space. Radio, telephone, and television signals now bounce into space and back. Any drive through the American countryside will reveal numbers of TV dish antennas receiving direct signals into homes from satellites orbiting the earth.

Now, for the first time, it is technologically possible to put a man on Mars. It will be expensive; but if we cooperate with other nations—Great Britain, France, Germany, Canada, Japan, India, China, Russia—the cost will be divided and the benefits will multiply.

Why Mars? Why not a joint effort to feed the hungry in Africa, or provide water in Bangladesh? Why not clothe and house the refugees along the Thai border, or throw our resources behind Mother Theresa in Calcutta? Why spend billions on space exploration when the United States and the Soviet Union could, in partnership, help house, educate, provide medical care for, and make increasingly self-reliant every citizen of the planet? I only wish that could be accomplished. But history, both past and present, gives no hope it could ever be done. We are consumed by the pursuit of geopolitical advantages. Afghanistan, Czechoslovakia, Poland, Estonia—the list goes on and on. We have simply too little trust. But the changing political realities are—especially after the 1987 Washington summit—that a joint mission to Mars is well within the bounds of political possibility. Carl Sagan, the visionary astronomer from Cornell, who testified about this to our committee, has written, "A major cooperative success in space could serve as an inspiration and spearhead for joint enterprises on earth." A joint mission just might be a start.

The critics of Mars exploration are right in one sense. It's not enough to go simply "because it's there." The romantic notion of swashbuckling adventurers, winging their way like Buck Rogers to faraway planets, is no longer the only reason to go. Nevertheless, the Soviets seem fascinated by the possibility there may be life on Mars. And while there is no scientific reason to believe this is so, Vyacheslav Balebanov, scientific deputy director of Moscow's Institute of Space Research, says the Russian people are dedicated to reaching this neighboring planet. "Our children won't make it, but our grandchildren will be there," he says. I cannot help but admire that kind of determination. A joint Mars project excites both adventurer and scientist alike.

Doctor Sagan believes that whether we cooperate or not, the Soviet Union is going to Mars. Long before *Sputnik,* Soviet scientists and astronomers declared their long-term intention to plant a colony on the red planet. So far, despite unmanned landings on the moon and Venus, they have not been able to develop a Mars lander—as we did so successfully and dramatically when the *Viking* lander sent back crisp photographs of the Martian surface in 1976. However, their spacecraft launch scheduled in 1988 will put satellites into orbit around Mars, operating in close proximity to both Phobos and Deimos, Mars's two small moons. Early in the next decade another Soviet Mars mission is planned. Most scientists believe it is impossible for the Soviets to actually land a man on Mars before the end of the century, but many believe that they may use 1992, the seventy-fifth anniversary of the Russian Revolution, for some surprise mission to Mars.

The year 1992 has significance to those of us in the Western world as well. It is the five hundredth anniversary of Christopher Columbus's discovery of the New World. Regardless of the political motivations of the King and Queen of Spain, that discovery was a necessary step to the linking of the continents. The Planetary Society and many others wonder what could be more fitting for 1992 than the commitment to a global program which crosses all lines for the purpose of the exploration and eventual settlement of another New World?

It's time for Americans to dream again—to be challenged again. Tip O'Neill, former Speaker of the House of Representatives, told me about those early days of America's space ventures, when everyone from the firemen at the Cape to the President of the United States felt personally responsible for our attempt to put a man in space. O'Neill, then a young Boston congressman, said he was at the White House during the countdown of America's first manned spaceflight. He said he had never seen President Kennedy so nervous. The Soviets had already surprised us three weeks earlier by launching Yuri Gagarin for one orbit. Our entire nation was determined to catch up and pass the Russians.

"The President," O'Neill told me, "was like a cat on a hot tin roof—pacing and pacing, back and forth." He knew America's leadership and prestige were on the line. After Alan Shepard successfully flew the suborbital mission, Kennedy greeted him as a national hero. Our nation once again had a dream— an attainable goal.

We need to dream of interplanetary spacecraft assembled in earth orbit at the American space station, and images beamed daily to earth live on television news. We need to dream of seeing that spaceship blast off from the space station, heading for Mars and back, manned by an international crew including dedicated Americans and Russians. When our people and theirs discover that men of widely diverse political and religious beliefs can not only live and work together, and risk life together, I believe something will begin to happen in the spirit of those of us who are watching but remain earthbound.

Very few know it, but the U.S. and the Russians are constantly pooling resources on search-and-rescue missions involving downed aircraft and lost ships at sea. More than one thousand lives have already been saved through this humanitarian cooperation. How much more good can be done through cooperation in space!

Besides these symbolic gestures, which may seem sentimental (although I believe they go much deeper), there is much to do on Mars that will benefit all humankind. Sagan suggests this joint crew would carry out experiments essential to "later expeditions by extracting water, oxygen, and hydrogen from the hydrated rocks and sand and from the underground permafrost. They would test out Martian materials for eventual bases and settlements there." He talks of a "roving vehicle wandering down an ancient river valley, the crew with geological hammers, cameras, and analytic instruments at the ready. Every day the explorers could rove to their own horizon, their discoveries televised back to earth at the speed of light."

Impossible? Mere dreams? I don't think so. As I have said, I believe a joint mission is not merely possible, but visionary. It is time for us to lift up our eyes beyond our changing political boundaries and see Earth as I saw it from space—one world, created by God, populated by people destined not to destroy each other or the planet on which they live, but to colonize other worlds and become a multi-planet species.

A joint human mission to Mars would help remake the politics of Planet Earth.

Already, both superpowers have active international space programs. The Soviet Union has carried twelve foreign nationals aboard its spacecraft and has achieved the desired public relations and political goals it sought. The U.S. has flown eight foreign nationals aboard the space shuttle, with tremendous results in foreign goodwill.

When NASA launched a satellite for communications within the Arab world, it invited Saudi Arabia to select an astronaut. The Saudis chose a member of the royal family, Prince Sultan bin Aziz, himself a jet fighter pilot in the Saudi Air Force. For the seven days of the mission, 100 million Moslems from Morocco to Indonesia were riveted to their TV sets. To say they were interested or excited about the mission is a clear understatement. They were ecstatic!

The goodwill for America was extraordinary and has been replicated each time we've been able to use our space technology for international understanding. Rodolfo Neri from Mexico flew on *Atlantis* just before our mission—and returned to his country a conquering hero feted by the Mexican president. Immediately before was a Spacelab mission dedicated to scientific experiments planned and run by the European Space Agency and flying two Germans and one Dutchman.

France has sent two astronauts into space—one on the

American shuttle and the other on the Soviet *Soyuz*. Both trained together for both missions, and each served as the backup on the other's mission.

In all, nineteen nationalities have observed Planet Earth from the perspective of space.

When Franklin Chang-Diaz, a naturalized American but a native of Costa Rica, flew on our mission, the U.S. State Department arranged for a live TV hookup from the *Columbia* to San Jose, the capital city of Costa Rica. Thousands in that small nation crowded to their TV sets as Franklin conducted a conversation in Spanish with the Costa Rican president. Almost the whole of the government was present for this historic interview. At one point, President Luis Alberto Monge said that a *campesino* (farmer) had asked him to ask what astronauts eat. As fate would have it, we had just been eating from that package of tortillas Franklin had brought along and which were taped to the wall. In response, Franklin reached for the tortillas and held them in front of the TV camera to the amazement, delight, and laughter of almost everyone in Costa Rica.

Need I say more about the public relations value of our space program among other nations?

From the very beginning of the space age, the United States has indicated a desire to work with other nations in space exploration and research. We have entered into over one thousand agreements with one hundred countries for cooperative efforts in space. We pioneered in drafting the principles that led to the Outer Space Treaty in 1967. We also played a lead role in formulating the document "The Peaceful Uses of Outer Space" for the United Nations Committee.

There are four additional UN space treaties concerning the rescue and return of astronauts, liability damages, registration of objects, and the Moon Treaty (which the U.S. and the Soviet Union have not signed). The future is ripe for further agreement on such matters as space rescue, nuclear reactor safety, standardized docking mechanisms, and cleaning up space debris.

The International Telecommunication Satellite Organization (INTELSAT) and the International Maritime Satellite Organization (INMARSAT) were both set up by the United States. We have long advocated the exchange of information from weather satellites. Our Landsat remote sensing system is used by many other nations as well as by U.S. scientists. As the Russians invited other nations to share in the use of their spacecraft to explore Halley's Comet, so we have invited international participation in a large number of scientific projects in space, such as the Hubble Space Telescope, the *Galileo* probe to Jupiter, the Infrared Astronomy Satellite, and a number of others.

In the mid-1990s we will launch the largest cooperative international space project in history. This permanently occupied space structure will be a home not only for American scientists, but for our European, Japanese, and Canadian partners as well—all of whom will contribute substantially in the investment and in key pieces of technology. The station will grow and evolve, and will be operational for thirty years. It is the beginning of a new era of international cooperation in space.

A delicate issue, however, is the fact that the international participation will be at a time when the station may be used for some U.S. defense research purposes. Additionally sensitive will be the fact that our partners will also be our competitors, particularly in commercial space products. The space station agreement will be an excellent way to test our ability to handle relationships that are both competitive and collaborative.

Not only will America greatly benefit from having economic and scientific help in building and operating space projects, we will also benefit as we attract the world's best minds to participate in our programs. In the area of global remote sensing, for instance, we have been cooperating with more than one hundred other nations. Through this we gained broad acceptance of the principle of freedom to observe the earth from space. As a result, international forums now accept the U.S. position that there should be no limitations on the rights of all nations to acquire data from space; in other words, space, like the oceans, belongs to all humankind.

This policy has invigorated many other nations' efforts to get involved with space exploration, research, and technology. France, Germany, Britain, and Italy all have strong space programs. France has deployed an earth-based remote sensing satellite named *Spot*. Germany, which was the prime developer of the 1 billion dollar Spacelab for the shuttle, continues to use that technology. Italy leads in technology for very high frequency communications satellites.

The Japanese founded their space program in cooperation with the United States. Most of their satellites have been built by U.S. industry and launched by the Japanese for meteorology and communications purposes. Japan is now building its own launch vehicle, which will use higher efficiency liquid fuels. Eventually, it will be a competitor to our American ELVs.

The People's Republic of China launched its first satellite in 1970. Then in 1984, it placed a communications satellite in geostationary orbit. It is now marketing its Long March 3 rocket internationally and is offering attractive government-subsidized prices to drum up business.

The U.S. has coordinated efforts in space with a number of other nations, such as India and Indonesia. The Indonesian satellite is a vital communication link for that developing nation, which is spread out over twenty-three thousand islands.

While we must protect ourselves in the global marketplace, only good can come from cooperating with these emerging space nations that are seeking to help their own people through space exploration. America's role should be to provide steady and consistent leadership in joint ventures.

Entrepreneurs in Space

In the mid to late 1990s the American space station will be operational. This technological achievement will be the home for teams of scientists, astronomers, doctors, and engineers from many nations who will live and work in space. It will be an advanced research facility, with laboratories provided by our allies. Not only will it be a platform to explore the heavens, but it will be our primary base to explore the hidden treasures of the earth. For it is here that scientists will provide us with priceless medical and scientific knowledge about the human body.

The space station, while under the auspices of NASA, will be mostly designed and built by American aerospace companies. It will be yet another example of the partnership between private enterprise and government in the research and development of high technology.

In August 1986 the White House finally conceded that it would agree to the construction of a shuttle to replace the *Challenger*. But it also set a policy that henceforth the shuttles would carry only military and scientific cargoes, and NASA would no longer be permitted to solicit new commercial satellite payloads. Those with commercial payloads previously scheduled to fly on the space shuttle were forced to look elsewhere for launch opportunities. The decision fell like a bombshell, for it was viewed by many as a radical alteration in the direction of America's space program. Under the circumstances created by the loss of *Challenger,* I agreed with the policy, and believed it was wise to use the shuttle primarily for payloads that need human operators on board.

This plan was put together by a task force of officials representing several government agencies. It was resisted by a few of NASA's top brass who regarded their agency as America's sole space proprietor. But other NASA officials believed that, despite the shock waves, this could be the catalyst to force American industry into the launch business—which until then had been solely under NASA's control.

I saw that as a healthy philosophy, for the American tradition has always been for government to encourage business—rather than be in business. I had reservations about the President's "cold turkey" approach, for I felt that time should have been allowed for American industry to get its long-delayed satellites into space. Also, I feared the temptation to launch them on foreign rockets would be too great. Still, on the whole, I believed this was the way the nation should go. American industries would be the players, NASA would be the coach, the Department of Transportation would act as the commissioner, and the American People would be the owners.

But for the plan to work, the government needed to be a participant, and sometimes a partner in cooperation and funding. Sadly, the Reagan administration did not offer the decisive leadership needed to quickly stimulate a new space enterprise of commercial rockets. Their ideological zeal was not balanced by the pragmatism needed to set the wheels of the system in motion.

At the time of the decision, NASA had ninety commercial

communication satellites awaiting rides on the shuttle. Of these, forty-four were under contract for future shuttle launches. Companies hoping to launch forty others, while not having signed contracts, had deposited $100,000 each to stand in line. The Reagan plan permitted NASA to carry only about fifteen of these commercial payloads during the next decade. That meant a number of companies who wanted to put their payloads into space had to look elsewhere.

"What will happen?" some of my colleagues moaned. Russia, of course, immediately sent word it would be delighted to help American industry get its satellites into space. (I continue to find it interesting how Communist leaders preach against a capitalistic venture—until it benefits them.) The Chinese also wanted a piece of the cake. The big winner, many felt, would be Arianespace, a private commercial launching company incorporated under French law, whose shareholders include Western European manufacturers and banks and the French National Space Research Center (CNES). The company has an office less than a block from the White House and has multiple-launch facilities in Kourou, French Guiana, on the northern coast of South America—only a short hop across the Caribbean from Miami.

Unlike NASA, Arianespace relies exclusively on the use of expendable launch vehicles (ELVs) rather than manned space vehicles like our shuttle. America, of course, also uses ELVs. Our Delta, Atlas Centaur, and Titan rockets have been highly successful in placing satellites in orbit. However, in the early 1970s the government decided to phase out all its one-shot, expendable launch vehicles and make the shuttle the only U.S. launch system. This had great advantages in that the shuttle was supposed to be able to carry up to sixty-five thousand pounds into low earth orbit, where the standard Delta rocket was limited to a payload of about four thousand pounds. Now, however, under the Reagan administration, that option is closed.

Nevertheless, I believe America is getting back on track. American entrepreneurs are now scrambling to develop our own ELVs to get the growing number of commercial payloads into space. Some analysts believe the commercial space business could mushroom into a multi-billion-dollar-a-year industry by the year 2000.

In the past, private companies have felt there was no way they could compete with NASA in developing launch capabilities, because of NASA's huge advantages in technology and facilities—and its willingness to cut launch costs almost in half through government subsidies. Now not even the sky is the limit as America's aerospace giants jump into the race to provide rockets to carry payloads into space. The question is, can the private firms compete with the government subsidies of foreign launchers?

Unbelievably, in the light of this situation, the Air Force and NASA dragged their feet in approving a plan to allow private corporations to rent government launchpads and other facilities to support commercial space launches. This approval was needed to clear the way for companies with plans to enter the commercial launch business. Congress had given the Department of Transportation secretary authority to grant commercial access to government launch ranges back in 1984.

The new possibilities for commercial enterprise have excited a number of entrepreneurial corporations. Heading the list is Martin Marietta, which makes the Titan rockets in its Denver aerospace division. Titans have flown for more than two decades —with a success rate of 129 out of 134 launches. Its production line is in full operation. Its first commercial launch is scheduled in 1989, carrying J-C-SAT Z, a communications satellite.

Flagship of the Martin Marietta fleet will be the *Titan III,* which is capable of carrying payloads of up to thirty-two thousand pounds. Some of the satellites will be placed in low earth orbit, others in intermediate orbit, and others will be positioned thousands of miles into space in geostationary orbit, where they will remain fixed over one spot on the earth's surface.

The company is working with the U.S. Air Force to produce

Artist Robert McCall's interpretation of a space shuttle launch. [Photo courtesy Congressman Nelson]

a new fleet of larger Titan rockets designed to carry Air Force payloads into geostationary orbit as well. The Air Force plans to launch its first one sometime in 1989.

General Dynamics, maker of the Atlas—the nation's first ICBM—has been providing rockets to both NASA and the Air Force for years to place satellites in orbit. General Dynamics has restarted Atlas production, with the first rockets going back up in 1989. Plans are also on the drawing board to manufacture a Super Atlas G-Centaur, which would be able to carry even more than the largest European Ariane 3 rocket.

The third major ELV entrepreneur is McDonnell Douglas. While its Delta rockets can carry only lighter loads—up to four thousand pounds—they operate economically. Over the years they have had an excellent safety record (95 percent success rate for 179 launches). One rocket was lost, along with its fifty-seven-million-dollar weather satellite, in May 1987, but that accident was considered a fluke. A new version, the Delta II, won a DOD contract in which Air Force secretary Edward Aldridge specifically solicited bids to produce a vehicle that could be used to launch commercial satellites.

These big companies are but a few of a number of American manufacturers racing to get their rockets into space. Former astronaut Deke Slayton heads a Houston-based firm called Space Services, Inc. Space Services has already tested rockets from its southern Texas launch site and plans to carry payloads of about two thousand pounds into low earth orbit. Space Services has also made the news by contracting with a Florida-based group interested in using space as a burial ground. Thousands of people want the group to put the cremated ashes of loved ones into gold capsules and either release them in orbit high above the earth, or send them winging into outer space toward the proverbial edge of the universe.

A team from the Hughes Aircraft Company and the Boeing Aerospace Company proposed to the Air Force their plans to build a huge new rocket named after Greg Jarvis, the Hughes engineer who died aboard the *Challenger*. Using some of the same technology that produced the Saturn moon rockets, the Jarvis would be able to carry eighty-five thousand pounds of payload into low earth orbit—as opposed to the sixty-five thousand pounds the shuttle is now capable of carrying.

Undoubtedly, many additional ideas will be proposed by the aerospace industry to try to assure U.S. access to space.

Our mistake was in putting all our eggs in one basket. We spent all our time and money developing *THE* space transportation system. What we needed, instead, was a variety of systems—ELVs for most unmanned payloads, and the shuttle for the missions requiring human participation. This planning mistake has been costly to our country in terms of time, money, security, and prestige.

Exactly where do all these payloads go once they reach space? Most of the satellites and other payloads sent into space by today's rockets are placed in low earth orbit. Others are rocket propelled beyond, into geostationary orbit.

Low earth orbit is that band of space 150 miles to 500 miles above the surface of our planet. In this region, the various satellites and payloads circle the earth every ninety minutes— most operating between 175 and 250 miles out.

Leading the way in low earth orbit are those satellites that study the weather from their orbit, circling the globe over the earth's poles. Also traveling on these busy space freeways are remote sensing satellites that take X-ray, infrared, and ultraviolet photos and other measurements, as well as several Department of Defense secret spy satellites. Navigation and military communication satellites operate above and below the fringes of low earth orbit, a few dropping to about seventy miles above the surface of our planet at their lowest point.

Most of today's scientific exploration—both of space and looking back to earth—is done from low earth orbit. Solar Max, for instance, is studying the sun from low earth orbit. The gigantic Hubble Space Telescope, once it is launched, will occupy a permanent place in orbit about 320 miles above earth.

Farther above earth's surface, other satellites orbit. The Pentagon's Navstar Global Positioning System, an entire group of satellites, will circle earth at twelve thousand miles out when they are deployed.

Another type of satellite is those that go into geostationary orbit, occupying a narrow band of space 22,300 miles directly above the equator. Orbiting at the same speed as the earth's rotation, these satellites remain fixed over the same spot on the globe all the time, thus giving the appearance of standing still from earth's perspective. Most of these are communications satellites designed to relay signals to ground stations.

Following my return to Earth, I visited Rockwell International, the builder of the shuttle, as well as a number of other U.S. aerospace companies. I visited Lockheed, which assembled the Hubble Space Telescope, that will enable us to see farther into space than ever before. This telescope, lofted above the murk of earth's atmosphere into the crystalline clarity of space, may enable us to discover and understand the physical processes that drive certain types of stars, processes that seem to be more powerful than anything we know here on Earth. It will capture, on a ninety-four-inch mirror more flawless than any ever ground, the dim light of stars farther away than any ever seen from this planet. As I talked with managers and technicians, and inspected the production facilities of aerospace companies across the country, I began to understand the full dimensions of the national asset they represent.

American aerospace companies are constantly expanding the nation's capabilities by developing new technologies, new materials, and new ways of doing things. But the special value of the aerospace industry is not just that it teaches us new ways to do things; it also shows us new things to do.

A joint industry that combines the efforts of U.S. aerospace companies and the U.S. government is, I am convinced, an invaluable arrangement. No other country in the world has anything quite like our shared government/industry space work. The Japanese are quite successful in government/industry cooperation, but they are only beginning a national space program. The Soviets have no privately directed space effort; their program is totally run by the government. As a result, their space push is strong and, in many ways, more extensive than ours, yet they have not achieved the technological sophistication we have.

Comparable perhaps, is Europe, where the member nations of the European Space Agency have combined private and public efforts to produce a reliable commercial rocket—the Ariane. Despite a number of failures in 1986, they have been successful in garnering almost 50 percent of the world's commercial satellite business in the past year, though this is largely due to NASA's exclusion of further commercial payloads.

There is another business area related to launching satellites that has attracted the private investment of a significant amount of money in recent years. This is the development and production of "upper stages" for use in space launch vehicles. Upper stages are the rockets that are used to move satellites from the intermediate orbit provided by the space shuttle and ELVs to the final (frequently much higher) orbit that some satellites need to achieve in order to conduct their intended mission.

Examples of commercial upper stages are the PAM (Payload Assist Module) produced by McDonnell Douglas Corporation, and the TOS (Transfer Orbit Stage) being developed by Orbital Sciences Corporation. To date, more than thirty PAMs have been used to launch satellites, and another twenty-eight are on order to support future launches. The TOS has not yet been used for a satellite launch but it has been chosen to be the upper stage that will launch NASA's Advanced Communications Technology Satellite in 1989, and then the *Mars Observer* spacecraft in 1992.

Twenty-five years after man first ventured into space, hundreds of American companies are now directly involved in the space business. There is reason to believe that by the time another twenty-five years have passed, industrial activities in space may rival those of today's computer industry in terms of growth and success. By the year 2050, miles-wide solar arrays in space will probably be beaming power down to earth by microwave; mining operations will be taking place on asteroids as well as the moon; and there could well be a human colony living on Mars.

Exactly how quickly this new economic frontier opens depends in large part on the actions of the United States government, and also on what is done by the Soviet Union, Japan, France, and West Germany. Many fear that Congress and the administration could well respond to this challenge as King John of Portugal responded to Christopher Columbus, who sought financing for his exploration across the Atlantic to seek an unknown world. Portugal, because of pressing needs at home, turned a deaf ear to the explorer's pleadings. Rebuffed, Columbus was forced to turn to neighboring Spain. Queen Isabella, though faced with the same economic problems, had vision and foresight. Money was provided, and Columbus, a private entrepreneur, sailed westward. Our only hope is that the U.S. government will go the way of Spain—not Portugal.

Like the transcontinental railroads, which opened the West; like the federal highway system; and like our modern airline industry, which catapulted America into an era of rapid mobility, space ventures require investments beyond the capacity of the private sector. That means government help is necessary to subsidize our modern industrial Columbuses—not only in the form of NASA, which should continue to provide technology and tools, but in the form of government contracts and incentives to private corporations interested in space exploration, research, business, and development.

Satellite communications—the first commercial use of space— is already a mature industry. Communication satellites generate more than $3 billion a year from the transmission of television and radio broadcasts, telephone use, electronic mail, business data, and even such things as the publication of newspapers like *USA Today,* the *Wall Street Journal,* and a number of national magazines.

The second major space industry to affect our way of living, remote sensing, is at least a decade behind the first. Remote-sensing satellites, often called "spies in the sky," are used extensively by the military. However, these specialized satellites have numerous civilian uses as well. They relay the weather maps we see on our local news programs, enabling our weathermen to dramatically improve their forecasting ability and reduce deaths by warning us of approaching storms. They also detect air pollution, track the source of acid rain, measure ozone and other critical atmospheric elements, and give farmers accurate information to guide them in planting and harvesting.

Challenging issues are being raised by the prospect of commercial newsgathering from space. The U.S. news media discovered the value of remote sensing in April 1986, when the press used Landsat images to show the massive failure of the Chernobyl nuclear plant in the Soviet Union. Several American magazines have used remotely sensed images since 1974, but the Chernobyl accident was the first time Americans saw widespread use of media photographs from space.

The photographs of Chernobyl were available only because a Landsat satellite happened to be in the right orbit when the accident took place. For full media coverage it would cost up to $470 million to develop a "Mediasat" system composed of two satellites that could ensure same-day coverage of events around the globe. Such a system would cost an additional $15 million a year to operate.

A side issue has also been raised by national security experts who feel the use of remotely sensed data by the media in general would compromise certain U.S. national security activities and cause problems in foreign relations. But despite these problems, Mediasat will materialize, and it will be just a short time before America as well as other nations develop comprehensive remote sensing systems.

Commercially, the value of remote sensing satellites may be greatest in their ability to provide detailed pictures of the earth's surface. For instance, photographs from the five Landsat satellites launched by NASA since 1970 have proved invaluable in the mapping of remote areas. Because of them we now know the exact locations of lakes, islands, underwater shoals and reefs, pipelines, and electric power lines. We can also run rough population surveys, guide ships through iceberg-strewn northern seas, and even spot great schools of fish in the ocean.

Furthermore, satellite images are an invaluable aid in crop planning. For instance, following the Russian wheat deal of 1972 in which the U.S.S.R. bought 20 million tons of American wheat at low cost, the Department of Agriculture decided to begin monitoring the Russian crop by satellite. Since the United States exports as much as two thirds of the harvest of some crops, estimates of international supply and demand are critical to agricultural planning.

The Department of Agriculture is not the only organization interested in using space for agricultural purposes. In October 1987, NASA, Walt Disney World, and Kraft, Incorporated entered into an experiment designed to perfect the growing of food in space. At The Land, a giant six-acre greenhouse run by Kraft at Walt Disney World's Epcot Center, a new space agricultural exhibit opened, in which scientists began experiments that will teach us how to grow crops in orbit.

Using the extensive and sophisticated facilities at Epcot Center, the space agriculture experiment features six nine-foot-tall "grow racks" where lettuce, wheat, soybeans, potatoes, peppers, and sugar beets are raised hydroponically—in nutrient solutions rather than in soil. NASA scientists believe these vegetables can be raised inside a spacecraft on its way to Mars (the journey could take ten months one way), in America's space station, on a lunar base, or even in a greenhouse on Mars. This would enable space travelers to live long periods in space without having to return to earth for resupply.

"With a self-sustaining system people could survive long-duration spaceflights or even colonize distant planets," says Andrew Schuerger, a plant pathologist at The Land.

Another interesting project at The Land is an attempt to grow wheat and soybeans in a "lunar soil simulant"—a basaltic rock from Minnesota that is similar in mineral composition to moon soil. Dr. Henry Robitaille, agricultural manager at the exhibit, feels the lunar soil experiments may lead to the development of agricultural techniques that could be used by space colonists at a moon base. Imagine having Mrs. McGregor's cabbage patch growing on the moon—thanks to, of all people, Walt Disney!

As NASA astronaut Steve Hawley says, "It's not a question of whether or not we will do those things, but merely a question of when those type of endeavors will happen."

Landsat data find their most extensive commercial use, however, in mineral exploration. Geologists, petroleum engineers, and other scientists have learned to identify features that might point to reserves by studying satellite images of known oil, gas, and mineral deposits. Oil companies depend on satellite data to look for the folds and domes in the Earth capable of trapping oil or gas. Mineral experts search for clays often associated with uranium deposits, or plants that grow on tin or molybdenum deposits. Landsat's multispectral scanner records the reflection of light off the Earth with a sensitivity to color far surpassing that of the human eye. By enhancing colors digitally, explorers can detect features on the Earth's surface that are invisible to the eyes of researchers.

One use of this technology is in the creation of a grid network dividing the globe, with each unit about forty miles long and forty miles wide. Landsat can report on the vigor of crops in each unit. This is integrated with weather information, and subscribers to the service may receive up-to-date information by computer relay. Florida citrus growers save $35 million a year because satellite information tells them when to turn on the big burners in the citrus groves to protect them from frost.

Despite the exciting things already going on as a result of space research and development, most space scientists will not be satisfied until we are manufacturing a full range of products in space. These experts believe that space-based "materials processing"—that is, manufacturing of things such as drugs, alloys, and crystals—will literally change the way life is lived on earth.

We have already discussed the benefits of weightlessness to drug manufacture, but in fact gravity influences virtually every physical process on earth. When metals are mixed to form alloys, for example, the heavier metal always sinks to the bottom. When tiny bubbles are introduced into building materials to strengthen them, the bubbles always rise to the surface. As a result, the mixtures are never uniform and never as strong as they could be. Such problems would be eliminated if materials were manufactured in space.

For the time being, however, because of the present problem of hauling heavy materials into orbit, the only products that can bring a sufficiently high return on investment are pharmaceuticals and crystals. That is not to say a procedure may not be developed that will allow the production of heavier materials in space. Nor should it eliminate the possibility of developing in space a procedure that will give us the ability to manufacture space-researched materials on earth. Research and development of all these things should be continued by space scientists, both aboard the shuttle and eventually on the space station.

Another great advantage of manufacturing in space is that molds and containers are often unnecessary there. Crystals, for example, can be grown with no risk they will absorb alien molecules by touching a surface—even a base. Objects can be fashioned in perfect spheres without the normal distortion that comes when they rest on a surface.

The first commercial products manufactured in space were the tiny spheres NASA made for the National Bureau of Standards. The bureau sells these standard reference materials for use in measuring microscopic electronic components, such as those used for calibrating instruments like filters and porous membranes. The spheres that NASA manufactured were droplets of polystyrene one-twenty-five-hundredth of an inch in diameter—about the size of a red blood cell. There are about fifteen million or so in a small vial, and each vial, about the size of a little finger, sells for $400. Pharmaceutical companies use the spheres in counting blood cells. Scientists in other industries are now using them to measure particulate pollution and to produce finely ground products, such as paint pigments. Additional uses are being discovered every day.

It is also possible to produce large semiconducting crystals of exceptional purity in space. These crystals, made of materials like silicon and gallium arsenide, may be the basis of the future electronics industry in the United States. When sliced into wafers, printed with electronic circuits, and then diced into quarter-inch squares, these exceptional crystals could make the semiconductor chips that run every computer.

Gallium and arsenic, combined, conduct electrons ten times faster than the silicon that is used in today's computer chips, lasers, high-frequency antennas, fiber-optic switches, solar-power arrays, and other mysterious wonders of the high-tech electronic world. Both metals are highly resistant to heat and radiation, and their tremendous speed yields considerably more work per unit of weight.

When grown on Earth, however, gallium arsenide crystals suffer serious imperfections. Gravity forces impurities into the crystals that disrupt their evenness and ruin some of the circuits. According to companies such as the Harris Corporation, which is headquartered in my hometown of Melbourne, Florida, between 50 and 98 percent of all finished chips have to be discarded because of these flaws and defects caused by Earth's gravity.

However, if these crystals are grown in space, where there is no convection of liquids, they are nearly perfect. As such, the entire surface of a crystal, composed of several square inches, can be sliced off and made into one large superchip, with major gains in reliability and speed. Simple logic concludes that with the production of flawless crystals and virtually no rejects, the cost of chips will drop, consumers will benefit, and America's competitive position in the world computer market will be considerably strengthened. Koreans and Chinese may be able to produce cheaper running shoes and shirts because they use cheap labor, but America may be able to produce cheaper chips—meaning cheaper and more efficient computers—because of space technology, all run by well-paid, creative Americans. That is obviously a good return on the taxpayer's investment.

Crystal growth research in space has almost limitless possibilities. The Soviets know this and are experimenting extensively with crystal growth aboard their *Mir* space station. I have talked with several scientists who believe the production of gallium arsenide on orbit will allow the computer technicians of the next generation to put an entire computer on one wafer. Scientists contend that two or three $500-million spacecraft, outfitted as space factories and serviced every three months by the shuttle, could meet half the growth in U.S. semiconductor demand over the next decade.

Today, there are also American industries doing active research in the processing of collagen fibers for the repair and replacement of human connective tissues. Others are planning research that will lead to the manufacture of ultra-pure, bubble-free glass and glass-forming alloys. There is even experimentation with steels that float on water and other miracle alloys, which could totally revolutionize the building and transportation industries.

Obviously, these industries need more than the shuttle to conduct their research. The next step will be the orbiting space station, perhaps preceded by a commercial module. The U.S. station will be a space factory run by space scientists and robots. Manufacturing marketable amounts of medicines and crystals requires equipment weighing many tons, plus additional tons of material to be processed. It also requires constant, usually hourly, supervision. For economic reasons alone, the space station is the only way this can be done. And unless Congress and the administration drop the ball, we will have the space station by the mid-1990s.

Besides its scientific laboratories, the space station will include a repair shop for fixing defective satellites. In scenes straight out of the movie *2001,* a space vehicle will pull over to a dead satellite, take it in tow much as a wrecker from a garage pulls in a disabled car, and pull it back to the shop at the space station for repairs.

Such repairs will save American industry a staggering amount of money. Communications satellites cost close to $100 million each, while specialized scientific satellites cost from $60 million to $1 billion. There are more than one hundred operating satellites in orbit at the present time. Hundreds more are planned for the next decade. Like any piece of machinery, satellites break down and wear out. Because they are in zero gravity and not exposed to air pollution, they last much longer than they would on earth. But still, repairs are necessary and will be much, much cheaper than replacement.

Today, the average communications satellite lasts eight or ten years. As it dies, its last act is to move itself out of the way to make room for a new model. Those that fail prematurely are simply abandoned. Rescue or repair is impossible, because the shuttle is unable to get that far out into space. All this will change by the late 1990s, however, when it will become possible to service them.

The space station will also keep a supply of spare satellites on board for certain essential services, such as communications. For instance, if an important satellite goes dead, the crew could be there in less than three hours. Not only will they pull the old one in for repairs, they will set the spare in orbit at the same time—much as a repair shop might lend you a car until yours is fixed.

The possibilities of space repair and servicing are as limitless as they are on earth. Private enterprise will turn its creativity and entrepreneurial skills to power generation, food supplies, health care, orbital refueling, as well as providing trained personnel for research and development on the space station and the lunar station. A future company may consider an orbiting electric utility—a huge solar array, projected to cost more than a billion dollars, to supply power to an industrial park in space. NASA has awarded contracts to other entrepreneurs to develop a "space tug" to take payloads from the space station out to geosynchronous orbit. The tug will also be used to repair and retrieve satellites in high orbit.

Eventually, there will be large platforms that will house not only antennas and transponders for a range of communications services, but also observatories for scientific exploration and perhaps giant solar arrays for power generation. Of course, the assembly of such structures by private enterprise—with government help—will result in a new wave of economic activity on earth.

Much as Orville and Wilbur Wright dreamed of heavier-than-air flying machines, man continues to dream of all that can be accomplished in space. Some dreams have already come to pass; others will prove to be impossible—or perhaps merely impractical. Why should we not dream of mining operations on asteroids rich in precious minerals and 10,000-square-meter solar sails, driven by photons from the sun, for long space voyages? One company has already proposed self-replicating, solar-powered mining and manufacturing centers on the moon.

The use of outer space as a place of business has opened up a whole new vista of opportunity. Potential space commercialization ventures will be investments of billions per annum by the year 2000. The weightless environment of space, in which new commodities can be manufactured more efficiently than on earth, will undoubtedly be the next economic frontier for American companies—just as the West became the frontier of the last century, thanks to the opening of the railroads from the East.

When we first began the early flights into space, Congress did not anticipate that space would become a place of business. But the age of space commerce has arrived. Now we must anticipate the next steps and work to remove any barriers that might impede these exciting possibilities.

In 1985 I co-sponsored a bill in Congress that would extend business tax benefits to those companies whose place of business is in outer space rather than here on Earth. The 1986 tax law provides accelerated depreciation to be applied to business done in space. It was a recognition of the government's obligation to encourage space business.

Future legislation will ensure that space ventures are treated essentially the same as Earth ventures under our tax code. It is hoped that future administrations and Congresses will follow these suggestions and streamline regulations that otherwise would hamper private space ventures.

The United States—right now—has the potential to commercialize space. Despite the *Challenger* disaster, spaceflight in the shuttle has been highly successful. The United States, time after time, has developed marvelous new machines—from videocassette recorders to machine tools to semiconductors. Then we have let the Japanese and other innovative nations take the market from us. Most ideas on how to regain these lost markets call for some form of government intervention in the marketplace. But in the case of the space industry, not only is the government already in the business, it created the marketplace. One of the tasks of the President and the Congress is to determine just how much the government should remain in the space industry (not only actively, as with NASA, but by providing tax and tariff benefits) and how much it should turn projects over to private enterprise.

No matter how careful we are, putting objects into space means some of those objects will be lost. A major investment, such as a $270 million Landsat 4, can be lost as a result of faulty insulation on a wire. The satellite industry has had to write off one out of every six satellites launched since the mid-1970s. Its only protection is space insurance. In 1983, however, three major losses cost the satellite-insurance industry $300 million—more than the insurance company earned in premiums since it began issuing policies. That led to a huge rate increase. One of the ways the federal government can help the space industry is to act as insurer of last resort, just as the Federal Reserve acts as lender of last resort to protect banks from the risk of failure.

In short, just as those in the launch business know the real argument is not whether to use expendable rockets or manned shuttles, but how to use a combination of both; so the argument is not whether government or private industry should be in the space business but how both should cooperate. We should not look to the federal government to come up with new, fresh, innovative ideas. The very nature of government with its burdensome bureaucracy and pork-barrel politics prohibits it from doing much that is fresh and innovative. American industry, however, essentially free from those burdens, is in the position to take space by storm. Yet, for the reasons mentioned above, industry needs the support of government—both morally and financially.

Space enterprise is a new kind of challenge. As exciting as our short history has been in America, there will be many more new technology opportunities as we fly into the twenty-first century.

Space Spin-offs

The research and development for our nation's space program has produced technology that has transformed our lives remarkably. The microminiaturization that came from requirements to develop space equipment light in weight, small in volume, and exceptional in reliability, has changed our daily lifestyles in a revolutionary way and increased our quality of life. Here are but a few examples.

More than a million Americans suffer from juvenile diabetes, a disease that destroys the body's ability to control its blood sugar. It can provoke such serious complications as heart disease, kidney malfunction, and blindness. Until recently, it was controllable only by regular monitoring of blood sugar levels and regular injections of insulin.

Now, however, thanks to medical research in space, a new technology has emerged that may ultimately free diabetics and victims of other chronic diseases, (like leukemia and hormone disorders) from their restrictive lifestyles. NASA is currently working with private corporations and health care organizations—such as Johns Hopkins University's Applied Physics Laboratory; the National Institute of Child Health and Human Development; and the National Institute of Arthritis, Diabetes, and Digestive and Kidney Diseases—to develop a programmable, implantable medication system known as PIMS.

NASA and Johns Hopkins first proved that the concept would work. Then the Parker-Hannifin Corporation worked with the Marshall Space Flight Center to develop a pump that was capable of delivering doses as small as one-millionth of a liter. NASA's Goddard Space Flight Center contributed microelectronic technologies, and Wilson Great Batch developed the special batteries needed to power the PIMS. The result is a small device about the size of a woman's compact that gives accurate dosages of insulin automatically once implanted in the diabetic.

Today, the PIMS is a reality. It has performed well in long-term animal implants and has been implanted in humans. Prospects for the PIMS are excellent, and researchers are excited about the near-term possibilities for those afflicted with similar chronic diseases. Because the PIMS delivers medication continuously at optimum, variable rates, patients will not encounter overdosage or as much buildup of tolerance levels, nor will they experience the side effects that are often inherent in current injection procedures.

The PIMS will provide real benefits to a substantial number of handicapped Americans. What's more, it is a product that private industry can successfully market. This is an example of how space technology, effectively applied, can relieve the suffering of many.

The space program has actually spun off more helpful technical products than any other program in the history of the nation. The Apollo program, for instance, invested $20 billion into the computer, semiconductor, and aerospace industries with tremendous spin-off results.

Integrated circuit costs were reduced from an average of fifty dollars each to two dollars each—leading the nation into a thriving semiconductor market.

The demand for computers that were powerful, fast, and reliable—yet small and energy efficient—pushed U.S. computer technology ahead by a decade. As a result, computers have become one of the nation's top growth industries. Computers have so transformed our society that the "micromillenium" is now being hailed as the second industrial revolution.

The early satellites of the 1960s set the pattern for more than fifty commercial and research communications satellites launched during the subsequent fifteen years. Private enterprise has now invested well over $1 billion in Comsats, with a growth trend that promises another doubling in the next few years. One global communications satellite, Intelsat, is being used by one hundred countries, with revenues that exceed $200 million a year. Despite inflation, international telephone rates are cheaper than ever.

Thousands of lives and billions of dollars have been saved by improved weather forecasting, early storm and flood warnings, and reports on wind conditions and iceberg hazards to shippers using the sea lanes. Advice to farmers on when to plant, irrigate, fertilize, and spread insecticide saved the farm industry more than a billion dollars last year. Altogether, the accuracy of weather forecasting saves U.S. citizens $5.5 billion yearly and saves an estimated $15 billion worldwide.

In general, NASA calculates that for each billion spent on NASA research and development, 60,000 to 100,000 new jobs are created, and a net return is made to the economy of seven to fourteen billion dollars. A Chase Econometrics study has shown that more than 400,000 Americans are employed as a result of the space industry.

And that is only what has taken place in the past. Just as computers are spawning the second industrial revolution, I believe that space industrialization during the 1990s and beyond will become the third industrial revolution. In communications alone, various satellite services that will be commercialized in the next decade to provide for radio, television, telephone, navigation, and other industries will create up to 100 billion dollars in new business, annually, and several million new jobs.

What are some of the benefits consumers can expect? Education courses televised via satellite could be produced at a minimal cost. Wrist transceivers operating through satellites could provide private, personal communications between any two individuals for about thirty cents a call. Space production of higher-temperature turbine blades could save airlines up to $6 billion over ten years. Production of electronic devices in space using containerless processing to avoid impurities could be a billion-dollar-a-year industry in the next ten years.

And, as we have seen, space-produced pharmaceuticals will totally revolutionize the medical industry. For instance, in only two or three shuttle flights, it is possible to produce enough urokinase (for dissolving blood clots) to benefit humanity immeasurably.

However, the greatest benefits for mankind will be those we stumble onto serendipitously—things we know nothing about today, but will discover as we explore what we do know.

Recently, the secretary of Health and Human Services invited me to speak to a group of chief executive officers of major U.S. corporations about the applications of space technology for the benefit of the handicapped. I quoted from a recent report released by the congressional Office of Technology Assessment (OTA) which confirmed that effective use of both low-tech and high-tech can help more older Americans live independently.

According to the report, "Technology and Aging in America," new computer-based technologies can assist the severely disabled and those suffering from chronic medical problems. These include such remarkable inventions as programmable wheelchairs, voice-activated robots, and a variety of prosthetic devices. According to OTA, these technologies can help improve the health and functional abilities of senior citizens and possibly reduce health care expenditures.

Expanded support for biomedical research will speed progress toward new treatments, cures, and even preventative measures for chronic, debilitating diseases that affect growing numbers of Americans over age seventy-five. The resulting reduction in suffering, dependency, and health care expenses could be significant, says the OTA report.

Telecommunication applications in the home, such as video-cassette players and personal computers, can provide information on health habits specifically developed for older persons. Similarly, two-way audiovisual telecommunications systems can provide information and instructions about self-health care. These systems could also directly link patients' homes and physicians' offices for two-way communication and for monitoring medications and vital signs, such as blood pressure. Also, computers can make needed improvements in monitoring prescription drug intake and in reporting over-the-counter medicine use by older consumers.

In the workplace, opportunities for home-based work through the "electronic cottage" may evolve for older Americans. Although labor force participation rates of the elderly continue to decline, OTA finds support in the senior community for innovative employment arrangements and options.

Each year NASA prints an illustrated publication called *Spinoff* (available from the Centralized Technical Services Group, Box 8757, Baltimore/Washington International Airport, Maryland 21240). There are more than 30,000 applications of space technology providing incredible benefits for those of us who live on earth. Here is a list of seventeen of the most recent, adapted from a NASA folder called "Space Program Benefits."

Insulin Infusion Pump

For years diabetics have been tied to a rigid schedule in which most of life's ordinary functions centered around insulin injections. Today, according to NASA, more than 12,000 diabetics are free from these restrictions because they use what is called "pump therapy." This insulin pump, not much bigger than a credit card, houses a microprocessor, a long-life battery, a reservoir for the insulin, and a syringe. The pump delivers insulin, into the system at a preprogrammed, correct rate, giving diabetics new freedom as well as better control of blood sugar levels.

Reading Machine for the Blind

A device that converts regular inkprint into a readable, vibrating form that is perceptible to the sense of touch enables blind persons to read almost anything in print—not just braille transcriptions. A blind reader moves a miniature camera across a line of print with one hand, and with the fingers of the other hand senses a vibrating image of the letters the camera is viewing on a special screen. A related spin-off is the Paper Money Identifier—a small device the size of a cigarette pack that scans paper money and generates an audible signal identifying the denomination.

Vehicle Controller for the Handicapped

A spin-off of the Apollo lunar landings is a one-handed "joy stick," the kind used on the Lunar Rover, which allows a handicapped person to accelerate, brake and steer an automobile with one hand. It is possible to adapt this unistick system to an ordinary vehicle giving marvelous new freedom to persons with no lower limb control and only limited use of their arms.

Window into the Human Body

Using Magnetic Resonance Imaging, doctors can now "see" into bones and provide "maps" of the human body. This provides invaluable diagnostic information to physicians and surgeons.

Weather Forecasting

As mentioned elsewhere in this book, weather forecasting through weather satellites is now saving lives and dollars. NASA points out, for instance, that in 1900, long before the advent of weather satellites, a major hurricane struck Galveston, Texas, and took 6,000 lives. A similar hurricane struck in 1969 causing $1.4 billion in property damage; yet, thanks to weather satellite forecasts, only 256 people lost their lives—and most of those could have been spared if they had heeded the early warnings to evacuate the area.

Voice-Controlled Wheelchair and Manipulator

Based on robot technology developed for space-related programs, a voice-controlled wheelchair and its manipulator are now almost ready for severely handicapped persons. A computer translates commands into electrical signals that activate appropriate motors and cause the wheelchair to do exactly what it is told. The manipulator picks up objects, opens doors, turns knobs and does many other functions.

Speech Auto-cuer

A speech analyzing device presents automatically-derived visual cues to a wearable eyeglass display which, in combination with lip reading, enables accurate speech perception by deaf people. This remarkable device, which will help 1.8 million deaf people in the United States, was developed by a coalition of government, industries, and colleges. Support was provided by NASA and the Veterans Administration.

Water Recycling

Thanks to the National Space Technology Laboratories at Bay St. Louis, Mississippi, certain aquatic plants are now converting sewage effluents to clean water — at a fraction of the cost of conventional sewage treatment facilities. These plants are already at work in a number of smaller towns, in San Diego, California, and at Disney World's Epcot Center at Orlando, Florida.

Scratch-Resistant Eye Glasses

Using space technology, a major producer of sunglasses has now produced a plastic lens with glass-like scratch resistance.

Advanced Wheelchair

Langley Research Center, Hampton, Virginia, teamed with the University of Virginia's Rehabilitation Engineering Center, and developed a twenty-five-pound collapsible wheelchair that offers the strength and weight-bearing capability of a fifty-pound stainless steel wheelchair.

Laser Heart Surgery

Many doctors believe the use of laser heart surgery, a technology transfer from aerospace research, may virtually eliminate the need for coronary bypass surgery in the future. The experimental laser system is able to clean clogged arteries non-surgically and with unprecedented precision.

Flame-Resistant Materials

Originally developed to minimize fire hazards in the space shuttle, new flame-resistant materials that do not burn or smoke are now being used in airplanes, ships, buses and rapid transit cars. Toxic smoke, produced from burning materials, is often the major cause of fire fatalities.

Dental Braces

Millions of dental patients are rejoicing over a new type of wire material, called Nitinol, which is helping reduce the number of brace changes, due to its exceptional elasticity.

Search and Rescue

Since 1982 more than 850 lives have been saved from boating, aircraft and automotive incidents, because satellites "listen" continuously on emergency frequencies used by these vehicles. Within minutes of an emergency message a computer identifies the location of the transmitting source within a three-mile area. International cooperation is involved as the United States, Canada, France, the Soviet Union (all co-founders) work with Bulgaria, Denmark, Finland, Norway and the United Kingdom to aid in speedy search and rescue of victims in downed airplanes, capsized boats and other emergency situations.

Anti-Corrosion Paint

In an effort to reduce maintenance costs on gantries and other structures at the Kennedy Space Center, NASA has developed a superior coating that not only resists salt corrosion but protects structures from the extreme heat and thermal shock created by rapid temperature changes during launch times. Now used in a paint, this inorganic coating bonds to steel and creates a hard ceramic finish with superior adhesion and abrasion resistance.

Advanced Turboprop

One drawback to highly efficient turboprop engines has been that propeller-tip speed limitations have held down airplane speeds. Now, wind tunnel tests have shown that prop-fans driven by advanced engines can power commercial transports to speeds equal to those of jet airliners—at fuel savings up to 40 percent.

Breathing System for Firefighters

A broad range of fire-fighting equipment has been developed by NASA. The latest is a breathing apparatus that protects from smoke inhalation. The traditional system was heavy, cumbersome, and restricting. Many firefighters preferred not to use it at all. The new system weighs only twenty pounds and includes a face mask, frame and harness, a warning device and an air bottle. Today, every major manufacturer of breathing apparatus is producing units that incorporate space technology in some form.

Space exploration continues to produce spin-offs, not only from NASA's laboratories but from the labs of many American companies—large and small. Civilization has no choice but to continue to be creative in the application of technology in all segments of our society—in our homes, in private business, and in government. The advances we have made in the last decade can help improve not only the quality of life for the nation's elderly, but for all Americans.

Understanding Our Beginnings, Charting Our Future

The Infrared Astronomy Satellite already has discovered what may be another solar system within our existing galaxy of stars. When the United States launches the Hubble Space Telescope into Earth orbit, new and clearer sightings of stars and other planets will tell more clearly the story of the universe. I am convinced that these future scientific discoveries will continue to reveal that there is a magnificent order to this universe.

The search for other life is perhaps one of the most difficult endeavors to justify in dollars and cents, yet it is one of the most fundamental instincts in human nature—to reach out. This question has led scientists to begin to search for radio signals that would reveal intelligent life in the distant universe. Relatively crude experiments by radio astronomer Frank Drake in 1960 have led to progressively more sophisticated searches as our computer technology has allowed us to process millions of bits of data instantaneously, looking for tell-tale signs. NASA's new ambitious program called SETI (Search for Extraterrestrial Intelligence) will expand the number of radio frequency wavelengths searched by ten billionfold.

Recently, in a test demonstration of some of the prototype technologies, scientists easily detected a one-watt signal from the Pioneer 10 spacecraft that is now over three billion miles away. This is equivalent to detecting a signal one hundredth the strength of a household light bulb at the very edge of the solar system.

Why should we spend the money to undertake this search now, not next year or the year after that? The answer is troublesome. Activities within our radio frequency spectrum are expanding. Very soon our radio frequency spectrum will be so noisy that we will be unable to detect any alien signal.

This question also has profound theological significance. In commenting on NASA's SETI study, Theodore Hesburg, President of the University of Notre Dame, said:

> There are few questions that more excite the curiosity, the imagination and the exploratory bent of modern man than the one posed in this study: Are we humans alone in this vast universe? The question is usually expressed in terms of other possible intelligent beings on other planets. The philosopher in me would want to believe that if there are other intelligent beings, they are also free, and will use that freedom to try to find us. The basic problem to which this study is addressed is similar: Will we use our freedom to find them? What priority should this search have for modern man, everywhere?

America's interplanetary exploration has vastly broadened our understanding of the universe. In the early 1970s, the U.S. launched *Pioneers 10* and *11*, which have investigated several of the planets in the solar system, sending back new pictures of Saturn and Jupiter. *Pioneer 10* has now passed outside of the solar system, beyond Pluto, the farthest planet, and is still sending weak signals back to the Jet Propulsion Laboratory in Pasadena. Should any intelligent life ever encounter this spacecraft, it will find a metal plate engraved with a sketch of man and woman scaled to size along the craft's side, and a description showing which planet in the solar system the craft originated from. Carl Sagan designed the plate so that it could be understood by any other intelligent beings.

In 1975 we launched *Viking* on a mission to land on Mars, take pictures, and analyze the Martian soil for evidence of life. All these dramatic data were sent back to earth. And although no trace of life was found, the possibility continues to exert a powerful hold on man's imagination. Indeed, the search for Martian life is a major goal of the Soviet space program, as we have seen.

From the space shuttle we will launch the *Galileo* mission, a highly sophisticated spacecraft that will fly around the planet Jupiter, photographing its moons and sending a probe into the Jovian atmosphere until the pressure destroys it. Also, we will send a mission to Venus to map its cloud-covered terrain with radar, sending back the images that cannot be obtained otherwise. In the 1970s the Soviets sent several missions to Venus, but still not much is known because of its perpetual concealment from visual probes.

Following the fruitful cooperation of participants in the international Halley's Comet watch, the United States is now planning a rendezvous with another comet and asteroid to learn about these little-known travelers in the solar system. Theories abound. There is a hypothesis, for instance, that comets could be responsible for both the origin of life and the demise of some of its forms on this planet. The hypothesis suggests that millions of years ago comets struck the earth carrying complex biological molecules and it was these that began the chemical reaction that led to the formation of life. A well-established theory holds that in the distant past, a comet or asteroid collided with earth with such force that a veil of suspended dust blocked out the sun and led to the extinction of the dinosaurs.

When people ask me "Why should we explore space?" I answer in part, "Because it is our nature." Man must continue to satisfy his hunger for knowledge and an understanding of creation.

Hundreds of years ago when man first thought the world was flat, the theories of a round globe were laughed at. Galileo was roundly scoffed at when he said he saw moons around the planet Jupiter. Now we are going to explore those moons through the probing eye of the *Galileo* spacecraft.

Americans are an exploring people. Having been founded by explorers, it remains in our blood to pioneer the unknown. Beyond the scientific benefits, the simple romantic fascination with another world is enough motive to force us to go there. We must continue, for as Solomon said in Proverbs: "Where there is no vision, the people perish."

After the space station, our most ambitious undertaking will be what *U.S. News and World Report* called "man's inevitable trip to Mars." In late 1987, a large group of space scientists gathered at the University of Colorado in a "Case for Mars" conference. Some of our most distinguished scientists and pioneers in the field of aerospace, as well as several NASA astronauts, attended. While granting that the Soviets have a more ambitious program (they want to land a man on Mars in the first decade of the next century), nearly everyone who attended the conference was enthusiastic about America's ongoing participation. The cost will be awesome, probably $50 billion or more. The humans who make the trip can plan on being away from earth for two to three years.

This project was proposed as far back as 1969, when a White House task force endorsed a man-to-Mars shot. In 1986 President Reagan's National Commission on Space again listed Mars as an eventual target—a goal that was given the backing of former astronaut Sally Ride in her final paper to NASA before returning to Stanford University. Even NASA administrator James Fletcher has said, "I believe we should go, and I'm confident we will go."

There is much yet to be done. Sophisticated space suits must be designed, since Mars is colder than Antarctica, and its thin air has almost no breathable oxygen. Although there appears to be no life on Mars, frozen beneath its rocky, sandy surface may be large reserves of water that may one day sustain humans living on the planet.

As now envisioned, a journey to Mars will begin with a blast-off from America's space station, thereby lessening the dangers and the difficulties of leaving from Earth. Loaded with fuel and supplies, the spacecraft will travel for months on its 100-million-mile journey. In one plan, as the spacecraft approaches Mars, it will separate into three sections that will land on the Martian surface or on Phobos or Deimos, the planet's two small moons. Mars's relatively friendly environment will allow astronauts to spend several months exploring the planet, sending scientific information back to earth. A rocket will then lift the Mars lander from the surface to begin its year-long flight back on a long, circular route to intersect the earth's orbit around the sun.

Later missions to Mars will carry prefabricated buildings and greenhouses to establish a permanent base. Because the atmosphere on Mars is mostly carbon dioxide, which is essential for plant growth, and since there may be water beneath the surface, scientists feel that a human outpost could become self-sustaining; the carbon dioxide would feed the plants, which, in turn, would give off the oxygen essential for human life. The water could be decomposed to produce fuel.

A new concept for space travel has recently been presented by one of my fellow crew members, Franklin Chang-Diaz. As transportation technology was the key element that permitted the ocean-going explorations of the globe five hundred years ago and the westward settlement of our nation 150 years ago, so Franklin's technological theory, as outlined below, could be the single most important element to foster future exploration of outer space.

Using our current technology, it will take us almost a year

to reach Mars—and five centuries to reach the closest star. Even if we could move through space at the speed of light (186,000 miles per second) it would still take four and one-third years to reach the closest *star*. Mars, on the other hand, could be reached in as little as four and one-third minutes, and Pluto—our most distant planet—in about five and one-third hours, if we could travel at the speed of light.

Obviously, we are a long way from that kind of speed—despite the "time warps" so beloved in Hollywood where, going by Einstein's theory of relativity, spacecraft can move at the speed of light and theoretically go backward in time. (Doctor Wumbug was able to do this, you remember, with his famous time machine in the comic strip "Alley Oop.") But today's scientists are not working in the fantasy land of movie and comic strips, but with real technology. Doctor Chang-Diaz's proposal for the development of a revolutionary new propulsion technique could provide the necessary breakthrough into feasible space travel.

Doctor Chang-Diaz has proposed a series of experiments at MIT in which a super-hot ball of gas called a *plasma* will be created by microwave energy and then confined within a magnetic field. At full temperature, the plasma (which is a form of matter in which a gas becomes so hot that the electrons in its atoms fly out of orbit, leaving behind the positively charged nucleus) will reach a temperature of tens of millions of degrees. When used in a future propulsion system, this superheated ball of plasma will be injected with liquid hydrogen. The hydrogen would then be expelled through a nozzle to produce thrust. The resulting speed could decrease our flight time from earth to Mars to just a month or so and could possibly reduce the time required for an unmanned space probe to reach the nearest star to about fifty years.

I have encouraged Franklin with his proposal, believing it is mandatory we explore this idea—and other concepts—in order to achieve the breakthrough necessary to conquer space. It once took a family almost a year to cross America using the most modern transportation available—a covered wagon. Now, that same family can fly from Atlanta to Los Angeles in great safety and comfort in approximately four hours. Why not expect this same kind of breakthrough for spaceflight?

There are many problems to be worked out. A prime worry is the health of the astronauts, who will be subjected to long periods of weightlessness, which takes a toll on the heart, muscles, and bones. However, tests are already under way to plan for this. At the Biosphere II project near Tucson, eight persons will be placed in a hermetically sealed, two-acre structure for two years. They will produce their own food and recycle all materials to see whether long space flights are feasible.

Much more will be learned from robotic technology like that in the U.S. *Mars Observer* spacecraft that will be launched in 1992 to orbit the red planet and study its surface and climate.

There are other huge programs planned for the coming decade. The big astronomy satellites—the Space Telescope, the Advanced X-Ray Observatory, the Space Infrared Telescope Facility, and the Gamma Ray Observatory—are all designed for maintenance by crews from the shuttle and the space station. Repairs on such things as the scientific instruments, radio antennas, and the star-trackers, and refrigerants used to keep the telescope mirrors and instruments at an even temperature will all be handled by astronauts on orbit. Of course, these observatories are enormously expensive—the Space Telescope project alone costs more than $1.4 billion. But the benefits more than justify the investment.

The Space Telescope will be the equivalent of having eyes 10 billion times more sensitive to light than the eyes of the keenest astronaut. It will have the ability to read a newspaper headline 200 miles away, detect a lighted match 10,000 miles away, or observe a camera flash on the moon 240,000 miles overhead. It will routinely outperform the great two-hundred-inch telescope at Mount Palomar, California (the largest in the world) by a factor of ten.

The telescope will give us the ability to study objects some 10 billion light years away, allowing astronomers a glimpse of what the universe looked like in that era. A light year is the distance light travels in one year—about 6 trillion miles. Multiply that by 10 billion and you have the range of the space telescope.

"With the Space Telescope, we're increasing astronomical capability more than it's ever been increased since Galileo started using a telescope," says project scientist Edward Weiler.

All this will be possible because of the near-perfect shape and incredible reflective power of the ninety-four-inch mirror that is at the heart of the instrument. The twenty-five-thousand-pound telescope, which had been scheduled to be launched in May 1986, is housed in the world's largest "clean room" at Lockheed Missile and Space Company's Sunnyvale, California plant. The filtered atmosphere of the room is completely replaced every two minutes to prevent any chance of dust reaching the sensitive mirror surface. Currently, it is costing NASA 8 million dollars a month to store and maintain the forty-three-foot instrument during the long delay in shuttle flights that followed the *Challenger* explosion. Scientists, however, say the cost is worth it when compared to the ultimate payoff.

Astronomers believe that by enabling us to study the universe as it was 10 billion or so years ago, the Space Telescope should give new and exciting understanding to just how the galaxies, the largest of the cosmic structures, evolved. It will also give us the ability to fine-tune techniques by which astronomical distances are measured.

The telescope was named for Edwin P. Hubble who was the first astronomer to substantiate that the universe is expanding. Building on his discovery, modern astronomers call the measure of the rate of that expansion *Hubble's constant*. It relates an object's speed away from the center of the universe to its distance from that center.

This theory is built on what many scientists call the Big Bang concept—a concept that at some point in time and space this universe came into being instantly. Since then it has continued to expand. Assuming this expansion has been at a constant rate, scientists, using the Hubble constant, believe they can calculate the age of the cosmos. Figures vary, but latest calculations put that age at 10 billion years.

Using the telescope, scientists hope to come up with answers to fundamental questions about whether the universe will continue to expand forever, or if the expansion might one day reverse itself, leading to a "Big Crunch" as all the matter in the universe rushes together.

Of more interest to the ordinary layman, the telescope will take routine *Voyager*-class photographs of the planets in Earth's solar system.

Equally exciting is the possibility of discovering other planets like our earth, orbiting other stars like our sun. What strange and powerful forces will be discovered if such planets do exist—as most astronomers believe? The idea of other planets with intelligent life has long excited man's imagination. With the Space Telescope it is very possible that discovery will be made. What kind of life is out there? Are there people in need of help? Are there people who can help us? Will we be able to communicate?

The other observatories will help answer fundamental scientific questions asked by astronomers concerning Gamma rays, X rays, matter and anti-matter. The Gamma Ray Observatory, for instance, which is designed to give fascinating pictures of the ancient universe, may provide clues to many of the nagging scientific questions. For instance, Where is the anti-matter in the universe? If matter and anti-matter are equivalent, as today's scientists believe, we should find them in equal amounts in the early seasons of the universe. Today's universe, however, seems to be composed almost entirely of matter—not anti-matter. Why can we not observe the anti-matter universe as well?

This universe will always be a mystery. For every known we discover, we unearth a hundred unknowns—beckoning us to further discoveries.

We have no choice but to continue our exploration—back to our Alpha, forward to our Omega.

Tragedy and Triumph—
Reaching for the Stars

There has been much success in America's space program. There has also been failure. The loss of the *Challenger* and its crew left the entire nation not only in a state of grief, but in stunned confusion. Why had it happened? Who was to blame?

The space shuttle represents a revolutionary departure from the expendable rockets that were the launchers for the first manned flights of Mercury, Gemini, and Apollo. The cone-shaped manned capsules of those programs were designed to provide the highest ratio of payload to weight. The blunt ends generated maximum drag during reentry with some lift for steering. The heat shields of the capsules were made of a material that was destroyed during the spacecraft's fiery descent through the atmosphere.

Mercury was America's first manned space program. Alan Shepard's suborbital flight in May 1961 opened the door to an entirely new era for the nation—and the world. Shortly after Shepard splashed down in the Atlantic Ocean, President Kennedy proposed to the Congress the bold, new initiative that became known as Apollo: "I believe that this nation should commit itself to achieving the goal, before this decade is out, of landing a man on the moon and returning him safely to earth."

Before Apollo, however, the two-man Gemini spacecraft in 1965 and 1966 had improved our mastery of technology and our skills, such as maneuvers in space, rendezvous and docking, and extravehicular activities. We discovered that we could function in space for long periods of time with no harmful aftereffects. The photographs from the Gemini era taught us a lot about the earth's geography, environment, and resources.

America then sent unmanned probes to reconnoiter the moon for Apollo. *Ranger* showed the first closeup lunar photos. Lunar orbiters provided detailed information on lunar topography, gravity, and environment. Surveyors that landed softly on the moon showed that its surface could support the weight of an Apollo landing craft, and that there would not be an appreciable dust cloud. Meanwhile, we started to push outward into the solar system to learn more about ourselves, our universe, and the technology of spacecraft design.

Technology and human skill finally came together when Frank Borman, James Lovell, Jr., and William Anders orbited the moon ten times, only seventy miles above its barren surface. Then, in July 1969, in one of the most extraordinary achievements in history, Neil Armstrong, wearing a space suit, climbed down the ladder of a lunar lander and planted his foot in the Sea of Tranquillity. It happened just eight years after the first manned spacecraft had circled the earth and was followed by five more moon landings.

Apollo vastly expanded our knowledge of the moon and the Earth. Six Apollo expeditions explored the moon. Our astronauts worked effectively and even drove a vehicle on the lunar surface. Experimental equipment was left behind that kept sending data back to Earth long after the astronauts departed.

Skylab was America's first space station. Three American astronauts lived and worked in it for periods lasting twenty-eight, fifty-nine, and finally, eighty-four days. The crew performed a host of experiments in Skylab that provided extraordinary opportunities for surveying and understanding Earth and the sun. Our early attempts at manufacturing products in space were conducted there.

The *Apollo/Soyuz* test project was the world's first international manned space mission and included the highly symbolic rendezvous and docking of American and Soviet spacecraft. In that historic flight, Tom Stafford, Deke Slayton, and Vance Brand lifted off from Kennedy Space Center on July 15, 1975, the same day the Russian *Soyuz* lifted off from a secret space center deep in the heart of the Soviet Union. *Apollo* then docked in space with the *Soyuz,* and our crew participated with cosmonauts Alexi Leonov and Valery Kubasov in activities for nine days, during 138 earth orbits, before the two teams separated and returned to their respective countries.

The U.S. unmanned program has been equally successful. It started with our first satellite, *Explorer I,* and followed with the space missions of a large number of extraordinary planetary explorers—the Mariners, the Pioneers, the Vikings and the Voyagers.

But the triumph has not been without tragedy. Such tragedy in the heavens was foretold as far back as Greek mythology. On the island of Crete in ancient Greece, as legend has it, two of King Minos's subjects wanted to fly. They constructed wings made of wax and feathers. Daedalus and his son, Icarus, soared about the sky, defying the ancient mythical gods. Icarus, however, was not happy with suborbital flight. He wanted to go higher and higher. Daedalus warned him against this, but the young man's venturesome spirit overrode his obedience to his father. As he flew higher, he passed too close to the sun. The wax holding the feathers in his wings melted, and he fell into the sea.

Man will continue to go higher and higher, but not without sometimes falling back into the sea—as *Challenger* did. Tragedy is always a companion of triumph and is the price that must be paid by all who venture beyond the realm of the known into the unknown. Just as Columbus ran the risk of sailing off the edge of the earth, so today's space travelers run the risk of death in order to reach new worlds beyond our own limited environment.

Spaceflight is inherently risky. It is universally felt that it was a miracle that we had fifty-five space missions without a fatality in flight. The Soviets have lost four cosmonauts in flight—that we know of. America had previously lost three astronauts on the pad in the *Apollo 1* fire. Four more astronauts—Theodore Freeman, Charles Bassett, Elliot See, and Clifton Williams—were lost during training accidents. There are 1,192 parts of the space shuttle, which, if any one of them failed, would likely mean the loss of the vehicle and the crew. Spaceflight is a risky business, and the astronauts all agree these are acceptable risks. But there is no excuse for bad management and poor communications. It is those areas NASA is now struggling to change and improve.

The whole idea of spaceflight had become almost routine to the general public. Television anchormen sneered at NASA when launches were scrubbed for safety reasons. Politicians and entertainers alike showed up at the launch site in their finest clothes, preening before the TV cameras and newspaper photographers, giving virtually no thought to the risks being taken by those aboard the spaceship. These same people then roundly criticized NASA when the launch did not go according to their schedule.

The launch schedule itself was building to an astonishing goal of one shuttle launch every two weeks. This was supposed to happen on a NASA budget with less than half the buying power of budgets during the Apollo program.

Through it all, the battle raged between the scientists and politicians as to whether America should be using manned shuttles or expendable rockets, whether our primary goals should be to explore space or defend it, and whether it was really worth the expenditure of money and the risk of life when we had so many other priorities, such as feeding the hungry, caring for the sick, and defending our nation.

Much has been written about the mistakes that were made by NASA and its contractors, by the administration, and by the Congress, that led to the giant explosion ten miles high in the Florida sky on January 28, 1986. "It was an accident that was waiting to happen . . ." wrote the Rogers Commission in their report on *Challenger*. The board of inquiry uncovered what some called "an astonishing record of callous risk-taking, muddled management, and cover-your-ass bureaucracy." The fact is, the threads of disaster were there long before *Challenger*.

The Rogers Commission and our Science and Technology Committee's investigation found that the loss of *Challenger* was caused by the aft field joint on the right-hand solid rocket motor. The failure of this joint was due to faulty design. Neither NASA nor Morton Thiokol fully understood the operation of the joint nor of the flexible O-rings that were supposed to seal against the metal joint to prevent the hot gasses from escaping. The testing and certification programs were inadequate and faulty. Safety programs in NASA were not given proper emphasis.

The investigation further found that NASA's near impossible goal of achieving twenty-four flights a year contributed to unsafe launch conditions. The committee, the Congress, the administration, and the press all contributed to this pressure by accepting a high flight rate as a realistic goal and then judging NASA's success by it.

Furthermore, NASA attempted to evolve from a research-and-development agency into a competitive business operation that exuded an aura of success. The agency's confident posture led others to believe that the space shuttle was fully "operational," a line that was bought by the Congress and our committee as well as by the White House and President Reagan.

Unreasonable goals should never again be allowed to thwart safety.

The Rogers Commission and our committee found a flawed

decision-making process used by NASA and Morton Thiokol, in which ideas were either not communicated or miscommunicated. Communication was so unbelievably poor that the top NASA management, who had the final say of "go" or "no go" for launch, did not know about two Thiokol engineers' strenuous objections to the *Challenger*'s launch.

It is inexcusable that Thiokol management would override their own engineers and announce that the *Challenger* was safe to launch. The Rogers Commission concluded that this reversal was done to accede to pressure from the Marshall Space Flight Center management.

During our committee's investigation, I wondered why the Thiokol engineers did not worry about the stiffening of the O-rings on *Columbia*'s attempted launch of January 6, when it was 42° Fahrenheit. As it turned out, we were scrubbed for a different reason.

At *Columbia*'s actual launch the O-ring temperature was 58° Fahrenheit. Inspection of our solid rocket boosters revealed erosion of the O-rings. At that point, the engineers wondered why the O-rings' previous thermal distress had occurred during the past two January flights (in 1985 and 1986). What was common to January? The answer was: cold weather. The Thiokol engineers had had their warning before cold weather became a factor in *Challenger*'s launch.

If NASA management had only consulted its shuttle flight history when the temperature dipped so low that January night, it would have been clear that they should cancel the launch. Incredibly, the twenty-four-flight history revealed that only three flights out of twenty showed any O-ring thermal distress when the temperature was 66° Fahrenheit or above. But all four flights with O-ring temperature at 63° Fahrenheit or below had thermal distress. The clue should have been recognized.

Communication problems are not unique to NASA, but they hit NASA with a vengeance. Directives and information were going from top to bottom, but not the other way around— from the grass roots to management. In addition, the Marshall

Flight Center, according to the Rogers Commission, wanted to contain any serious problems and not communicate them to others in NASA. Its response was to insulate and isolate itself.

Communication on another issue was just as bad. Rockwell, the orbiter's developer, issued an ambiguous warning that flying the orbiter might be unsafe because of the ice all over the launch tower. But the statement was not clearly worded and was misunderstood.

Back in the LCC, George Abbey worried about his flight crew. He asked whether his friend Rocco Petrone, president of Rockwell's Space Transportation Division, had said it was okay to launch. "Yes," came the answer. But Rocco had not said yes.

A certain superiority and arrogance was to blame. NASA believed in itself. Why shouldn't it? It had had twenty-five years of success. And it expected others to believe in it, too. NASA expected Congress to rubber-stamp what it wanted; if NASA didn't get what it wanted, it would generally try to do what it wanted anyway. If NASA did not like something in a congressional spending bill, the agency had been known to wait until it was too late to change course and then explain to Congress that it was impossible to follow Congress's directive.

For example, Congress continually urged NASA to modify the shuttle to make it capable of spending more time on orbit. Despite the obvious technical benefits, NASA found reasons to avoid this improvement year after year, primarily because one small group within NASA believed that an extended duration shuttle would threaten the rationale for the space station. A more recent example is NASA's refusal to follow a strong recommendation by our Committee to place a *Mars Observer* spacecraft on an expendable launch vehicle in 1990. NASA unrealistically insisted it must be flown on the space shuttle and refused to follow our advice over our vigorous protest. We wanted the mission to launch at its projected 1990 date. NASA stalled until it became too late to get the spacecraft built for a

1990 launch. They then announced that they would do the mission in 1992.

And Congress acquiesced. Well, NASA had always been so right . . .

A mindset developed within NASA: it was not accountable—not to anyone nor to any institution. NASA managers carved out fiefdoms and were, in effect, operating on their own.

The U.S. Congress had a greater responsibility to hold NASA more accountable than it did. But Congress has always had a friendly relationship with NASA. In the early years the infant agency relied on congressional stalwarts to provide the funds for the space spectaculars. Under strong direction from Presidents Kennedy and Johnson, the money flowed. In the Nixon administration, the funds were cut back and the Apollo program to the moon terminated. The Nixon administration provided only limited funds for the development of the space shuttle.

There were cost overruns in the development of the shuttle, but money was always provided, even if reluctantly. After six years without an American in orbit, the success of the space shuttle seemed to rekindle Congress's willingness to approve NASA's recommendations. NASA usually got what it wanted, and always had a direct line to the president.

In the congressional appropriations process for a NASA budget, the president proposes and the Congress disposes. The Committee on Science and Technology and its Subcommittee on Space write the legislation to authorize the funds to be spent by NASA. The NASA bill outlines specific programs, such as the development of the Space Telescope, and tells how much is to be spent on them. Over the years, there has been little disagreement between NASA's requests and the Congress's actions.

The Congress generally has provided NASA with adequate funding to do its job well.

In addition to its budgetary responsibility, the Science and

Technology Committee also has oversight responsibility to see that NASA is doing its job. And yet a congressional committee cannot possibly micromanage NASA. Even if the committee had poked and prodded every day at NASA's headquarters and field centers, it is doubtful that the faulty design of *Challenger*'s solid rocket booster would have been detected.

But the committee should have tried to hold NASA more accountable than it did. After turning in success after success, NASA was doing virtually what it wanted, when it wanted, and congressional oversight was no more than a matter for NASA to tolerate.

Even today, after the chastening experience of the *Challenger* accident, it is still institutionally difficult for NASA to hold itself accountable to Congress.

There is a great deal of talk about the necessity of making a new commitment to space. Not true. America has already committed herself to space. The contract has been signed in the blood of her fallen and cosigned by those willing to run future risks. Our new world is, in fact, being directed by what we have already accomplished. The question lies in our priorities.

Most meaningful, perhaps, is the use of space to obtain scientific data. However, our prime reason for commitment can be summed up in the words of a Soviet space scientist: "Man is evolving into space and is going to operate there." Regardless of the problems, space is our next frontier. To neglect it would be as foolish as saying to Lewis and Clark, "We have everything we want back East. There's no need to go beyond the Mississippi."

What is America's primary mission in space? Do we have a goal? A vision for the future? And what can we do to implement it?

Sally Ride analyzed four future goals for the space program:

· Studies of earth
· Exploring the planets

· A moon base
· A manned trip to Mars

Doctor Ride also posed a penetrating question about leadership, calling for a new perspective in setting goals. She summed up by saying we should keep our eye on the doughnut, not the hole. Larry Martz, writing in *Newsweek* magazine, said Dr. Ride's report was "the beginning of wisdom, and the basis for a program we can live with" (*Newsweek*, August 17, 1987).

I agree. In our democratic system, any program as big as NASA is bound to find itself bogged down in compromise, bureaucratic red tape, and the struggle to flow with political and economic trends. That's not necessarily bad. The democratic process, as cumbersome as it is, demands that NASA keep its structure flexible and expandable. Now, in the spirit of Sally Ride's parting remark about the doughnut, NASA is being forced to reexamine its goals and is, perhaps for the first time in a long time, looking to the American People for direction.

The American adventure is a story about heroes, about discovery, about exploration, about people who forge ahead. That is the nature of our country. We have always been a nation that is restless unless pressing the unknown. We have always had a frontier to expand: westward, inward, upward.

Nothing has symbolized the character of the American People as explorers, as discoverers, as adventurers, like the space program. This drive to reach new limits is expressed in the language of our test pilots who speak of "pushing the envelope." It was captured in the spirit of Christa McAuliffe, who said, "We must continue to reach for the stars."

We must. If America ever abandoned her space ventures, then we would die as a nation, becoming second rate in our own eyes as well as in the eyes of the world.

Senator John Glenn, our first astronaut to orbit earth, answered that in his comments on the *Challenger* tragedy. "The final four words that came from the *Challenger* just seconds before the explosion were 'Go at throttle up.' And in my judgment, those four words are far more than just a courageous epitaph. They are America's history. They are America's destiny. And they will once again turn tragedy into triumph." Now it is time to move beyond our tragedies to the expected triumphs of the future, to determine our major goals and enter into a national resolve to build on our experience and explore the unknown.

I believe our next major space goal should be the completion of the space station in the 1990s, then on to the planet Mars with humans aboard early in the next century.

While all this is going on, we will continue to observe and measure our own planet. Looking back at Earth from the perspective of space is instructive for our future conduct. We can see the expanding desert from space and try to find new sources of water under the sand. We can identify the specific location of crop disease to prevent its spread. Even the magnitude of urban sprawl can be measured and planned as we face the reality of the decaying inner cities. Once this is done, we can use space-age materials in their reconstruction. What we learn from space will help us appreciate and protect our planet.

The afternoon of the *Challenger* accident, the President cancelled his State of the Union message and the entire nation went into mourning. The spirit of America had been dashed against the rocks of adversity. Dashed, but not broken. We had been knocked down, but not knocked out.

The tragedy of the *Challenger* shook the nation to its roots. But now the tree is coming alive, new leaves are budding, and fruit is on the way. America is not only back, she is looking forward. An entire generation is standing on the threshold, eager to move ahead.

Shuttle Flight History

Launch Date and Duration	Mission and Vehicle	Crew Members	Comments
4-12-81 2.25 days	STS-1 Columbia	John Young Robert Crippen	First orbital flight of the space shuttle
11-12-81 2.25 days	STS-2 Columbia	Joe Engle Richard Truly	Second orbital flight. Test of remote manipular system. Mission cut to two days by fuel cell failure
3-22-82 8 days	STS-3 Columbia	Jack Lousma Gordon Fullerton	Student experiments; test of hardware for electrophoresis experiments. Landing site changed to White Sands, NM, because of water on lake bed at Edwards AFB. Landing delayed one day because of bad weather at alternate landing site

Launch Date and Duration	Mission and Vehicle	Crew Members	Comments
6-27-82 7.04 days	STS-4 *Columbia*	Tom Mattingly Henry Hartsfield	1st flight to carry a Dept. of Defense payload. 1st flight to use electrophoresis
11-11-82 5.08 days	STS-5 *Columbia*	Vance Brand Robert Overmyer Wiliam Lenoir Joseph Allen	1st deployment of satellites
4-04-83 5 days	STS-6 *Challenger*	Paul Weitz Karol Bobko Donald Peterson Story Musgrave	1st flight of *Challenger*, 1st shuttle EVA (Peterson, Musgrave) satellite initially failed to reach geosynchronous orbit because of guidance failure. Later raised to proper orbit using attitude and maneuvering thrusters
6-18-83 6.08 days	STS-7 *Challenger*	Robert Crippen Rick Hauck Sally Ride John Fabian Norman Thagard	1st American woman in space (Sally Ride). Use of remote arm to deploy and retrieve shuttle pallet. Scheduled landing at KSC waved off because of bad weather. Landing at Edwards AFB
8-30-83 6.04 days	STS-8 *Challenger*	Richard Truly Dan Brandenstein Guion Bluford Dale Gardner Bill Thornton	1st shuttle night launch and landing

Launch Date and Duration	Mission and Vehicle	Crew Members	Comments
11-28-83 10.32 days	STS-9 *Columbia*	John Young Brewster Shaw Robert Parker Owen Garriott Byron Lichtenberg Ulf Merbold	Two-shift 24-hour operations; Space-lab 1. 1st non-U.S. crewmember aboard (Merbold, West Germany)
2-03-84 7.97 days	STS-41B *Challenger*	Vance Brand Hoot Gibson Bruce McCandless Robert Stewart Ron McNair	1st KSC landing. Both satellites failed to reach geosynchronous orbit. Both re-trieved on STS-51A and returned to Earth for refur-bishment.
4-06-84 6.99 days	STS-41C *Challenger*	Robert Crippen Francis Scobee Terry Hart James van Hoften Pinky Nelson	Rendezvous, re-pair, and redeploy of Solar Max satel-lite. Highest alti-tude to date (269 nautical miles)
8-30-84 6.04 days	STS-41D *Discovery*	Henry Hartsfield Michael Coats Richard Mullane Steve Hawley Judy Resnik Charles Walker	1st "Frisbee-type" satellite deploy-ment; 1st commer-cial payload specialist (Charles Walker). 2d Amer-ican woman in space
10-05-84 8.23 days	STS-41G *Challenger*	Robert Crippen Jon McBride David Leestma Sally Ride Kathy Sullivan Paul Scully-Power Marc Garneau	1st American women to walk in space. 1st seven-person crew; 1st time for two women in space; 1st American or-bital fuel transfer; 1st Canadian crew-man (Garneau). KSC landing

Launch Date and Duration	Mission and Vehicle	Crew Members	Comments
11-08-84 7.99 days	STS-51A *Discovery*	Rick Hauck David Walker Dale Gardner Joseph Allen Anna Fisher	Two spacewalks to retrieve Indonesian satellite and WESTAR VI, lost 9 months before. KSC landing
1-24-85 3.06 days	STS-51C *Discovery*	Tom Mattingly Loren Shriver Ellison Onizuka James Buchli Gary Payton	Mission dedicated to DOD. KSC landing
4-12-85 7 days	STS-51D *Discovery*	Karol Bobko Don Williams Rhea Seddon Jeff Hoffman David Griggs Charles Walker Jake Garn	Satellite failed to activate when deployed. Unscheduled spacewalk to attach "fly swatters" in attempt to trip activation switch. 1st American heart images in flight. U.S. senator aboard as payload specialist
4-29-85 6.96 days	STS-51B *Challenger*	Robert Overmyer Fred Gregory Don Lind Norman Thagard Bill Thornton Lodewijk van den Berg Taylor Wang	Extensive Spacelab experiments. Animal tests caused contamination
6-17-85 7.07 days	STS-51G *Discovery*	Dan Brandenstein John Creighton Shannon Lucid John Fabian Steven Nagel Patrick Baudry Sultan S.A. Al-Saud	French experiments on board. Arabian prince as payload specialist

Launch Date and Duration	Mission and Vehicle	Crew Members	Comments
7-29-85 7.95 days	STS-51F *Challenger*	Gordon Fullerton Roy Bridges Story Musgrave Anthony England Karl Henize Loren Acton John-David Bartoe	Around-the-clock astronomy studies. Spacelab 2
8-27-85 7.10 days	STS-51I *Discovery*	Joe Engle Richard Covey James van Hoften John Lounge Bill Fisher	Rendezvous with failed satellite from April flight. Spacewalk for cap- ture, repair, and redeployment
10-03-85 4.07 days	STS-51J *Atlantis*	Karol Bobko Ronald Grabe Robert Stewart David Hilmers William Pailes	1st flight of *Atlan- tis*. 2d dedicated DOD flight
10-30-85 7 days	STS-61A *Challenger*	Henry Hartsfield Steven Nagel Bonnie Dunbar Guion Bluford James Buchli Reichard Furrer Wubbo Ockels Ernst Messerschmid	1st 8-person crew. 1st foreign dedi- cated Spacelab (West Germany)
11-26-85 6.87 days	STS-61B *Atlantis*	Brewster Shaw Bryan O'Connor Mary Cleave Sherwood Spring Jerry Ross Charles Walker Rodolfo Neri	Two spacewalks for assembly and evaluation of space station materials

Launch Date and Duration	Mission and Vehicle	Crew Members	Comments
1-12-86 6.09 days	STS-61C *Columbia*	Hoot Gibson Charlie Bolden Franklin Chang-Diaz Pinky Nelson Steve Hawley Bob Cenker Bill Nelson	RCA communication satellite deployed. Landing at KSC delayed two days and waved off because of bad weather. Landing at Edwards AFB. U.S. Congressman Nelson aboard as payload specialist.
1-28-86	STS-51L *Challenger*	Dick Scobee Michael Smith Judy Resnik Ellison Onizuka Ron McNair Greg Jarvis Christa McAuliffe	Explosion destroys crew and orbiter seventy-three seconds into flight.

Index

Abbey, George, 9, 10, 21, 84, 109
  described, 214–16
  launch of *Challenger* and, 225,
    294
Adamson, Jim, 84, 180
Advanced Communications
    Technology Satellite, 256
Advanced X-Ray Observatory, 284
Agena target vehicles, 212
Agriculture, 259–60, 270
Air Force Institute of Technology,
    215
Air sickness, 64, 128, 183, 189–92
Aldridge, Edward, 221, 253
Aldrin, Buzz, 212
Alligators, 54
Alloys made in space, 261, 263
Altitude chamber, 51–52
America's mission in space, 296–98
Anders, William, 184, 289
Andrews Air Force Base, 51, 181
Anemia, 203
Anti-corrosion paint, 276

Anti-matter, 286
Apollo program, 269–70, 273,
    288–89, 295
Apollo 1 disaster, 14–15, 178, 184,
    291
Apollo 8, 184
Apollo 10, 9
Apollo 11, 28
Apollo 13, 15, 205–6
Apollo/Soyuz mission, 228, 229, 230,
    238, 290
Aquarius, 206
Arianespace, 250
Ariane 3 rocket, 253, 256
Arlington National Cemetery,
    184–85
Armstrong, Neil, 28, 200, 289
Astronauts, 25
  chief, *see* Young, John
  civilian, *see* Civilian astronauts
  complaints from, 54, 102, 103,
    212–14
  number of, 204–5

Astronauts *(continued)*
  quarters for, 208–9
  selection and assignment of,
     214–16
  see also individual astronauts
Astronaut Support Person (ASP)
     (Cape crusaders), 106, 109,
     219, 220
Astronaut training, 40–93
  altitude chamber, 51–52
  astronaut instructor, 85
  "the bag," 43, 91
  congressional duties and, 44, 51,
     65, 88
  disorientation, 73
  emergency escapes, 68, 70,
     71–73
  for experiments in space, 64–65,
     82, 93
  firefighting, 70–71
  flying skills, 77–81
  other astronauts and, 53–62
  physical conditioning, 25, 32, 40,
     88, 219
  physical exam prior to, 41, 43
  press conferences during, 82–83
  psychiatric exam prior to, 44, 46
  quarantine and, 92–93
  routine, 62
  shuttle mockup, 65–68
  shuttle simulators, 55, 58
  space food and, 47, 50–51,
     83–84
  space gear and, 46–47
  teamwork and, 73–74
  weightlessness, 63–65, 284
Atlanta Chiefs, 217
Atlantis, 188, 215, 220, 244
Atlas Centaur rocket, 103, 250, 253
Aziz, Prince Sultan bin, 244

"Bag, the," 43, 91
Balebanov, Vyacheslav, 241–42
"Barbecue configuration," 149
Bassett, Charles, 291

Baylor University College of
     Medicine, 216
Beatty, Becky, 186
Beckman, Ken, 23
Beggs, Jim, 30–31, 220–26
  flight assignments and, 40–41, 52
  Graham and, 221–23
  invitation from, 35–36
"Bends, the," 51
Beta cells, 202–3
Bible, 123, 281
Big Bang concept, 285–86
Biosphere II, 284
Blood deterioration experiments,
     192–94
Blood pressure tests, 161, 197–98
Boeing Aerospace Company,
     253–54
Bolden, Charlie, 62, 65, 93, 205
  described, 5, 54–55
  helium and nitrogen leaks and,
     113–14, 177
  postponed launches and, 13, 17,
     19, 25, 97, 101–2
  in space, 126, 167–70
Borman, Frank, 184, 289
Brand, Vance, 228
Breathing system for firefighters,
     276–77
Brooklyn Polytechnic Institute, 207
Bugg, Charles, 187
Bungo, Michael W., 189, 195, 197
Bush, George, 181–82

California Citrus Association, 136
Canada, 241, 246
Canavalin, 188–89
Cancer research, 186–89
Cape crusaders, 106, 109, 219, 220
Capsule Communicator
     (CAPCOM), 97, 106, 117,
     160, 162, 208
Carter, Manley Lanier "Sonny," 217,
     219, 220
Cavert, Tillman and Ellen, 94

Celebrity status, 25–26
Cenker, Bob, 16, 67, 99, 109
  described, 7, 59, 62
  in space, 118, 120, 125–26, 131,
    133
Center for Blood Research, 193
Central Florida Blood Bank, 193
Chaffee, Roger, 14–15, 178
Challenger disaster, 59, 82, 175–85,
    189, 253, 288–98
  changes at NASA due to, 213–14,
    216, 225, 291
  crew of, 178–80
  Glenn on, 297–98
  investigation into, 54, 183, 212,
    291–96
  memorial to, 183–84
  Morgan and, 37
  O-rings and, 100, 292, 293
  reaction to, 38, 288, 297–98
  recovery of debris from, 219, 220
  viewed on television, 176–78
Challenger shuttle, 84, 96, 101, 176
  assignment on, 41, 52
  decision to launch, 223, 225
  McAuliffe's teaching from,
    74–77
  replacement for, 248–49
Chang-Diaz, Franklin, 16, 55, 93,
    109
  as Costa Rican hero, 94, 245
  described, 5, 58
  plasma propulsion system and,
    282–84
  postponed launch and, 96–99
  in space, 117–20, 126, 129, 158
Charles, John, 197
Chase Econometrics, 270
Chernobyl accident, 258
Cheyenne Mountain, 44
China, 241, 247, 250
Civilian astronauts, 31–38
  Challenger disaster and, 37–38
  NASA invitation, 35–36
  opinions on, 37–38
  qualification for, 31

subcommittee chairmanship and,
    32, 35
  training for, *see* Astronaut
    training
Claustrophobia, 43, 91
Coelho, Tony, 181
Cohen, Aaron, 216
Columbia mission (on orbit), 104–71
  See also Columbia mission
    (pre-launch)
  bathing, 140
  checklist, 136, 138
  close confines on, 142
  dangers associated with, 163, 183
  deorbit burn, 165–66
  deorbit preparation,
    157–62
  discussion of personal feelings,
    142
  experimental rocket firing and,
    163–64
  external fuel tank separation, 117
  first flight of, 30
  G forces, 115
  as a glider, 168–70
  hair washing, 140–41
  heads up display, 169
  helium leak, 113–14, 177
  initial tasks, 122–23
  landing, 168–70
  launch, 103, 111–17
  main engine critical point, 108,
    115
  Max Q, 114
  nitrogen leak, 141
  OMS burns, 118–19, 120, 126,
    162, 163, 183
  reaction control system jets,
    163–64, 166, 167
  research on, *see* Space research
  returning to earth, 157–71
  rocket booster separation,
    114–15
  satellite launch, 125–26, 189
  shuttle portable on-board
    computer, 149

Columbia mission (on orbit)
     (continued)
   sleeping, 131, 133, 143, 145, 160
   space food, 126, 133–36, 160–62
   space gear, 140
   space toilet, 123, 125, 141, 168
   stowage bags, 122
   tape recorders on, 142, 143
   temperature, 149, 164–65
   vernier rockets, 120, 162
   views from, 121, 123, 138,
        144–52, 160, 161, 165
   water dump, 138, 140
   zero gravity, *see* Zero gravity
Columbia mission (pre-launch):
   See also Columbia mission (on-orbit)
   assignment on, 52
   at one with, 10–11
   automatic countdown for, 16–19,
        24, 110–11
   checks, 109–10
   crew of, 5–7, 53–62
   crew badge of, 84, 86–88
   dangers associated with, 13–14,
        15, 105, 107–8
   described, 10, 12, 16, 109
   emergency landing strips for, 58,
        97, 100, 107
   escape system on, 14
   experiments on, 64–65, 82, 93
   items carried aboard, 4–5, 105–6
   launching of, 103, 111–17
   launch window for, 17–18, 19, 99,
        101
   official designation of, 54
   postponed launches of, 3–20, 22,
        25, 95–103
   quarantine prior to launches of,
        3–7, 21–24, 92–94, 104
   shutting down, 19
   weather and, 101–3, 293
Columbia shuttle:
   firsts established by, 211–12
   maiden voyage of, 209
Columbus, Christopher, 143, 231,
     242

Communications satellites,
     240–41, 257–58, 264,
     270–71
Computer chips, 262–63
Computers, 269–70
Comsats, 270
Concanavalin, 188–89
Cosmos military satellites, 233
Costa Rica, 94, 215
Cremated ashes in space, 4, 253
Crew badge, 84, 86–88
Crippen, Bob, 209, 211
Crop planning, 259–60, 270
Crystal research and manufacture,
     161, 186–89, 161–63
Culbertson, Phil, 223

Daedalus, 290
Dalmane, 131
Dangers of space travel, 13–14, 15,
     105, 107–8, 163, 185
   see also Challenger disaster
Davis, Jeff, 195
Defense contracts, 46
Deimos, 238, 242, 282
Delta rocket, 250, 253
DeLucas, Larry, 64, 187
Dental braces, 275–76
Diabetes, 202–3
Dickerson, David, 65, 83
Discovery, 59
Disney, Walt, 84, 88, 260
Disney World, 84, 88, 259–60, 275
Drake, Frank, 278
Duke, Charlie, 9, 212

Eastern Test Range, 30
Edwards Air Force Base, 54, 58, 73,
     136, 193
   Columbia's landing at, 162,
        165–70
Egypt, 145
Einstein, Albert, 283
Eisenhower, Dwight D., 239

Electrophoresis, 200–203
Ellington Field, 77–78
Emergency escapes:
  crash landing in the sea and,
    107–8
  postlanding, 72–73
  prelaunch, 14, 68, 70, 71–72
Emergency landing strips, 58, 97,
    100, 107
Emory University, 217
Energia rocket, 235
Enterprise, 91
Entrepreneurs in space, 248–67
  agriculture and, 259–60
  communications satellites and,
    257–58
  exclusion of private enterprise
    from shuttle missions and,
    248–50, 256
  foreign rockets and, 250
  General Dynamics, 253
  government-industry
    partnership and, 248, 249,
    251, 253, 255, 257, 266–67
  Harris Corporation, 262
  Hughes-Boeing, 253–54
  insurance for, 266–67
  legislation for, 266
  McDonnell Douglas, 253
  manufacturing and, 261–66
  mapping and, 258-60
  Martin Marietta, 251, 253
  potential for, 256–57, 263, 265
  remote sensing and, 258–60
  repairing satellites, 264–65
  Space Services, Inc., 253
  space stations and, 263–65
  upper stages and, 256
  see also Arianespace
Entry interface, 166
Epcot Center, 259–60, 275
Erithropoiten, 203
Ethiopia, 151, 152–55
European Space Agency, 244, 256
Exceptional Scientific Achievement
    Medal, 216

Exercising in space, 195
  tests of, 194–97
Expendable launch vehicles (ELVs),
    250–54
Experiments in space, *see* Space
    research
Explorer, 27, 290
Extraterrestrial intelligence,
    278–79, 286

F-15 jets, 32
F-16 jets, 32, 115, 221
Falcoln Air Force Station, 213
Firefighting training, 70–71
Fixed-based simulator, 58
Flame-resistant materials, 275
Fletcher, James, 38, 225, 281
"Flight of Mercy," 152–53
Florida Citrus Commission, 83
Florida Times Union, 152–53
France, 241, 244–45, 247, 250, 257
Freeman, Theodore, 291
French Guiana, 250
French National Space Research
    Center (CNES), 250
Fuller, Craig, 182
Fuqua, Don, 3, 181

Gagarin, Yury, 123, 229, 243
Galileo, 281, 285
Galileo probe, 246, 280, 281
Gallium arsenide, 262, 263
Gamma Ray Observatory, 284, 286
Garn, Jake, 25–26, 38
  Challenger disaster and, 180, 181,
    182
  following in the footsteps of, 32,
    35, 65, 83, 84
Garneau, Marc, 211
Gemini program, 288, 289
Gemini 3, 9
Gemini 4, 176
Gemini 10, 212
General Dynamics Corporation,
    220–21, 222

General Dynamics Corporation
  (*continued*)
  ELV rockets and, 253
Geostationary orbit, 251, 255
G forces, 96, 115, 166, 168, 230
Gibson, Robert L. "Hoot," 97, 183
  astronaut training and, 55, 62,
    68, 71, 72, 93
  Atlantis and, 215, 220
  described, 5, 53–54, 109
  on landing in the sea, 107–8
  lift-off, 111, 113–14
  postponed launches and, 13, 17,
    18, 19, 22, 25, 101
  reentry of *Columbia* and, 166–70
  in space, 126, 141, 165
  T-38s and, 77–81
Glenn, John, 15, 27, 81, 181
  on the *Challenger* disaster,
    297–98
Global Climate and Environmental
    Change Initiative, 235
Goddard Space Flight Center, 269
Goldwater, Barry, 81
Gorbachev, Mikhail, 234–35
Graham, Bill, 221–23, 225
Great Britain, 241, 247
Great Grapefruit Controversy, 85,
    135–36
Greene, Jay, 205–8
Gregory, Fred, 97, 106–7, 117, 160
Griffin, Gerry, 213
Griffin, Richard, 213
Grissom, Virgil "Gus," 9, 14–15,
    178, 184–85, 212
Gromyko, Andrei, 229, 232–35
Grumman, 46
G suit, 46–47, 158, 167
Gunter, Nancy, 175, 208–9

Halley's Comet, 189, 238, 246, 280
Handel, George Frederick, 143
Harris Corporation, 262
Hart, Charles, 10
Hartsfield, Henry, 54

Harvard University, 221
Hawley, Steve, 55, 65, 98, 136, 183,
    260
  described, 5, 59
  launch and, 105, 106, 110, 111
  in space, 126, 133, 162, 195
Heads up display (HUD), 169
Herres, General, 44
Hesburg, Theodore, 279
Hoffa, Jimmy, 239
Holter Monitor, 197
Homestead Act, 28
House of Representatives, 20–23
  astronaut training and votes in,
    44, 51, 65, 88
  Challenger disaster and, 175,
    181–82, 185
  timing of flights and votes in,
    40–41, 52
House Science and Technology
    Committee, 3, 30, 182
  chairmanships and, 35, 53
  Challenger disaster and, 292–96
  Space Science and Applications
    Subcommittee, 7, 32, 35–36,
    44, 194
Houston Post, 103
Hubble, Edwin P., 285
Hubble's constant, 285–86
Hubble Space Telescope, 246, 254,
    255, 278, 284–85, 286, 295
Hughes Aircraft Company, 52,
    253–54
Huntoon, Carolyn, 216
Huntoon, Harrison, 216
Hypergolic propellant, 164
Hypoxia, 51–52

Icarus, 290
India, 241, 247
Indian River grapefruit, 83,
    135–36
Indonesia, 247
Infrared Astronomy Satellite, 246
Infrared (IR) camera, 161

Insulin infusion pump, 272–73
Intelsat, 270
Intermediate orbit, 251, 255
International Astronomical Society, 184
International cooperation in space, 227–47
  costs and, 231, 238
  existing, 244–47
  Mars and, 237–44
  recommendations on, 237–38
  search-and-rescue missions and, 243
  Soviet advances and, 235, 237, 239
  weapons and, 232–34, 239, 240, 246
International Maritime Satellite Organization (INMARSAT), 246
International Space Year, 235
International Telecommunication Satellite Organization (INTELSAT), 246
Isabella, Queen, 231, 257
Israel, 145, 147–48
Italy, 247

Japan, 241, 246, 255–56, 257, 266
Jarvis, Greg, 52, 74, 178, 253
Jarvis rocket, 253–54
J-C-SAT Z satellite, 251
Jet Propulsion Laboratory, 280
John Deere Tractor Company, 64
Johns Hopkins University, 269
Johnson, Lyndon B., 55, 295
Johnson Space Center (JSC), 13, 21, 70, 204, 225
  astronaut training at, 44, 55, 63, 72
  Building 9A, 65–70
  Media Services branch, 216–17
  physical exams at, 41, 43
  press secretary at, 65
Jupiter, 239, 246, 279, 280, 281

KC-135 airplane, 63–65, 74, 120, 121, 178, 187
Keillor, Garrison, 59
Keller, Helen, 185
Kennedy, John F., 14, 28, 182, 200, 243, 288, 295
Kennedy Space Center (KSC), 3–20, 54, 58, 193
  astronaut quarters at, 208–9
  prelaunch escape training at, 71–72
Kidney stone research, 198
Kraft, Incorporated, 259–60
Kubasov, Valery, 228, 290

Lake Wobegon Days (Keillor), 59
Land, The, 259–60
Landsat remote sensing system, 246, 258–60, 266–67
Langley Research Center, 275
Laser heart surgery, 275
Launch Control Center (LCC), 9, 16, 98, 113, 207
Leestma, Dave, 211
Leonov, Alexi, 228, 229–30, 290
Liberty Bell, 184
Lightning, 101–3, 151–52
Lockheed Missile and Space Company, 255, 285
Long March 3 rocket, 247
Lovell, James, Jr., 184, 206, 289
Low earth orbit, 251, 254
Lunar soil simulant, 260

McAuliffe, Christa, vii, 37, 52, 178, 181, 184, 297
  described, 74
  lesson plans of, 74–77
  life insurance on, 74
McBride, Jon, 211
McCain, John, 81
McDivitt, James, 176
McDonnell Douglas, 38, 188, 203, 256

McDonnell Douglas *(continued)*
ELV rockets and, 253
McGuire, Dr., 44, 46, 142
McNair, Ron, 178, 180
Magee, John Gillespie, Jr., vii
Magellan, 239
Magnetic Resonance Imaging, 273
Mali, 152, 155
Mariner, 290
Mark, Hans, 221
Mars, 234, 237–44, 259, 280–84
Soviet obsession with, 241–42,
280, 281
Marshall Space Flight Center, 64,
186, 225, 230, 269, 293–94
Mars Observer, 256, 284, 294
Mars Sample Return mission, 234
Martin Marietta, 251, 253
Martz, Larry, 297
Massachusetts Institute of
Technology (MIT), 58, 220,
283
Max Q, 114
Mayfield, Bob, 76
Mediasat system, 258
Melbourne High School, 27–28
Mercury program, 288
Merritt Island, 28, 30
Messiah (Handel), 143
Mexico, 244
Michener, James, 119–20, 227–28,
230, 240
Microminiaturization, 268–71
Middle East, 145–48
Militarizing space, 200, 232–34,
239, 240, 246, 254, 258
Mineral exploration, 260
Mir space station, 230, 233, 235,
263
Mission Control, 97, 106, 113
Columbia on orbit and, 117, 141
Columbia's return and, 157, 158,
161, 165
director of, 205–8
Monge, Luis Alberto, 245
Monroe, Vaughn, 138

Moon landings, 9, 28, 200, 212, 289
Moon Treaty, 245
Moore, Jesse, 3, 4, 52, 225, 229
Morgan, Barbara, 37, 38, 74
Morton Thiokol, 225, 292, 293
Motion-based simulator, 55, 58
Motion sickness, 64, 128, 183,
189–92
Mount Sinai, 10, 145–47

NASA 1, 22
National Aeronautics and Space
Administration (NASA):
astronaut training and, *see*
Astronaut training
chief astronaut, *see* Young, John
civilian astronauts and, 30–39
complaints from astronauts, 54,
102, 103, 212–14
Congress and, 292, 294–96
customers of, 7, 38, 44, 125
flight director, 207–8
investigation of, 54, 183, 212,
291–96
lost data, 198
NASAese, xi–xvi, 63, 76
pay of employees, 204–7
personalities and politics at,
204–26
PIMS and, 268–69
pressure on, 16–17, 291–96
pride of, 4, 292
private industry's launching of
satellites and, 249–54
problems on *Columbia* and,
19–20, 99, 100
product endorsements and, 83
professionalism of, 24–25
shakeup at, post-*Challenger*,
213–14, 216, 225, 291
Teacher in Space program of, 37,
38, 74–77
National Bureau of Standards,
261–62
National Institutes of Health, 269

National Research Council, 231
National Space Technology
   Laboratories, 274
Navstar Global Positioning System,
   255
Nelson, Bill:
   astronaut training and, *see*
      Astronaut training
   background of, 10, 27–30
   Challenger disaster and, 175–85
   as civilian astronaut, *see* Civilian
      astronauts
   Columbia and, *see Columbia*
      mission flight assignment,
      40–41, 52
   in Moscow, 194, 228–38
   parents of, 94
Nelson, Billy, 9, 17, 88, 91, 181
   illness of, 23
Nelson, George "Pinky," 55, 63, 65,
   84, 93, 99, 109
   described, 5, 7, 59
   experiments and, 189, 193
   on risk of manned spaceflight,
      185
   in space, 126, 129, 133, 151, 158,
      160, 166, 167, 168
Nelson, Grace, 110
   astronaut training and, 88, 91
   Challenger disaster and, 180, 181,
      182
   postponed launch and, 3, 9, 11,
      16, 17, 23–24
   return of *Columbia* and, 162, 168,
      170
   starvation in Africa and, 152–55
Nelson, Jane Ellen, 10
Nelson, Nan Ellen, 9, 17, 181
   tape made by, 4, 88, 106, 143
Neri, Rodolfo, 244
Netherlands, 244
Newsweek magazine, 297
Nicogosian, Arnold, 194
1992, 242
Nitinol, 275–76
Nixon, Richard, 295

North American Air Defense
   Command Center
   (NORAD), 44, 66

Oberg, James, 233
Office of Technology Assessment
   (OTA), 271–72
O'Neill, Tip, 242–43
Onizuka, Ellison, 178, 180
Operations and Checkout Building
   (O&C), 9
Orbital Sciences Corporation, 256
Orbiter maneuvering system
   (OMS), 118–19, 120, 126,
   162, 163, 183
Osterblum, Bob, 7
Osterblum, Ryan, 7
Otolithic stones, 128, 192
Outer Space Treaty, 245

Paine, Thomas O., 228, 237–38
Paper Money Identifier, 273
Pappas, Ike, 22
Parabola flight maneuver, 63–65,
   74
Parker-Hannifin Corporation, 269
Participation mystique, 10–11
Patrick Air Force Base, 104
Payload Assist Module (PAM), 256
Personal Rescue System, 43
Petrone, Rocco, 225, 294
Pharmaceutical research and
   manufacture, 200–203, 261,
   262
Phobos, 238, 242, 282
Phobos probes, 237
Piccard, Auguste, 114
Pioneer 10, 279–80, 290
Planetary Society, 242
Plasma propulsion system, 282–84
Pluto, 279, 283
Polystyrene spheres made in space,
   261–62
Precision approach phased
   indicator (PAPI), 169

President's National Commission
  on Space, 228–29, 281
Proctoscopic exam, 41, 43
Programmable, implantable
  medication system (PIMS),
  268–69
Protein chemistry research, 186–89
Psychiatric exam, 44, 46
Purine nucleoside phosphorylase
  (PNP), 188

Radio Corporation of America
  (RCA), 59
  as NASA customer, 7, 99, 125
Ranger, 289
Rapp, Rita, 83, 84
Reaction control system (RCS) jets,
  163–64, 166, 167
Reading machine for the blind, 273
Reagan, Ronald, 37, 43, 220, 221,
  225, 232, 281, 292
  entrepreneurs in space and,
  248–49, 250
Redstone rocket, 27
Regan, Don, 222
Remote serving satellite, 246,
  258–60
Resnik, Judy, 178, 180
Ride, Sally, 5, 59, 211
  recommendations for the space
  program, 237, 281, 296–97
Robitaille, Henry, 260
Rockwell International, 255, 294
Rogers Commission, 54, 292–94
  on *Columbia* scrub, 99–100
Russian cosmonauts, 17, 123, 191,
  194, 228–32

Sagan, Carl, 241, 242, 243, 280
Sagdeyev, Roald, 234
Saint Catherine's Monastery, 147
Saliva testing, 202
Salyut 7, 17, 229,231–32
Santy, Pat, 195

SATCOM satellite, 125–26, 189
Satellites, 59, 99
  communication, 240–41,
  257–58, 264, 270–71
  insurance for, 266–67
  international cooperation, 246
  launching of, 125–26, 189
  manipulator arm replica, 65–66
  military, 233–34
  NASA backlog for launching of,
  249–50
  orbit distance and, 251, 254–55
  private industry's launching of,
  249–54
  remote sensing, 258–60
  repair of defective, 264–65
  viewed from earth, 147
  weather, 258, 260, 270, 274
Saturn, 279
Saturn V rocket, 9, 28, 205, 254
Saudi Arabia, 244
Schuerger, Andrew, 260
Scobee, Dick, 76, 175, 178, 180, 209
Scobee, June, 180
Scratch-resistant eye glasses, 275
Scully-Power, Paul, 211
Search-and-rescue missions, 243,
  276
Search for Extraterrestrial
  Intelligence (SETI), 278–79
Seddon, Rhea, 5, 59, 183
See, Elliot, 291
Selfridge, Thomas, 185
Semiconductors, 269–70
  crystals as, 262–63
Shepard, Alan, 27, 200, 243, 288
Shepherd, Bill, 106–7
  described, 220
Shuttle missions, 9, 299–304
  brake systems on, 54, 97
  exclusion of private enterprise
  from, 248–49
  first, 30
  flight history of, 299–304
  launch schedule of, 291, 292
  official designation of, 221

ordinary citizens on, 30–39
outside temperature and, 100,
   293–94
safety record of, 15
scientific versus military
   objectives of, 200
space trash and, 66–67
storage and, 67–68
thunderstorms and, 101–3
see also specific missions
Shuttle portable on-board
   computer (SPOC), 149
Shuttle simulators, 55
  fixed-based, 58
  interior mockups, 65–68
  manipulator arm, 65–66
  motion-based, 55, 58
  training aircraft, 77, 168, 169
Silica tiles, 149
  damage to, 223, 225
  on reentry, 167
  as space trash, 138
Skylab, 200, 202, 209, 289–90
Skylab Medical Experiments
   Altitude Test, 209
Slayton, Deke, 27, 228, 229, 253,
   290
Sleep restraint, 131, 133, 145
Smith, Bill, 187
Smith, Mike, 76, 178, 180
Solar Max satellite, 59, 254
Solar system, 278–87
Solovyov, Vladimir, 237
Soviet Academy of Sciences, 231
Soviet Institute of Atomic Energy,
   234
Soviet Space Medicine Institute,
   194
Soviet Space Research Institute,
   231, 234, 241
Soviet Union, 17, 123, 191, 194,
   228–45
  economics of space and, 250,
    256, 257, 263
  Mars and, 241–42, 280, 281
Soyuz, 230, 245, 290

Space (Michener), 119–20, 227–28,
   230, 240
Space Act, 30–31
Space adaptation syndrome (SAS),
   128, 183, 189–92
Space Cooperation Pact, 238–39
Space food, 47, 50–51, 83–84, 126,
   133–36, 160–61, 162
Space gear, 46–47, 95, 140
Space helmet, 47, 73
Space Infrared Telescope Facility,
   284
Space insurance, 266–67
Spacelab, 244, 247
Space Motion Sickness (SMS), 128
Space research, 82, 161, 186–203
  anemia, 203
  blood deterioration, 192–94
  blood pressure, 161, 197–98
  changes in total body water, 198
  detailed secondary objectives, 18?
  diabetes, 202–3
  emphasis on science, 200
  growing protein crystals, 161,
   186–89
  pharmaceutical, 200–203
  saliva testing, 202
  space adaptation syndrome, 183,
   189–92
  stress tests, 194–97
  training for, 64–65, 93
  urokinase, 202
Space Services, Inc., 253
Space shuttle, *see* Shuttle missions
Space spin-offs, 268–77
  advanced turboprop, 276
  advanced wheelchair, 275
  anti-corrosion paint, 276
  breathing system for firefighters,
   276–77
  communications satellites,
   270–71
  computers, 269–70
  for consumers, 271
  dental braces, 275–76
  employment and, 270

Space-spinoffs *(continued)*
  flame-resistant materials, 275
  insulin infusion pump, 272–73
  laser heart surgery, 275
  PIMS, 268–69
  reading machine for the blind,
    273
  scratch-resistant eye glasses, 275
  search and rescue, 276
  speech auto-cuer, 274
  vehicle controller for the
    handicapped, 273
  voice-controlled wheelchair and
    manipulator, 274
  water recycling, 274–75
  weather forecasting, 274
  window into the human body,
    273
Space stations, 198, 200–202
  described, 248, 263–65
  Soviet, 17, 229–32
Space Telescope, 246, 254, 255,
  278, 284–85, 286, 295
Space toilet, 123, 125, 141, 168
Space trash, 66–67
  ice as, 121
  pieces of tiles, 138
  water dump and, 138, 140
Space tug, 265
Space weapons, 200, 232–34, 239,
  240, 246, 254, 258
Speech auto-cuer, 274
"Spies in the sky," 258
Spinoff, 272
Spot, 247
Sputnik, 27, 239
Stafford, Tom, 228, 229, 290
Star City, 229–30
Starvation in Africa, 152–55
Stewart, Troy, 11, 95
Strategic Defense Initiative (SDI)
  (Star Wars), 232
Stress test, 41
  in space, 194–97
STS-7, mission, 209
STS-9, mission, 212, 221

STS-41C, mission, 209, 221
STS-41D, mission, 68
STS-51L, mission, *see Challenger*
  disaster
STS-61C, mission, 54, 221
  see also Columbia
Sullivan, Kathy, 211
Super Atlas G-Centaur, 253
Surgenor, Douglas, 193

T-38 jets, 77–81, 191
Teacher in Space program, 37, 38,
  74–77, 181
Thomas, Gene, 101, 110
Thornton, Bill, 192, 195
Time magazine, 233
Titan rocket, 250, 251, 253
Titan III, 251
Today, 184
Tracking and data relay satellite
  system (TDRSS), 195
Training, *see* Astronaut training
TransAmerican Cargo Airlines, 153
Transfer Orbit Stage (TOS), 256
Treadmill exercise, 194–97
Turboprop, advanced, 276

United Nations (UN), 245
U.S. Air Force, 30, 221
  cooperation with private
    industry, 251, 253
  Space Command, 213
U.S. Attorney for the Southern
  District of California, 220,
  222, 225–26
U.S. Department of Agriculture,
  259
U.S. Department of Defense, 44,
  46, 215, 253, 254
U.S. Department of Justice,
  225–26
U.S. Department of
  Transportation, 249, 251

U.S. Naval Academy, 55, 215, 220, 221
U.S. Navy Fighter Weapons School, 219
Universe, 155–56, 278–87
University of Alabama at Birmingham, 64, 82, 186, 187
University of Colorado, 44, 281
University of Virginia, 275
Upper stages rockets, 256
Uranus, 183–84
Urokinase, 202, 271
USA Today, 4, 38
U.S. News & World Report, 281
USS *Forrestal*, 217

Vanguard rocket, 27
van Hoften, "Ox," 59
Vehicle Assembly Building (VAB), 9
  described, 96
  road to launch pad from, 11
Vehicle controller for the handicapped, 273
Venus, 239, 280
Vernier rockets, 120, 162
Viking, 242, 280, 290
Voice-controlled wheelchair and manipulator, 274
Volcanoes, 149, 161
Voyager, 183, 290

Waite, Jack, 170, 171
Walker, Charlie, 38, 188, 202
Walk in space, 176
Ward, Doug, 216–17
Washington, Harold, 153
Washington Summit, 235, 241

Waste collection system (WCS), 125, 168
Water dump, 138, 140
Water recycling, 274–75
WCPX-TV, 152
Weather satellites, 258, 260, 270, 274
Weightlessness, *see* Zero gravity
Weiler, Edward, 285
Weinberger, Caspar, 233
West Germany, 241, 244, 247, 257
Wheelchair, advanced, 275
White, Edward, 14–15, 176
  on risks in space program, 178
White Room, 12, 72, 96, 98
Williams, Clifton, 291
Window into the human body, 273
World Vision, 153
Wright brothers, 185, 265

Young, John, 9, 101, 209
  criticism of NASA, 102, 212–14
  described, 211–14
  weather surveillance plane and, 10, 16, 17, 18

Zero gravity, 115–43
  body fluids and, 118, 122, 123, 158, 197–98
  experiments, *see* Space research
  footloops and, 126, 129
  M&M game, 129
  reentry from space and, 166–69
  sleeping, 131, 133, 141
  Space Motion Sickness and, 128
  space toilet and, 123, 125
  spine and, 141
  training under, 63–65, 74, 178, 284